MW00610078

"Eva Gold and Steve Zahm's hear. ... traordinary and beautifully written book. Within a rich, robust, and deeply relational theoretical framework, they offer new methodology and timeless wisdom, weaving together topics of great interest to contemporary Gestalt therapists. For example, the integration of mindfulness and relationality demonstrates their fundamental unity, adding breadth and depth to our understanding of each. Ultimately the authors reach deeply into the causes of human suffering, pointing to ways that a Buddhist psychology informed Gestalt therapy can address change at the most fundamental level. I found the explorations in this important new text inspiring, and I highly recommend it to every humanistically oriented psychotherapist." —Peter Cole, LCSW. Co-director of the Sierra Institute for Contemporary Gestalt Therapy, Assistant Clinical Professor of Psychiatry, UC Davis School of Medicine, and co-author of *New Directions in Gestalt Group Therapy: Relational Ground, Authentic Self*

"I loved this book and highly recommend it for its very accessible, seamless, and profound interweaving of both the theoretical and methodological convergences of Buddhist psychology and Gestalt therapy. BPGT brings together the universal understanding of Eastern wisdom with Western psychology's relative approach to individual psychodynamics. In laying out this comprehensive and novel integration, Gold and Zahm make an important contribution offering new directions for the expansion of human potential." —Bob Edelstein, LMFT, MFT. Founder and President of the Existential-Humanistic Northwest professional organization.

"This book offers an elegant and highly readable integration of Buddhist psychology and Gestalt therapy. Gold and Zahm's Buddhist psychology informed Gestalt therapy (BPGT) model expands Gestalt therapy's reach, while remaining true to its basic principles. I particularly liked the many clear clinical examples illustrating how this integration actually works in therapy sessions. The ideas are simple, profound, and easily implemented. By the end of the book, I was so excited by the new possibilities offered, that I was trying its methods on myself. If you are planning to buy one new book on Gestalt therapy this year, I recommend this one." —Elinor Greenberg, PhD, CGP. Author of *Borderline, Narcissistic, and Schizoid Adaptations: The Pursuit of Love, Admiration, and Safety*. Faculty of the New York Institute for Gestalt Therapy, faculty of the Gestalt Center for Psychotherapy and Training, and an Associate Editor of *Gestalt Review*

BUDDHIST PSYCHOLOGY
& GESTALT THERAPY
INTEGRATED

Buddhist Psychology & Gestalt Therapy Integrated

Psychotherapy for the 21st Century

Foreword by ERVING POLSTER

EVA GOLD
STEPHEN ZAHM

METTA PRESS | PORTLAND, OREGON

Metta Press

Buddhist Psychology & Gestalt Therapy Integrated

Copyright 2018 by Eva Gold and Stephen Zahm

All rights reserved. No part of this publication may be reproduced, stored in a retrieval system, or transmitted, in any form or by any means, electronic, mechanical, photocopying, recording, or otherwise, without the prior written permission of the publisher.

Printed in the United States of America on acid-free paper

ISBN-13: 978-1-7324920-0-4 (pbk)

ISBN-13: 978-1-7324920-1-1 (ebk)

Library of Congress Control Number: 2018907419

Every effort has been made to trace the ownership of copyrighted material. Information that will enable the publisher to rectify any error or omission in subsequent reprints will be welcome. In such cases, please contact the publisher.

BOOK DESIGN by *The Frontispiece*

We dedicate this book to our parents, our first and most important teachers...

To my mother Lil who embodied selflessness, and showed me how to meet old age, sickness, and death with grace, and to my father William who taught me very early about compassion for others in simple but profound acts that I have never forgotten.
–EG

To my dad Nate who, through his example and way of being, taught me about the inherent value and equality of all people, and to my mom Bernice (Buddie) whose capacity for contact and connection infused my earliest beginnings and beyond.
–SZ

ABOUT THE AUTHORS

Eva Gold PsyD, a psychologist in private practice, is a founding co-director of and senior faculty at Gestalt Therapy Training Center—Northwest in Portland, Oregon. Her current practice is primarily working with psychotherapists, including mentoring, consultation and supervision. Dr. Gold taught Gestalt therapy for fifteen years as an Adjunct Assistant Professor at Pacific University School of Professional Psychology. She is the author and co-author of many articles and chapters on Gestalt therapy theory and practice. A student of Buddhist psychology and an Insight meditation practitioner for nearly twenty years, she trains and presents nationally and internationally on the intersection of Buddhist psychology and Gestalt therapy.

Steve Zahm PhD, a psychologist in private practice in Portland, Oregon and Vancouver, Washington is a founding co-director of and senior faculty at Gestalt Therapy Training Center—Northwest. His practice includes consultation, supervision, and both individual and couples therapy. He taught Gestalt therapy for almost four decades as an Adjunct Professor at Pacific University School of Professional Psychology. Dr. Zahm is the author and co-author of many articles and chapters on Gestalt therapy theory and practice. A student of Buddhist psychology and an Insight meditation practitioner for many years, he trains and presents nationally and internationally on the intersection of Buddhist psychology and Gestalt therapy.

CONTENTS

FOREWORD

One of life's common challenges is the merger of any distinct identity with another that appears manifestly different. In this book, Eva Gold and Steve Zahm take on this age-old task of making sense of diversity by exploring the parallels of ancient Buddhism and contemporary Gestalt therapy. In articulating their common ground, they expand and enrich each perspective.

Drs. Gold and Zahm have both been deeply involved in Gestalt therapy since the 1970s—for all of their professional careers—as psychotherapists, teachers, trainers, and writers. As long-time meditation practitioners and students of Buddhist psychology, they have also brought their exploration of the intersection of these two approaches to the international Gestalt therapy community in many conference workshop presentations over the past decade, and they have pioneered integrating Buddhist psychology and mindfulness into Gestalt therapy training. Thus they are well positioned to take on the ambitious task of this exploration and integration. This book reflects their depth of understanding of each system as they creatively consider what each offers, where they converge, how they are different, and the expansive potential of the proposed synthesis. The result is a pathway to incorporating the broad views of Buddhist psychology and the expanded awareness of meditative experience into Gestalt therapy's richly diverse perspective.

Buddhism's broad focus is on addressing the needs of ordinary human existence. As the authors say, Buddhist psychology attends to the human condition we all find ourselves in, and it offers practices as well as an orienting path that provides ongoing and lifelong guidance. Buddhist meditation has been used since ancient times as a major instrument for penetrating the barriers to full experience, leading people to a mind-filling sensibility allowing elemental connection. Much as psychotherapy had to address barriers, so too did the Buddhist system create methods and ethos for guiding people through these to a deeper connection with and understanding of life experience. This integrative imperative resonates with the human reflex toward wholeness and reflects Gestalt therapy's ultimate goal as well. Gestalt therapy and mindfulness meditation are also both grounded in the removal of distraction from fundamental raw experience, the stuff from which wholeness is formed.

As an heir to Freudian psychoanalysis, Gestalt therapy transcends this narrowly clinical purpose in its particular unfolding of individual existence. It seeks to evoke revelatory meaningfulness that inspires sharp attention to the elemental details underlying the complexity in every person's life. Reaching beyond concern with symptom removal, Gestalt therapy has emphasized two key facets. First, the quality of people's contact to each other is given central status. Second, a sharpened awareness of sensations, emotions, purpose, and meaning is the vehicle for arousal and recognition of the essential ground of existence. For Gestalt therapy, the accentuation of awareness led to the concept of the awareness continuum. That is, if one is faithfully aware in each moment of his or her immediate experience, a succession of such experiences will inevitably lead to where one needs to go. This faith in fluidity fits well with Buddhism's reach beyond idiomatic concerns to reveal the vitality of raw energy and the capacity to be value-free, to be harmonious with personal phenomena, and to access this essence.

Paralleling the meditative pointedness of Buddhism, the founders of Gestalt therapy proposed a focus that shifted the psychotherapeutic purpose from the understanding of one's life to the direct experience of it, a focus shared with the Eastern philosophies. Gestalt therapy offered the concept of focused attention to increase awareness as the key to psychotherapeutic treatment, in contrast to the prevailing goal of insight. This introduced to the psychotherapeutic community a new priority—the management of attention. Through the expansion and amplification of attention, people would be led to enriched existence, not only through the resolution of acute psychological problems, but through the restorative effect of deep absorption in the flow of life experience. That represented a historically pivotal shift from Freudian intellectualism into the ever-present fundamental need of people to pay sharp attention to the details of their existence. This elemental shift in priorities allowed the psychotherapist to see the power of attention as a basic human instrument, leading incidentally to insight, but offering a biologically promised reward of enchantment with raw living.

Enter Gold and Zahm, bringing their depth of knowledge of each of these approaches, spelling out each viewpoint, and detailing how they converge. The authors make some surprising comparisons that highlight the overlapping characteristics of these two systems, and they have taken this theoretical and methodological syncopation and given both systems new dimension. This new dimension makes explicit, therefore more impactful, the impelling nature of amplified attention to the simplicities of direct recognition of narrowly targeted experience. However, it also tackles the concomitant complexity of human motives, contradictions, disappointments, celebrations, and all the manifold stimuli, which make our lives recognizable as the lives we live every day.

I will mention just a few of these comparisons to offer a taste of how the authors provide an enlarged outreach to the human experience. When they explicate the details of Gestalt therapy's process, they provide testimony not only to its individual psychological focus, but also to its role in enabling people to experience the aware human existence. In both systems, this human existence is understood as a distillation of a large and ubiquitous need for wholeness, the purity of which is perpetually violated by reflexive limiting constructions and the distracting requirements of everyday living. The authors' expanded Gestalt therapy perspective incorporating Buddhist psychology offers an added focal point for attention and increases awareness of a broader perspective on the human dilemma and potential for psychological freedom.

Another overlapping perspective that the authors consider relates to the concept of self. Both Buddhist psychology and Gestalt therapy understand self as a natural but humanly-based construction, created as a particular and specialized function of the mind to organize experiences and give them abstract and shorthand meanings, providing each person with a running commentary on his or her existence. One of the greatest senses of merger of these two perspectives is their emphasis on the misunderstanding of fundamental existence through the distractions of accident, personal distortions, and self-negating emotional priorities. Mistaken ideas of self-reification and created identifications are seen in Buddhism as contributors to mind-created suffering and barriers to freedom, flexibility, and awakened living. In Gestalt therapy, the self-experience is the object of revision. The classification of self provides clarity and gives life to otherwise isolated characteristics. However, it is also understood that this classification may blur the clarity of primal awareness and be distorted, creating emotional disturbance. However, as Gold and Zahm make clear, both systems join in being grounded in the concept of disturbance as error, and in seeing the fundamental ground of existence as wholeness. Each system offers a path back to this essential wholeness by addressing the how of its derailment.

Commonalities aside, self is clearly accentuated more in Gestalt therapy as a natural configurational process; one that keeps the person oriented and provides meaning to otherwise elusive implications of life's events. These identifying experiences illuminate a person's essence of what he or she *is*. However, in Gestalt therapy, self-process is understood to be fluid, and the possibility of transformation, comparable to that pointed to by Buddhism, arises through this absence of fixity. That is, I may have an Ambitious Self but it is not Me. Nor is any other description of the self etched in stone. This fluidity creates its own variation of a possibility for dissolving a stiff identity and prioritizing immediacy of awareness.

Both Buddhist psychology and Gestalt therapy attempt to illuminate self-experience. Buddhist psychology slants more toward mistaken notions of a fixed or permanent self-reification and created identification taken as real. Gestalt therapy is more focused on limiting self-concepts, those limitations of ego functioning that result in constricted living. The two perspectives are not so far removed from each other in the fundamental need for one to take stock of one's character. And as Gold and Zahm point out, in both cases, the value is placed on rising beyond fixities to experience the ever-present rawness of direct experience and its accompanying sense of Being. Importantly, in both systems there is a vigilance against falling fixedly in love with one's self-classification, recognizing instead the essence of existential fluidity and the freedom to move beyond a transitory portrayal of self into a deeper experience of a content-free energy reservoir.

These two realms, the expanded possibilities of wholeness

offered by focus on immediate experience and directed attention, and reaching beyond fixed and limited notions of self, are only a few of the high points of the larger synchronization of these two seminal influences that the authors explore. This recognition of the familial relationship of the systems and the wealth of observations about their convergences contribute to an increased dimensionalism for Gestalt therapy. I highly recommend this book to any clinician interested in an expanded understanding and perspective of what is possible in a humanistic, experiential, and existential psychotherapy, free of limiting notions of what can be included in psychotherapeutic exploration. In showing the common ground traveled, and in developing this proposed synthesis of these two approaches, the authors contribute to an enriched, unified, and more far-reaching understanding, rising beyond what each independently offers—much as two eyes, each seeing on its own, is empowered by its union with the other.

Erving Polster, PhD
La Jolla, California

ACKNOWLEDGMENTS

These acknowledgements reflect the web of interconnection that sustains us. A deep bow of gratitude to all of those we mention here, and to so many more.

We are grateful beyond words for our Gestalt therapy teachers, Isadore From, Bob Martin, Erv Polster, and Miriam Polster. Their way of being and what they taught has shaped us not only as therapists, teachers, and writers, but also as human beings. Their support, wisdom and depth of knowledge continue to guide us, and are the foundation on which this book is built.

Our retreat experiences, especially those at Spirit Rock Meditation Center and Vajrapani Institute Retreat Center, have been invaluable, and we appreciate those who have created and sustain these sacred retreat spaces. We are grateful to all of our Buddhist teachers, who have freely offered us their teachings, including Eugene Cash, Ruth Denison, Kate Dresher, Mary Grace Orr, Adrienne Ross, and John Travis. A deep bow to Gil Fronsdal a guiding teacher to both of us over many years and many retreats. Thanks also to Pat O'Shea for initially pointing us toward these retreats and teachers.

Gestalt therapy colleagues around the world have been an essential support. We appreciate the efforts of those who make the Association for the Advancement of Gestalt Therapy (AAGT) international conferences happen, allowing this important contact and connection. To those who have attended our conference presentations, we have benefited from your encouragement and enthusiastic embrace of our developing ideas. Your eagerness to read the book has kept us going! We are indebted to Brian Arnell for literally handing us Ruth Wolfert's 2000 British Gestalt Journal article at the Philadelphia 2010 conference, and to Ruth Wolfert for writing an article that inspired another level of our own exploration. We are grateful to our partner Jon Frew for many years of collaboration in teaching and training. Our students and trainees have also been active participants in the exploration, expansion, and clarification of these ideas and their application.

For reading, editing and feedback we thank Kate Dresher, Tuck Kantor, Bruce Kenofer, Brad Larsen-Sanchez, Susan Matheson, Gretchen Newmark, Barbara Rassow, and Marian Sandmaier. We also deeply appreciate Daniel Berman, Al Bernstein, and Barbara Zahm who each read the entire manuscript, offering their unique perspective and encouragement. Steve thanks his peer consultation group, Bob Edelstein, Robert King, Paul Rakoczy, Daniel Schiff, and Stephan Tobin for their ideas, intellectual rigor, and emotional support, and adds appreciation to Daniel and Stephan for feedback on specific chapters.

Consultant Jane Friedman gave us guidance in essential decisions, including referring us to Emma Hall and Kevin Barrett Kane at The Frontispiece who brought expertise and patience to the entire book design process. Our assistant extraordinaire Pauline Dutton kept the ship of our lives afloat, allowing us to focus on writing. Joshin Yamada (our "MacNinja") rescued us in computer emergencies, and offered essential technical support.

Much love and deep gratitude always to our amazing family and incomparable friends for loving support and patience with our busyness and unavailability when we were frequently "working on the book." And to the *bodhisattva* Metta, constantly at our side while we worked, sustaining us with a calming presence, tail wags, and his pure embodiment of love.

INTRODUCTION

> *The theory of Gestalt therapy takes as its centerpiece two ideas. The first is that the proper focus in psychology is the experiential present moment ... the here and now of living. The second ... is that we are inextricably caught in a web of relationship with all things.*
>
> —Joel Latner, *The Gestalt Therapy Book*

> *Buddhism is not a philosophy, not just a description of the world. It is a practical means for dealing with our lives and the problem of our suffering and happiness.*
>
> —Jack Kornfield, *Living Dharma*

WE WERE FIRST INTRODUCED to mindfulness practice at an Insight (*Vipassana*) meditation retreat in 1979. As Gestalt therapists we were both struck by the common ground this practice shared with our psychotherapy approach. The instruction to focus attention on the details of present moment experience and bodily sensation, not to change experience but to invite an expanded awareness, was very familiar territory! Also, the same things that had drawn us both to Gestalt therapy, including the value placed on this direct experiencing, and grounding in an organic process of healing and transformation, made this meditation approach feel like a natural home. Although this interest had been sparked, it was not until twenty years later that we began to delve more deeply into a study of Buddhist psychology through reading and workshops with Buddhist teachers. At the same time, we both began more regular daily meditation practice and attendance at Insight meditation retreats. As we learned and practiced, our initial interest in the common ground of these two systems blossomed, resulting in a number of conference presentations, development of a model for integrating Buddhist psychology in Gestalt therapy training, and now this book.

How is it that this ancient Eastern wisdom tradition and a contemporary Western psychotherapy share so much common ground? From our perspective, it is not surprising because although they evolved at different times, and in very different cultures, both systems are pragmatic, and both rely on direct observation rather than abstract or theoretical concepts to understand human existence and our psychological dynamics. Both observe what we do and how we do it, and both offer methods to increase awareness of these phenomena. It makes sense that the perspective gleaned from this kind of direct observation and immediate verifiable experience—whether 2600 years ago or sixty-six years ago—results in a similar viewpoint and understanding.

Buddhist psychology and Gestalt therapy both recognize the human potential for growth and actualization that is available to us as we free ourselves from restrictive patterns, beliefs, and self-concepts. In both systems, focused attention leads to increased awareness, illuminating a path toward more freedom from these limitations. Both approaches also rest on the natural transformation made possible by attending to and connecting with actual present experience. The two systems share a broadly holistic perspective in which everything is included—cognition, sensation, emotion, and embodiment. Existential realities are also encompassed in both, including our interconnectedness in the field of which we are a part, and our responsibility in the moment-to-moment creation of experience and choices.

Buddhist psychology practices and Gestalt therapy methods

each create conditions for more connection with our actual lived experience. Neither system has the aim of self-improvement with a predetermined agenda nor of attaining an idealized version of ourselves. Rather, the aim is embodiment of and intimacy with our authentic lived experience. This attention to the actuality of our moment-to-moment existence allows healing, growth, and transformation. Both approaches contribute to ameliorating our suffering, but do not stop there. They both also support the natural human capacity for increased awareness and understanding that lead to heightened vitality, well-being, and being more present and awake in our lives.

Buddhist psychology views and Gestalt therapy theory intersect in fundamental ways. Gestalt therapy is based on a model of health, not pathology, which includes belief in the capacity for natural regulation. This is in harmony with the Buddhist view of human nature, and the understanding that our fundamental psychological health and wholeness, while they may be obscured, are the ground of our human existence. There are also parallels between the two systems' understanding of the important concept of "self," not as a reified and solid entity, but as fluid process. These two systems also share an understanding of the subjectivity of experience and how it is created. They converge in how they conceptualize suffering and its cause, as well as in the understanding of what is curative or beneficial. Both systems are grounded in a fundamental recognition of interconnectedness and interdependence.

The methods of mindfulness meditation and Gestalt therapy's approach also have much in common. They share an empirical stance, prioritizing observation and direct experience over concepts. They both recognize the benefit of being present with and increasing awareness of "what is." Each includes ways to slow down and attend more closely to perceptual processes, so that the nuances of experience are revealed. Gestalt therapy originally brought this perspective to the field of psychotherapy, influencing its evolution. It turned a finely tuned attention to the details of immediate experience, taking nothing for granted. It introduced methods for focused attention on present contacting, enabling an enlivened rediscovery of one's existence through direct sense data. This created an entry point into previously inaccessible areas of understanding, more clarity of perception, empowerment for action, and openness to experience previously avoided or out of awareness (Polster & Polster, 1999).

This also describes the essence of mindfulness. Mindfulness meditation methods cultivate a capacity for focusing "bare attention" on what is arising in the present in the body and mind, revealing the flow of moment-to-moment experience as it unfolds, in the service of clearly seeing what is revealed. As we increase awareness in this process, we not only connect deeply and directly with our own hearts and minds, but with the truth of our human situation. Mindfulness meditation and Gestalt therapy both highlight the wisdom and self-understanding available to us through attention to immediate experience just as it is.

Importantly, the perspective we present here values the holistic integrity of each of these systems. Rather than taking mindfulness out of context, we place it within the body of teachings of Buddhist psychology in which it is embedded and consider its original aims. Nor are we proposing layering another system on top of Gestalt therapy. Rather, we clarify and articulate the fundamental convergences of the two systems. These convergences are then the ground for presenting Gestalt therapy as a clinical application of aspects of Buddhist psychology and mindfulness. They are also the ground for exploring how Buddhist psychology views and meditation practices can support us as Gestalt therapists, enhancing qualities and skills that our method relies on, and supporting our phenomenological, dialogical, and field perspectives.

Although this intersectionality is key in our integration, the other essential ingredient is how the two systems diverge in their central concerns and emphases, and their ultimate aims. The fact that Buddhist psychology and Gestalt therapy have convergent paradigms, and are centered in compatible views and methods, makes our proposed integration a natural one. However, it is in their differences that we find the rich possibilities to be mined from a psychotherapy approach that can encompass both. Each system offers something that the other does not, and each contributes to the process of psychological growth, healing, and transformation.

Gestalt therapy, like Western psychotherapy generally, focuses on individual emotional, psychological, and relational issues. The increased awareness that is fostered within the therapeutic relationship helps patients connect with what they feel and what they want, facilitates resolving psychological issues and internal conflict, and leads to growth and change in their relationship with themselves and in their contact in relationship. When successful, Gestalt therapy leads to not only symptom relief, but to transformation of self-experience that opens a door to more authentic, engaged contact with others and the world.

Buddhist psychology's central concerns are different. Its views and practices are universally applicable to the overall human condition, going beyond our individual psychology. It is centered in the understanding that we are capable of greater well-being, clarity, wisdom, and compassion than we ordinarily conceive of or experience. Its path supports us in accessing and developing these capacities with practices that lead to greater awareness and insight into the universal truths of existence. It points us toward developing understanding of the causes and conditions that contribute to the creation of suffering, and ultimately to freedom from it. As we find more freedom from limiting concepts and identifications, we develop the wisdom, along with compassion for others and ourselves that supports more skillful action in the world, and the ability to be more present and awake in our lives. The ultimate aim is for all of our experience to be met and held with wisdom and clear awareness.

Our vision in bringing these two systems together is to create an integrated approach, a psychotherapy for the 21st century. This *Buddhist psychology informed Gestalt therapy* (BPGT) includes the individual and relational, but also the universal perspective, and encompasses both the aims of Gestalt therapy and the aims of Buddhist psychology. It includes Gestalt therapy's humanistic, existential, experiential psychotherapy perspective, and its methods for addressing the suffering engendered by our individual and relational psychological issues, and for expanding our capacity to live life richly and deeply. And it does not stop there. It also includes Buddhist psychology's broad view of the human situation, its perspective on suffering and the possibility of freeing ourselves from it, as well as cultivation of our innate capacities including wisdom, compassion, and love.

In this exploration we outline an approach to personal growth and transformation that allows Gestalt therapy to even more fully realize the promise of its phenomenological, field, and dialogical foundations. This integration remains faithful to Gestalt therapy's fundamentals, and at the same time it broadens Gestalt therapy's perspective and scope. This opens another level of therapeutic exploration that includes increasing awareness of the processes that result in suffering. We consider an expanded view of natural regulation. We also look at integrating experiments involving meditation practices and the cultivation of beneficial qualities, along with other elements of the Buddhist path, encompassing Buddhist psychology's enlarged view of what constitutes mental and emotional health.

This book is intended for academics, students, psychotherapy trainees, counselors, psychiatrists, psychiatric nurse practitioners, psychologists, social workers and psychotherapists of any stripe. Meditation teachers as well as Buddhist chaplains curious about ways to address individual psychological issues may also find it of benefit. With its comprehensive overviews of each approach, it is accessible for those new to these ideas and also in-depth enough to add understanding for those with previous knowledge and experience of Buddhist psychology and Gestalt therapy. It offers specifics for psychotherapists of any theoretical orientation who are interested in integrating aspects of these views and practices into clinical work. For Gestalt therapists who have not yet discovered the rich possibilities in Buddhist psychology and its meditation practices to support and enhance Gestalt therapy work, we lay out the terrain to be explored. And for all those intrigued by the possibility of an expanded, integrated psychotherapy system, we offer theoretical support for this integration, along with methods for its application that we hope offer ideas, support and direction for taking the exploration further. The training model we present, based on the Buddhist psychology and Gestalt therapy training program we have offered for the past ten years, will be of particular interest to Gestalt therapy trainers as well as to any teachers, trainers, or supervisors interested in incorporating these important and powerful ways of teaching and cultivating therapeutic skills for the next generation of psychotherapists.

Each section of the book creates the ground for the next. Part I is an introduction to and overview of Buddhist psychology views and meditation methods, and Part II covers Gestalt therapy theory and practice. Part III details the convergences of these two systems' views and methods, along with the clinical implications of these convergences. Part IV explores an expansion into new directions for Gestalt therapy, a Buddhist psychology informed Gestalt therapy (BPGT) approach. Part IV also incudes an integrated model for psychotherapist training.

We discuss how this integration enhances the therapist's personal and professional growth and the overall training experience, as well as laying the groundwork for practicing from a BPGT perspective.

As in any process of putting evolving ideas onto the page where they appear static, these words reflect a particular point in our understanding of the intersection of these two rich and multifaceted systems. As you read, we encourage you to consider this as a living co-created process, an invitation to engage in your own exploration. We are happy to have the opportunity to share this path that has been, and continues to be, so rich for us. And we are grateful to all of you whose interest in increasing awareness and expanding our human potential leads you to meet us here. We wish you wisdom and compassion in your work, and ease and joy on your own transformative journey.

BUDDHIST PSYCHOLOGY
& GESTALT THERAPY
INTEGRATED

PART I

Buddhist Psychology & Meditation Practices

1

Introduction to Buddhist Psychology

> *Early Buddhist thought has little interest in conceptual speculation ... choosing instead to cleave to a rigorous empirical phenomenology. What one can actually see unfolding under scrutiny of the moment is considered to be of far more interest and use than theorizing from abstractions.*
>
> ——Andrew Olendzki, "The Roots of Mindfulness"

AN IN-DEPTH UNDERSTANDING of Buddhism requires a lifetime of study and practice. Some say many lifetimes! Although Western psychology has focused primarily on its meditative practices, particularly mindfulness, Buddhist psychology like Gestalt therapy, is a complete, dynamic and interrelated system for growth and transformation. In this section, we outline Buddhist psychology views, and the path of which mindfulness is an essential element, but only one element. This broad perspective includes the original aim of Buddhist psychology. That is, the radical psychological transformation that can lead us toward more wisdom, compassion, and ultimately freedom from suffering.

Following this introduction, Chapters 2 and 3 outline the basics of Buddhist psychology views and practices. The Buddhist literature is too vast to allow a comprehensive or in-depth consideration here. Instead, we outline basic concepts and practices most relevant for what we reference later in the book. Our study and practice has been primarily through Western teachers and writers in the Insight (*Vipassana*) tradition that derives from Theravada Buddhism, and these chapters reflect our own understanding and distillation of this perspective. These ideas are basic to appreciating the convergences of Buddhist psychology and Gestalt therapy that we lay out, and the integration that we propose.

Importantly, it is not possible to fully grasp these views and practices through an intellectual understanding alone. Just as reading a description of a sunset is not the same as watching a sunset, Buddhist psychology, like Gestalt therapy, relies on the experiential. If you are not already practicing meditation, we recommend exploring the various meditation practices offered here, as well as others that can be found through the resources section at the end of this book. Exploring guided meditations, listening to talks by Buddhist teachers, and reading will allow you to continue to expand your knowledge and appreciation of the power, depth, and breadth of these teachings and practices.

A Buddhist Psychology Perspective

Buddhism is often described as a major world religion, and many people and cultures around the world practice it as a religion or as a spiritual path. However, many Buddhist practitioners, writers, and teachers emphasize that what Buddhism offers is a *psychological* understanding of the human heart and mind and the situation we find ourselves in. Buddhist practices allow us to understand suffering, and it offers methods for alleviating that suffering, as well as for enhancing well-being. Buddhism is non-theistic, relying on no deities, gods, or belief systems. Rather, its views and practices offer a path of inquiry that places primary importance on experiential understanding; the change that occurs in this process is a psychological one that involves feelings, thoughts, and behavior. In addition to meditation practices, other aspects of the Buddhist path include practicing non-harming and skillful ways of being, and the cultivation of qualities like wisdom and compassion, all considered necessary, from the Buddhist psychology perspective, to mental health and well-being.

Buddhism's psychological understanding is based in a surprisingly postmodern view of human consciousness, grounded in a process perspective of "noncentralized, interdependent systems for processing sense data and constructing identity" (Olendzki, 2005, p. 242). This basic understanding is that the nature of our human existence includes inevitable pain, the impossibility of lasting pleasure, and a tendency to not fully or clearly see or understand the reality of either our situation or ourselves. Because of this perspective and the emphasis on awareness and direct experience, the problems or questions posed by this tradition, and the remedies it points us toward, are psychologically oriented. Buddhist psychology doctrine offers observations of the nature of mind rather than an imposed belief system. In the words of Tibetan Buddhist teacher Lama Yeshe, "Buddhist teachings are basically applied psychology. Buddhism teaches the nature of suffering at the mental level and the methods for its eradication" (Yeshe, 1998, p. 55).

The Dalai Lama also describes Buddhist teachings as a science of mind not a religion. He has said that if there are conflicts between Buddhist ideas and scientific facts, then Buddhism must reconsider its position. Many Buddhist teachers and writers also emphasize that the same awakened state attained by the Buddha is available to us all. According to one legend, when the Buddha was asked, "What are you? Are you a man? Are you a god?" the Buddha replied, "I am awake." The Sanskrit word "buddha" translates as "one who is awake." Psychologist and Buddhist teacher Jack Kornfield, who has had a major influence in translating Buddhist psychology teachings and practices for

Western practitioners, posits that actually "Buddhism is not a religion according to its dictionary meaning because it has no center in God…. Buddhism is a system of philosophy, coordinated with a code of morality, physical and mental" (Kornfield, 1996, p. 238).

Buddhist practices can take us from the experience of suffering based on misunderstanding and confusion to more insight, clarity and, ultimately, inner freedom. This shift is understood to occur via a radical psychological transformation. Buddhist psychology encourages focusing on our physical and mental processes and the ways we can understand these. References to suffering in Buddhist teachings refer to mental suffering created in our minds, suffering that we have the ability to transform. Psychological and existential suffering are related to causes and conditions that include basic human impulses, like the reflex to seek pleasure and avoid pain. If these remain out of awareness, we are at their mercy. If we can see and understand them and their effect clearly, we can impact the causes and conditions that lead to our suffering or to our well-being. Following this path, we gain awareness of our own psychological functioning, as well as understanding universal human experience more deeply.

Buddhist psychology, like Gestalt therapy, is broad and inclusive, addressing the body, cognition, emotion, and consciousness. The practices support inquiry into direct experience, just as experiential psychotherapy does. Buddhist psychology is also practical and pragmatic, offering guidelines for living. These guide us away from thoughts and actions that contribute to unnecessary suffering for ourselves and others and point us toward ways of being that enhance our own and others' well-being. Beliefs are not required for this, but what is required is the willingness to look deeply into our own experience. Discovering the truth of the teachings through direct experience is a cornerstone of the practices. Buddhist psychology, like Gestalt therapy, stresses the importance of understanding "what is happening here and now ... comprehending our present experiences, what we are in this very moment, our fundamental nature" (Yeshe, 1998, p.26). Thus, many Buddhist practitioners, teachers, and scholars, particularly in the West, emphasize the primacy of psychological exploration and transformation in both Buddhist teachings and practices. This secular view aligns with our perspective. From this viewpoint, what we propose integrating in psychotherapy is not religion, and requires no adherence to any belief system. To maintain this clarity, throughout this book we refer to Buddhist psychology rather than Buddhism.

Still, this leaves us with the question of the relationship between what is generally considered psychological, and what is thought of as spiritual. As Western psychologists exploring integrating elements of this ancient Eastern wisdom tradition, do we have to consider the psychological and the spiritual as essentially separate and different aspects of our humanity? The Buddha's deep understanding about human experience clearly emerged from a profound ability to sustain inner contemplation, and to grasp important truths of human existence. And yet, according to many sources, the Buddha claimed only to be a teacher and to teach only one thing—suffering and the end of suffering. And the Buddha laid out this path in practical steps for anyone to follow. So, the perspective we take here is that rather than seeing psychological growth and spiritual transformation as necessarily distinct, we look at this as a unified path of development and evolution. To heal, grow, flourish, and reach our potential, we need to address both individual psychological issues and engage in study and practices that help us reach a deeper more expanded understanding of our human existence. This suggests a continuum of human development, rather than a psychological/spiritual division. For example, as Kornfield points out, Buddhist psychology includes iconic images, such as of the Buddha or of Kuan Yin—a symbol for one who is motivated by compassion for all beings. However, from a Buddhist psychology perspective, these likenesses do not have to be seen as icons to be worshipped but are rather symbols of qualities we aspire to and can ourselves embody, qualities such as love, wisdom and compassion (Kornfield, 2008). They can be viewed as part of the Buddhist psychology, "technology for changing consciousness" (Kornfield, 2008, p. 276). This is the ground for the integrated Buddhist psychology informed Gestalt therapy (BPGT) approach that we propose.

Some Western Buddhist teachers have emphasized meditation practices primarily and focused less on other aspects of the Buddhist path. And many Western psychologists have narrowed the focus even more to a secular mindfulness practice, often aimed at symptom reduction. Although mindfulness meditation has many benefits, this narrowed focus leaves out aspects of the Buddhist psychology path and its practices that are seen as essential to mental health, well-being, and liberation. These teachings and practices are part of a unified path, and as a whole develop understanding and discernment, and help us put this knowledge into practice with skillful action. In this book we are interested in maintaining the integrity of this unified path as we explore this integration, and again this does not require a belief system or adherence to dogma. On the contrary, like experiential psychotherapies, Buddhist psychology supports personal exploration and experimentation. Buddhist teachings instruct students to both take the advice of wise teachers and to value the truth of their own experience.

Depending on our perspective, the Buddha can be seen as a "liberal, ethical reformer, a great secular humanist, a radical empiricist, an existential psychologist, or a proponent of a broad agnosticism" (Bodhi, 2005, p. 43). Buddhist ideas and practices have been extracted, interpreted, and practiced differently in different countries and diverse cultures throughout history. Often rituals and cultural overlays have been integrated, and different perspectives have emphasized different aspects of the teachings and practices. Western psychology is now engaged in this process as well, with its extraction, secularization, and embrace of practices like mindfulness. Inevitably we see through the lens of our current perspective and culture, and for both Western psychology and Buddhist psychology this current point of meeting provides rich opportunity for ongoing exploration.

Historical Context
Theravada Buddhism
When we refer to Buddhist psychology in this book, we are primarily referencing the teachings that have come from Theravada Buddhism, a significant Buddhist influence on the West. Theravada, which is translated "School of the Elders," is one of three major branches of Buddhism. It encompasses the first teachings of the Buddha, stretching from the earliest period of Buddhist history to about 100 years after the Buddha's death when the original Buddhist community divided into different schools, around 385 BCE.

Theravada Buddhists believe that these are the teachings that were originally given by the historical Buddha. This branch of Buddhism comes primarily from Southeast Asia, including Thailand and Burma (now Myanmar). The two other schools are Mahayana, which includes Zen Buddhism—originally from China and subsequently spreading to Korea and Japan—and Vajrayana, with its origins in Tibet. In each of these schools there are numerous other divisions. The founders of Gestalt therapy were exposed to and influenced by Zen Buddhism in Japan, and some of its principles were incorporated into Gestalt therapy. There are many similar and overlapping views and methods among the different schools of Buddhist practice, and often the differences are only in emphasis or focus. Although we also quote from teachers in both the Zen and Vajrayana traditions, this overview focuses on the basics of Buddhist psychology from the Theravada tradition, as taught by our Western teachers, and other writers.

The Buddha spent forty-five years teaching, and although disagreement among scholars exists, he likely did so somewhere between 530 and 485 BCE. The Buddha's discourses were memorized and recited by his followers, so that the teachings were passed on via an oral tradition until they were ultimately recorded in writing. In the 3rd century BCE, Buddhist missionaries brought the teachings of the Buddha to Sri Lanka. Theravada Buddhism also spread to other Southeast Asian countries around this time. The teachings were written down in a language that is now referred to as Pali, and this written record, likely created about 400 years after the death of the historical Buddha, is called the Pali Canon. These teachings have been the primal source for all the evolving streams of Buddhist doctrine and practice—the common heritage of the entire Buddhist tradition (Bodhi, 2005).

Theravada Buddhism is practiced throughout Southeast Asia, and it began to have a major impact in the West in the 1960s and 1970s as Westerners who studied and practiced in India, Thailand, and Burma brought their teachers and aspects of these teachings and methods to the United States and other Western countries. Teachers such as Jack Kornfield, Joseph Goldstein, Sharon Salzberg, and Jacqueline Mandell Schwartz, founders of the Insight Meditation Society in Barre, Massachusetts, in the 1970s, were instrumental in bringing Insight (*Vipassana*) meditation practices to the United States. Many Western health and mental health professionals learned from and were influenced by these and other teachers and were inspired by their experiences to bring these practices into their own work. Jon Kabat-Zinn, founder of the Stress Reduction Clinic and the Center for Mindfulness in Medicine, Health Care, and Society, began teaching Mindfulness Based Stress Reduction (MBSR) to patients at the University of Massachusetts Medical School in the late 1970s and was instrumental in bringing this modality into the mainstream of behavioral health practices, as well as pioneering research in these methods. More recently, mindfulness has become prominent in its influence on psychotherapy research and practice, healthcare, and business.

Life of the Buddha

Siddhartha Gautama, the historical Buddha, was reportedly born in Lumbini in what is now Nepal some time around 550 BCE. Siddhartha means "he who achieves his aim," and Gautama was the family name. He is referred to by this name until his enlightenment, after which he is referred to as the Buddha, the Awakened One. He is also referred to as Sakyamuni, which means "sage of the Sakyas" (Sakya is a clan name). His father was said to be a powerful leader, and his mother, who is believed to have died seven days after he was born, a princess by birth. In addition to documented facts related to Siddhartha Gautama's birth, many legends sprung up about this event, as well as others in his life. One popular image is the baby Siddhartha being born perfectly clean and on his feet, walking seven steps. Each place his feet touched the ground, a lotus flower grew, and he proclaimed this to be his last birth. It is said that many wondrous signs also accompanied this birth, such as stars and lights in the sky, and trees flowering out of season.

These, along with the stories of the Brahmin priests who were called to read the auspicious signs and tell the child's future, bear similarities to the stories surrounding the birth of Jesus Christ. These also reflect the ongoing psychology/ religion dichotomy of the Buddha as an ordinary person who achieved awakening, and as a being attended by supernatural events and miracles. Along these lines, there are also stories of the Buddha's lives prior to his last human birth. While many teachings emphasize that the Buddha's awakening is possible for all of us, there are those who believe he had been on the journey to enlightenment over many lifetimes, living out his destiny to become a great teacher for humankind. Again, it is useful to keep in mind that belief in the supernatural or miraculous is not required to benefit from these teachings and practices.

According to legend, at the time of the Buddha's birth, a seer foretold that he would either become a great leader or leave the palace to become a seeker of truth and wisdom, renouncing his worldly inheritance. Siddhartha Gautama's father, who wanted his son to become that great leader and inherit his kingdom, never allowed Siddhartha to leave his compound, or to witness any illness, death, or other suffering. As a result, Siddhartha lived his early life protected from painful aspects of human experience, surrounded by luxury. Reportedly, he was showered with every comfort and pleasure imaginable, living in one lavish palace during the rainy season and another during the dry season, surrounded by servants, beautiful women, lovely blooming gardens, and delectable food. However, at age 29 when he escaped the palace walls and saw an old person, a sick person, and a corpse, he immediately understood that no one escapes these fates. He is also said to have seen a wandering ascetic representing a path by which suffering could be overcome. These four people that Siddhartha saw are referred to as the Four Messengers. Soon afterward, he determined to understand the source of human suffering and how to alleviate it.

This story of the Buddha's early life can be seen as a metaphor for how we all live, sheltered within the delusion that we can protect ourselves from life's difficult realities. The process of psychologically waking up, whether through psychotherapy or meditation practices, requires leaving the protection of the "palace" of our limiting concepts, beliefs, and comfortable habits, along with the illusion of the safety that these provide, confronting the truths of our existence and developing greater awareness.

For many years Siddhartha Gautama reportedly tried a variety of practices, including an ascetic existence during which he ate so little that he almost died of starvation. He came to realize that this extreme practice was not the way to true understanding, and he decided instead to follow the Middle Way, a path of moderation. In Bodh Gaya, India, he resolved to sit under a bodhi tree until he gained enlightened understanding. It is said that he remembered a time from his childhood when he rested in the shade of a rose apple tree and felt a profound sense of peace and contentment. He realized that this feeling might point to what he was searching for. During his forty-nine days under the bodhi tree, Siddhartha is said to have battled the forces of Mara. Mara can be interpreted as either a literal demon, or as a metaphor for the psychological forces of doubt and temptation that must be fully understood and seen through in order to attain awakening and realize an end to suffering. Histories of the Buddha indicate that at the end of the forty-nine days, at the age of thirty-five, Siddhartha attained enlightenment.

The Buddha's teachings are referred to as the *dharma* (in Sanskrit) or *dhamma* (in Pali), and the Buddha's first *dharma* talk, in Deer Park in northern India, set out the Four Noble Truths. We discuss these in Chapter 2. It is generally agreed that the Buddha lived to be eighty years old. Some consider all of his teachings over the next forty-five years to be elaborations on this first discourse. These would impact millions of people, and they can offer us essential wisdom and guidance today, as relevant and profound as they were 2600 years ago.

As you read the following two chapters, particularly if you are unfamiliar with Buddhist psychology and meditation, we suggest you first read to get the big picture of the views and their connection to the practices. You may need to refer back to these chapters when we make reference to and discuss these concepts later in the book. This overview provides the needed foundation for considering the intersection of Buddhist psychology and Gestalt therapy and the clinical implications of this intersection as well as the proposed integration.

2

Buddhist Psychology Views

Our most insistent existential demand ... is the need
for freedom from harm, sorrow, and distress ... or the
need to achieve well-being and happiness. However ...
to avoid harm and secure our well-being ... we have
to understand the conditions on which they depend.
　　　—Bhikkhu Bodhi, *In the Buddha's Words: An*
　　　　　Anthology of Discourses from the Pali Canon

THE BUDDHA'S CENTRAL INSIGHT was that life's unavoidable pain is amplified by the workings of the human mind. No one can avoid the inevitable pain of being human, the inevitable losses of old age, sickness and death. But the Buddha recognized that events, situations, or experience—although they may be painful—do not themselves directly cause suffering. While pain, loss, and disappointment are part of life, the Buddha saw that how we relate to situations and to ourselves is what creates and perpetuates suffering. Freedom from this suffering is found in following the Buddha's prescriptive path.

Buddhist psychology makes this important distinction between *pain* and *suffering*. While pain is an intrinsic part of our human existence, the added mind-created suffering is in *how* we relate to our experiences and this pain. Responses that lead to suffering may take the form of rejecting our current experience, denying the reality we are faced with, or craving an ideal self or situation.

I'm not supposed to get sick—why me? Life is so unfair. I can't stand this; when will it get better? I can't survive without my partner—I never thought I'd end up divorced. I'm tired of feeling so depressed; why can't I just be happy? I am such a failure. I just have to be stronger; I have to get over this and move on. Will I ever be different? What is wrong with me?

The Buddha clarified this important distinction between pain and suffering in asking his disciples whether, if shot with an arrow, they would feel pain. Of course, they answered yes. He then asked: If a second arrow struck you, would that increase the pain? Once again, the answer was yes. He saw the "first arrow" as the physical pain or primary emotional pain that is part of being human. He saw the "second arrow" as one that we shoot at ourselves in reaction to the first, the optional suffering.

We regularly see this "second arrow" suffering in our psychotherapy patients.* For example, as we listen to the patient who is in pain and struggling with job stress, financial worries, or a troubled relationship, we hear an added layer of suffering in the form of self-criticalness and self-blame. The patient thinks she should be managing better, or she compares her life and accomplishments to others. We may see this "second arrow" suffering revealed in symptoms like anxiety, depression, stress, and addiction. This is the process that we investigate, work with, and have an impact on in psychotherapy. This is also the suffering addressed through Buddhist psychology's understanding and practices.

The desire to have things a certain way, or wanting things to be permanent when nothing is, are natural human reactions. We

---

* We use the word "patient" throughout this text, although some psychotherapists see "client" as reflecting a more humanistic or egalitarian view of the psychotherapy relationship. For us, patient, with its Latin root meaning "one who suffers," more closely describes those who engage in this intimate and healing relationship to ease suffering and restore well-being.

have evolved to seek comfort and pleasure and to avoid pain; our very survival depends on this. However, from Buddhist psychology's perspective, when these natural responses drive clinging and craving or aversion, they contribute to the causes and conditions that lead to suffering. We cling to things even as they are slipping through our fingers or grasp for something that is out of reach. Or we respond with aversion to something painful or unpleasant, and attempt to get rid of, ignore, or avoid it. It is in avoiding our pain, and in not seeing clearly the truth of this existence, that we shoot ourselves with the "second arrow" of suffering.

This process also drives the hatred, aggression, and greed that we see on a global scale wreaking havoc with our planet and our ability to live together in safety and harmony. Buddhist psychology holds out the promise of transformation of this personal and collective suffering. It offers a path that helps open our eyes to the givens or truths of existence, helping us see that suffering is in the opposition to how things are and proposing practices that cultivate qualities that are part of the antidote to suffering. From a Buddhist psychology perspective, not only freedom from suffering but also greater peace and joy are available to us if we follow this path.

In this chapter we outline Buddhist psychology views. First we describe the four truths, which address human suffering, then the eightfold path, a prescription for ending suffering. Next, we outline Buddhist psychology's understanding of the three characteristics of existence, and related to these the understanding of dependent origination and freedom from suffering. Then we describe the five aggregates, the eight worldly conditions (not to be confused with the eightfold path), the three refuges, the five precepts, and the four heart abodes. Buddhism has a lot of lists! No need to try to remember all of these. You can refer back to them as they come up in later chapters. Finally, we end this chapter with a discussion of Buddhist psychology's understanding of universal and relative reality.

Four Noble Truths
The first teaching the Buddha offered after his enlightenment was these four truths. They address human suffering and its cause; they let us know that freedom from suffering is possible; and they point us toward a path that can lead to this freedom.

1. *Suffering or unsatisfactoriness (dukkha) is inherent in human existence.*
This truth points to the reality that being born into this human body, we are subject to old age, sickness, and death. All that we strive for is impermanent, and we will ultimately lose everything. Even when we do attain comfort or satisfaction, it is temporary, as all conditioned phenomena are inherently unreliable in providing lasting security or satisfaction, and the most positive of circumstance and experience will ultimately change. Although this should not be interpreted to mean that all of living is only suffering, this basic unsatisfactoriness exists.

2. *The cause of suffering is ignorance that manifests as attachment—grasping, craving and clinging, or aversion.*
We misunderstand the truth of our situation and misperceive the nature of reality, failing to recognize the truths of existence. This results in the ongoing striving for experiences of satisfaction and pleasure or to avoid pain, based in greed, hatred, and delusion. Unaware of the futility of this strategy, our desires and preferences result in grasping or craving for what we do not have, clinging to what is impermanent, or aversion to and trying to get rid of what we have or what we experience that we do not want. Being in opposition to what is, we suffer.

3. *Freedom from suffering is possible.*

Although pain is inevitable, suffering is not. As we cultivate the conditions for wisdom and clear seeing, we discover how to live in harmony with what is, without adding the "second arrow" suffering. It is possible to find peace even within the reality of the truth of *dukkha*. This does not mean we will not experience pain or loss, or that we will not actively seek to change unjust conditions or alleviate painful circumstances for others or ourselves. Rather it means we meet experience without opposition, and we increase our capacity to act skillfully in light of the circumstances we face.

4. *The path to liberation and freedom from suffering is the eightfold path.*

The Buddha laid out this path, in which all eight factors point us toward freedom from suffering. The Buddha was not abstract or speculative, but empirical and pragmatic. The four truths actually follow the steps of a medical model. The Buddha diagnosed the problem and defined the cause, then determined the prognosis and prescribed the course of treatment.

Noble Eightfold Path

The Buddha's prescription for finding freedom from suffering and realizing our innate capacity for wisdom and compassion is the eightfold path. The path encourages us not to avoid or deny pain, but rather to meet, investigate, and deeply understand it. This parallels psychotherapy's view that what we have avoided has to be directly faced for there to be change or healing. This path is not a series of linear steps. Rather these eight components form a unified system, with each aspect supporting the others, and every element of the path contributing to mental health and well-being. They are "comparable to the intertwining strands of a single cable that requires the contributions of all the strands for maximum strength" (Bodhi, 1994, p. 13).

The first two aspects of the path involve wisdom and discernment—right view and right intention—seeing things as they are and intending to follow the path and to cultivate understanding. The next three aspects relate to right conduct in the world—speech, action, and livelihood. The last 3 parts of the path relate to meditative practices—energy, mindfulness, and concentration. Here we see that mindfulness practice is an important element of the path but does not stand alone. In this prescription each component of the path offers practices that cultivate and develop essential mental factors, behaviors, or qualities that support moving toward freedom from suffering.

With practice, the capacity for these ways of being and experiencing increase, so that following the path becomes a natural inclination, and we become more aware of the impact of our actions, behavior, and attitudes. Paying attention to what happens as we follow (or do not follow) the prescription, we see cause and effect more clearly. Engaging with the practices, and cultivating these qualities, allows us to develop a happier and more peaceful life that benefits others as well as ourselves.

1. Understanding/View

Right view involves directly apprehending the Four Truths and recognizing the three characteristics of existence (described below in the next section). Right view means understanding reality as it is; knowing that ignorance results in the attachment that leads to suffering and knowing that there is a path to peace and freedom. It includes seeing that actions have consequences. This view informs all aspects of the path.

2. *Intention*

This refers to the motivation for action, sometimes described as "aspiration." For example, understanding that craving leads to suffering encourages us to attend to its arising. We also aspire to live a life of non-harming, with an intention to learn and grow in our understanding. Right intention can be a commitment to walk this path, attending to all aspects of it.

3. *Speech*

Speech is powerful and can be beneficial or damaging. This aspect of the path invites us to look at our speech based on its potential benefit or harm to self and others. We can undertake this training by being willing to practice avoiding false, harsh, or malicious speech. We can consider whether what we say is honest, truthful, timely, and beneficial. The intention, as with all action, is also important—we may say something that is painful or difficult for someone to hear, but our intention can be either to help or to harm.

4. *Action*

Actions can result in benefit or harm to others and ourselves. Beneficial actions are also referred to as "right conduct." Generally, this aspect invites us to reflect on our actions and cultivate ways of being that are of benefit to ourselves and others and that do not contribute to harming.

5. *Livelihood*

In moving toward freedom from suffering, this aspect of the path points to the importance of earning our living at work that is legal, non-violent, and ideally that benefits both one's self and others without causing harm to people, animals, or the environment. In what we do every day, we can seek to embody qualities and behaviors that are beneficial, like honesty and fairness, with all those we come in contact with.

6. *Effort*

This is the mental discipline to notice and respond skillfully to the tendencies of the mind that impair the ability to practice all elements of the path. This includes the particular effort that contributes to supporting and maintaining meditation practice. In this, balance is a key element.

7. *Mindfulness*

The quality of mindfulness that is cultivated in mindfulness meditation involves the capacity for present moment awareness of what is happening as it is happening. It is the ability to observe present experience as it arises with a "bare attention," free of evaluation and judgment. This takes intentional training. The practices that strengthen and cultivate mindfulness can ultimately lead to clearly comprehending what is occurring here and now, and the nature of reality and phenomena. Mindfulness can be practiced in formal meditation, as well as in all our daily activities, to train the mind toward present moment awareness.

8. *Concentration*

The quality of concentration, the capacity to sustain focused attention on a single object, enhances stillness and clarity of mind. This ability is strengthened in concentration practices by bringing the mind back to the object of focus each time we become aware that attention has shifted, strengthening our ability for one-pointedness of attention. This practice can lead to experience in which the mind becomes clear, tranquil, and luminous. When integrated with mindfulness, concentration contributes to insight and wisdom.

Often Western practitioners and Western psychology focus exclusively on meditation, with the other path elements left out, losing the richness and depth of the entire path for supporting transformation. In Chapter 11 we will consider how additional path elements can be integrated into BPGT's expanded approach.

Three Characteristics of Existence (*Dharma* Seals)

According to Buddhist psychology, everything in our experience has these three characteristics or givens: impermanence (*anicca*), unsatisfactoriness (*dukkha*), and not-self (*anatta*). These marks of existence reflect Buddhist psychology's understanding of universal or absolute truth, and they relate directly to the four truths, providing a perspective on the nature of phenomena and suffering. These three characteristics are essentially interrelated. As we look at each one, we see the emergence of and interconnection with the others. While we can describe these concepts, they are also necessarily seen clearly and known directly through experience and meditative practices.

1. *Impermanence*

The very nature of existence is change. Everything that is born will also die. All things are the result of particular causes and conditions that are constantly in flux. We more easily notice impermanence (*anicca*) and this change process when it happens quickly. For example, over the course of a few days, we can see a bud first opening into a flower, then begin to whither, drop its petals, and die. Other change processes are slower and may be so gradual or subtle that we cannot detect them. It is hard to recognize how we are growing older each day, yet when we see someone whom we have not seen in twenty years, or look at childhood photographs of ourselves, impermanence is apparent. When we pay attention to beginnings and endings, we see they are everywhere. In meditation practice we can notice this with each breath.

2. Unsatisfactoriness

The Buddha made the reality of *dukkha* the foundation of his teaching, as described in the first noble truth. Although *dukkha* is sometimes translated as "suffering," there is no direct English translation that encompasses its full meaning. *Dukkha* goes beyond pain or unhappiness and refers to the unsatisfactoriness inherent in conditioned existence that runs through the lives of all but the enlightened (Bodhi, 1994). *Dukkha* is the inevitable emotional and physical pain and discomfort associated with having a body and experiencing birth, old age, sickness, and death. *Dukkha* is also in our reaction to the experiences of grief, sorrow, pain, and loss. Even life's beauty and happiness are fleeting, and all of our accomplishments can still leave us feeling we have not done enough. Then we age and die, losing everything.

The Buddha deeply understood the human reflex to seek comfort and pleasure and to avoid pain. Observing this, he recognized that while emotional and physical pain may be unavoidable, we also add unnecessary suffering as we move through life driven by this process but unaware of and therefore trapped within it. When we attempt to hold onto something that is impermanent, we suffer. Whenever we yearn for our experience to be other than what it is, we suffer. Actual peace and contentment are rare, or may always appear just out of our reach.

3. Not-Self

In Buddhist psychology, *anatta*, or not-self, refers to the absence of any essential, enduring, independent self-identity. Believing in a separate, essential self is seen as a misunderstanding. This view does not deny that every individual's life has a sense of personal continuity. However, this sense of self that we experience is actually understood from the Buddhist psychology perspective as being comprised of five psychosomatic aggregates (described in detail below). The "self" is understood as arising from the interplay of these aggregates rather than existing as any permanent, solid, ontological entity (Watson, 2000). If we attempt to find the essence of our self in either the body or mind, we find the interdependence of these aggregates. Due to our lack of awareness of the interdependent and impermanent nature of these aggregates and all phenomena, this dynamic experience of ever-changing processes is grasped as a solid, separate entity.

Buddhist psychology recognizes self as process, the "how" rather than the "what." Understanding not-self and the illusory nature of all phenomena does not mean that these phenomena do not exist or that we do not exist. It is our perception of our apparent solid and independent nature that is mistaken. From a Buddhist psychology perspective, then, we engage in a process of "selfing," in which a dynamic experience of constantly changing process is erroneously grasped as an entity that contains the ongoing experience.

In the course of development, a child learns to perceive the world as consisting of stable objects that can be known, and to gradually build an identity. "The sense of identity ... and the notion ... of the world is regarded by the Buddhist tradition as an elaborate construction project.... Ours is a universe of macroconstruction, in which the continually arising data of the senses ... are channeled into structures and organized into schemas that support an entirely synthetic sphere of meaning—a virtual reality"(Olendzki, 2005, p. 244). In mindfulness meditation, we begin to discover this process of construction. As we sit and pay attention to experience, we become more aware of the arising and passing away of thoughts, feelings, perceptions, and bodily sensations that we mistakenly take to be a single, coherent, separate, and continuous self.

Buddhist psychology distinguishes between a working sense of self or continuity, and a reified self-concept that we super-impose on this. Our sense of self is a combination of thoughts, feelings, perceptions, and sensations; we are a body, and have consciousness, but our sense of a self-identity is created. At any moment, a sense of self is a contingent and dependent phenom-enon. When we pay close attention to our experience in the moment, we discover that it is constantly shifting. Thoughts and feelings arise and pass away. We may be watching a sad movie at home and crying; but a moment later the movie ends, and we receive a phone call from an old friend and feel happy. We see that any particular self-experience does not stay fixed—another manifestation of impermanence.

Nagasena, a monk who lived in the 2nd century BCE, demon-strated the impossibility of finding the essence or independent existence of self by making a simple comparison. He pointed out that it is impossible to find the "essence" of a chariot. The chariot is made up of elements, not one of which is the essence of the vehicle—not the wheels, not the axle, not the seat. In order for the chariot to exist, all the parts are required. When all the parts are present and operational, the chariot exists and is a useful conveyance.

This, of course, doesn't mean that we don't each have a sense of personal history and continuity throughout our life-time, an "autobiographical self." I (Eva) remember my child-hood, and the dress I wore to my best friend's birthday party when I was five. If I look in the mirror at my sixty-six-year-old face, I see the eyes of the child in the photograph taken at that party. In Buddhist psychology the understanding of not-self in no way negates this sense of personal continuity and memory. Understanding the not-self view is essential, however, because our belief in a reified self, and our identification with it, becomes the ground of the "three poisons" of greed, hatred, and delusion—that engender suffering.

Dependent Origination

The idea of dependent origination elaborates further on the essential interrelatedness of the three characteristics of existence, impermanence, unsatisfactoriness, and not-self. This is the understanding that all phenomena arise only due to causes and conditions that also arise. Everything that exists is part of a complex web or field, never occurring in isolation. This recognition also aligns with Gestalt therapy's field theoretical understanding described in Chapter 5. Everything and everyone is dependent on particular conditions in order to exist. One way of understanding dependent origination is to think of life on earth, and what would happen to it without the sun, rain, or wind. All of these conditions are necessary to sustain life as it is. And because everything is in constant flux, things, including ourselves, constantly come into being and cease to be. It is not possible to separate anything that exists from its causes and conditions. As all conditioned things are transient and impermanent, they are essentially unsatisfactory and potentially a source of suffering. The three givens of impermanence, unsatisfactoriness, and not-self are reflected in the empirical truth of dependent origination.

Freedom from Suffering

The Buddha taught a path leading to ultimate freedom but also a path "leading to the various types of wholesome, mundane, happiness to which human beings aspire" (Bodhi, 2005, p. 45). Therefore, following the teachings that lead toward this ultimate freedom also "enables sentient beings to plant wholesome roots productive of happiness, peace, and security in the worldly dimension of their lives..." (Bodhi, 2005, p. 45). Believing that naturally transient things have an ability to bring lasting satisfaction leads to suffering. Seeking to maximize pleasure and to minimize pain is human nature, but left unexamined, these reflexive responses sentence us to the ongoing pursuit of short-term aims with necessarily limited results. Wisdom lies in recognizing this, and to whatever degree we gain insight into this process, we have more freedom. Following the eightfold path and its practices, we plant the seeds of happiness, peace, and less suffering.

Recognizing that there is no separate, essential, enduring self helps us see all of what arises in experience as less personal. If we understand what sustains *dukkha*, we can begin to free ourselves from being caught in identification and craving for the continuously arising objects of desire, which in Buddhist teaching is referred to as *samsara*. Recognizing the characteristics of existence, not just intellectually but via our own experience, points us toward the possibility of freedom as we see that nothing is permanent or fixed, including our experience of self. It is then possible to respond to both pleasurable and painful experience skillfully rather than reactively.

Five Aggregates (*Skandhas*)

Buddhist psychology breaks down all perception and experience, including what we conceive of as "self," into these component parts, or aggregates. From this perspective, all that exists is an ongoing flow of these five aggregates, interconnected phenomena that are always shifting and changing. What we perceive and who we experience ourselves to be is understood as aggregates in constant flux, producing any experience. Looking through this lens, we recognize the absence of fixed entities including "self." This perspective is key in Buddhist psychology's understanding as it allows the ground of identification and grasping to dissolve, creating freedom from attachment, and pointing toward a way out of suffering. In Chapter 7, we look at how this recognition of the aggregates converges with Gestalt therapy's understanding of self as process and with its field phenomenological view.

The five aggregates are: form, sense impression, perception, categorization, and consciousness. These are the building blocks involved in constructing our experience, including a sense of personal identity. These aggregates are the ground of both identification and appropriation—basic activities by which our sense of selfhood is established and maintained. They are co-arising, co-existing, and co-vanishing phenomena. As the aggregates arise, exist, and vanish, thoughts, feelings, and perceptions bubble up within us, transmitting energy and impressions. It is our continual grasping that allows us to mistake this flow for fixity, creating an apparently stable self to identify with, and a seemingly solid external reality (Wolfert, 2000).

1. *Form*

Form includes the body—the organs of perception (eye, ear, nose, tongue, skin)—and all material elements—the corresponding physical objects that can be seen, heard, smelled, tasted, and touched. The body is not a fixed entity, as it can seem to be, but a continuum of the aggregate of matter coexisting with life force. While any form, for example a rock, may appear solid and motionless, it is actually composed of sub-atomic particles in a state of perpetual flux. Similarly, we don't generally sense our own bodies as energy, movement and vibration, but in deeply concentrated states available to us in meditation, we can attune to the subtle nuances that allow this awareness.

2. *Sense Impression*

Sense impression is whatever we experience via the senses and can include an accompanying feeling tone. The feeling tone may be pleasant, leading to the desire to continue the experience. Or the feeling tone may be unpleasant, leading to aversion or the desire to avoid or get away from the experience. The feeling tone may also be neutral, eliciting neither of these responses.

3. Perception

Perception is the process whereby we turn random sensations that bombard our senses into a specific concept or recognized experience. This involves a number of associative functions that are learned gradually over time and conditioned by individual history, as well as by factors like language and culture, so that every experience is processed in light of previous experience and understanding. This means that there is no process of accurate and passive "registration" of an external world by the senses, but rather a creative construction and categorization. This understanding is also seen in Gestalt therapy's phenomenological perspective described in Chapter 5.

This process may include omitting or filling in details and is also influenced by needs and interests. For example, when listening to a song on the radio, we do not hear a random collection of sounds, but we make sense of the story of the lyrics and their relationship to the melody based on our understanding of language and musical structure. Because perception also involves our preferences and concepts or ideas about an experience and includes the capacity for memory and recollection, if the song is one we've heard before and recognize, we can use this information to decide whether to turn up the volume or change the station.

4. Categorization

Categorization is the active conditioned response to the pleasant, unpleasant, or neutral qualities of any experience. This is how we respond to what we perceive. Categorization is motivated and directed in a particular way based on past experience and a desire to maintain pleasant sensations and experiences or to avoid unpleasant sensations and experiences. This is grounded in the understanding that there is no objective external reality but that we bring motivation, past experience, and our patterns of perceiving and organizing to the sensory input we receive.

5. *Consciousness*
In addition to the sense organs (eye, ear, nose, tongue, skin), there is "mind consciousness," whose objects are ideas. Mind consciousness coordinates things based on past experience and is what allows us to recognize things. Simply taking in information through the sense organs is not enough to produce experience. Consciousness is the ability to be aware of and process that which is seen, heard, smelled, tasted, felt, or thought. It transforms the meeting of external stimuli and sense organs into personal experience. Consciousness can then be understood as an emergent, conditioned phenomenon, the manifestation of a series of momentary occurrences, and at the same time, it can be seen as the agent, instrument, and activity of awareness (Bodhi, 2000).

Eight Worldly Conditions
Living in this material world, we are constantly subject to eight worldly conditions. We encounter **gain and loss,** not only of material things but also of people and experiences we value, such as our loved ones or our health. We may experience **fame and disrepute** in dramatic or milder forms, including actual celebrity or simple acknowledgement of a success or accomplishment. A loss of face or a humiliating defeat can always follow. As to **praise and blame,** they are likely to accompany the above. Likewise with **happiness and pain,** most lives bring a share of each.

Buddhist psychology recognizes that these eight worldly conditions are part of being human. On the relative and material level, some people profit and some lose out; some are famous while others are unknown. We often see a famous person's fall from grace, or the pain of obscurity when someone's "fifteen minutes of fame" are over. While one person is praised, another is blamed. Thus, from the Buddhist psychology perspective, it is understood that we cannot expect to go through life knowing only gain, fame, praise, and happiness.

This is an important teaching, perhaps particularly for Westerners, who are inundated with messages that say we should always be happy and that we should create a life that is successful and gratifying, and that we are at fault if we do not accomplish this. This Buddhist psychology perspective can help us be more readily present for losses and disappointments and help us to accept the inevitabilities of life's ups and downs, with less self-recrimination when things do not go as we hope or expect. The path laid out by Buddhist psychology allows us to meet life's twists and turns "the ten thousand joys and the ten thousand sorrows" with grace, as we recognize how we react to all of the above and learn to notice when we add the "second arrow" of suffering.

Three Refuges

Humans seek refuge in relationships, accomplishments, wealth, material possessions, power, sense pleasures, and other worldly attainments. From a Buddhist psychology perspective, when we do this, we are looking for happiness in the wrong place, since it is not the satisfaction of the next desire that offers a lasting sense of peace or contentment. Not only are these sources of refuge impermanent and subject to the worldly conditions just described, but pursuing them can also stir up more craving and further striving. Buddhist psychology guides us toward looking for happiness where it actually can be found and sees only three sources of true refuge. One is **the Buddha,** or one's own capacity for awakening. Another is **the *dharma,*** the universal truth of the teachings that lead to liberation. The third is *sangha,* the community of other seekers on the path. Meditation and other path practices themselves can offer a refuge, often experienced as an island of "being" within a sea of "doing".

Five Precepts

Elaborating on aspects of the eightfold path, the five precepts guide practitioners toward choosing actions that will not lead to remorse, and that do not create added suffering. These precepts become part of the path, and commitment to them increases awareness of one's daily behavior and its impact. Following these precepts also creates fewer obstacles in the path to awakening. The precepts are based on an understanding of cause and effect, or *karma.* Although some Buddhist practitioners believe in *karma* being carried over from past lives and influencing one's current incarnation, this belief is not necessary for understanding that we reap what we sow. *Karma* is also not just about a particular action but also the intention behind the action. We can affect our own and others' suffering by understanding the motivation and intention of our actions. And, according to the Buddhist view, it is never too late to make reparations and start again. These guidelines are *not* considered "commandments" but are useful in training the mind toward skillful ways of being in the world, encouraging an intentional and conscious recognition of choices and their impact.

Lay practitioners may undertake the training to refrain from: harming living things; taking anything that is not freely given; sexual misconduct; false or harmful speech; and the harmful use of substances.

Four Heart Abodes (*Brahmaviharas*)

The potential for these beneficial qualities already exists within us. They do not have to be forced or imposed, but are available to be nurtured and cultivated. Specific meditations can deepen and illuminate these qualities, and they are also the natural fruits of cultivating mindfulness, and following the entire eightfold path.

1. *Metta* (Loving kindness)

Metta, or loving kindness, is the quality of wishing for the happiness and welfare of all beings, without exception, including oneself. Loving kindness is a quality cultivated in mindfulness meditation, and there are also specific loving kindness practices. An example of a loving kindness meditation is described in Chapter 3.

2. *Karuna* (Compassion)

Karuna is translated as "compassion," although some consider this an insufficient translation. The root of the word, *ru*, means, "to weep," and *karuna* refers to our ability to relate to the plight of another so directly that their pain affects us as if it were our own. Like *metta*, compassion arises when we enter into the subjectivity of others, and share their interiority in a deep and total way (Bodhi, 2005). This understanding that flows from a sense of oneness with all other beings and results in a wish for all beings to be free from suffering, increases naturally through mindfulness practice. An example of a compassion meditation is described in Chapter 3.

3. *Mudita* (Sympathetic Joy)

Mudita is sympathetic joy, the capacity to find happiness in the good fortune and virtue of others as well as oneself. This requires an absence of envy, jealousy, and greed, as well as an experiential sense of the truth of interconnectedness, so that another person's happiness or good fortune is experienced to the same degree as if it were our own. This quality is a natural outgrowth of all of the views and practices as they cultivate our recognition of interconnectedness.

4. *Upekkha* (Equanimity)

Upekkha, or equanimity, is a sense of balance that is not disturbed by internal or external circumstances. Mindfulness cultivates a sense of equanimity, allowing less reactivity as we navigate all the challenges in life, including difficult emotional terrain. When we are equanimous, we are not "for" or "against" any experience, but rather we meet our experience as it is. Of course, we still take action in the world and make assessments of what is beneficial and harmful. But action is mindful, free of clinging to desired outcomes. The understanding of not-self, which allows less identification with experiences that arise, supports equanimity.

These qualities are innate capacities we can all tap into and further develop. From a Western psychotherapeutic perspective, this aspect of Buddhist psychology offers potential for our work with patients. Western psychology has not focused as much on the active cultivation of specific beneficial qualities or states that can enhance well-being and create more resilience in responding to life's challenges. This perspective is considered in Chapter 11 as part of the BPGT approach.

Universal and Relative Understanding
Universal Reality or Truth

The Buddha recognized the universality of the three characteristics of experience described earlier—impermanence, unsatisfactoriness, and not-self. Ultimate or absolute truth (we use these terms interchangeably) refers to these universal givens.

The terms "absolute, "ultimate," or "universal" are meant as a contrast to "relative" and should not be confused with an absolute version of an objective reality. This universal or absolute dimension encompasses such existential realities as the universality of pain and loss in our human lifetimes, the truth of interconnectedness, and the selflessness of all things (Kornfield, 2008). Importantly in Buddhist psychology, these truths are to be apprehended experientially, not imposed as "the truth."

Later we point out how aspects of the universal perspective are also contained in Gestalt therapy, and in Chapter 11 we further explore how this universal understanding can be integrated in BPGT.

Relative Reality or Truth

Relative or personal reality is the material world of perceived and created form in which we live our daily lives. Our ability to function—even our very survival—depends on it. We live in a human form and have certain practicalities to deal with. Where and how will we live? What work will we choose? Who will do the laundry and pay the bills? Is it best to stay in a relationship or to leave it? The relative mind perceives and functions in the sensory world. This mind process is dualistic, and as our five senses supply information, we tend to categorize and interpret this information as good or bad, right or wrong. There are things we like and things we don't like. Even dealing with existential realities, Western psychotherapy's focus is generally on these important personal, relative aspects of life, not the "bigger picture" of universal truths.

Non-Dualistic View

In Buddhist psychology, although "universal" and relative" are used to clarify this distinction, it is also understood that the universal is experienced and addressed though our personal and relative existence. Again, the Buddha taught a path leading to awakening but also "paths leading to the various types of wholesome, mundane happiness to which humans aspire" (Bodhi, 2005, p. 45). Following these teachings can lead to ultimate liberation, but also enables people to plant roots that are likely to yield happiness, peace, and security in the worldly dimension of their lives. In this way the relative and universal are not seen as separable.

As we navigate the relative plane of our lives, we can gain essential perspective if we keep in mind the truth of the universal givens—impermanence, unsatisfactoriness, and not-self. The relative and absolute are equally important; however, the difficulty comes when we reify the relative as if it were absolute. In fact, our capacity for well-being and our appreciation for material existence can be even greater without the clinging that is driven by fear of loss. We can still pursue our aims, but we do so with equanimity and are less focused on the result than on the integrity of the process in which we are engaged. Meditation practice becomes one doorway through which we can more clearly see the universal truths of our existence as reflected in our moment-to-moment sensation, perception, and meaning-making.

So although Buddhist psychology makes the distinction between universal and relative reality, this is not seen as an actual dichotomy. Rather, the inseparability of the material world of form and the vast unknowable absolute is recognized. It is also understood that the absolute is not more important than the relative. They are simply "two sides of the same coin." According to Zen teacher Charlotte Joko Beck, "the phenomenal world of people, trees, and rugs, and the absolute world of pure unknowable nothing, of energy, are the same thing. Rather than pursuing a one-sided ideal, we need to bow to the absolute in the relative as well as to the relative in the absolute.

We need to honor everything" (Beck, 1995 p. 16).

While we need to make use of concepts and labels, at the same time we can know that these *are* concepts or labels, standing in for actual direct experience, or a more universal understanding. This is also scientifically supported. Quantum physics suggests that what we perceive as solid and separate is actually impermanent and interconnected, consistent with the Buddhist psychology view. It supports the understanding that the concepts we use do not reflect absolute reality, but they are rather "multi-level abstractions. Even such an elementary concept as chair is an abstract class, a categorization that is not real, but rather more or less useful... Physics has found no fixed elementary building blocks, no mini-entities on the micro level that combine to form the world we know; rather it has found a vast fluid field, an open system with a web of interconnections" (Wolfert, 2000 p. 78).

From the quantum perspective, the "chair" is mostly open space, shifting rapidly as energy changes form, particle to wave and wave to particle. All that exists is a field of causes and conditions that influence this, and the causes and conditions are themselves an impermanent and ever-shifting field. Recognizing this, the absolute nature of all things and the phenomena of impermanence and not-self become clearer. We begin to see how we reflexively reify what is actually a process, and we see that this process involves movement, impermanence, and not-self. Still, on a relative level, and from our ordinary point of view, we experience what we are sitting on as solid, and everyone will know what we mean if we say, "Please bring me a chair."

These Buddhist psychology views offer so much wisdom, depth, and insight into our human condition and the ways our minds work that they are worth studying, contemplating, and coming back to again and again. For further elucidation and deeper understanding, refer to the resources at the end of this book. From this ground of basic Buddhist psychology concepts, we now move to the practices. Although the concepts are critically important, the practices are equally vital, as they are what give rise to our direct, experiential understanding.

3

Insight Meditation Practices

> *Mindfulness is not only a technique or practice, but is concerned with the quality of wakeful presence and the willingness to learn.... It is saturated with sensitivity and curiosity, with the willingness to make peace with all moments and all things, and to be free wherever we are.*
>
> —Christina Feldman, *The Buddhist Path to Simplicity*

THE BUDDHA'S ESSENTIAL CONTRIBUTION to understanding our human condition was identifying the nature of mind-created suffering. Having seen into the cause of suffering, and after realizing its cessation through his own experience, he then offered teachings and practices to others. He suggested a path that, if pursued diligently, would lead to freedom from suffering, to well-being, and to profound peace. Insight, or *Vipassana*, meditation is one of these practices. *Vipassana*, a Pali word, literally translated means "clear seeing." In English, this is most often translated as "insight." Insight here refers to the ability to see clearly into the true nature of reality or phenomena and the three characteristics of experience.

This insight, along with the capacities that are cultivated by the other elements of the eightfold path, can lead to freedom from mind-created suffering. The terms *Vipassana* or "Insight" are often used interchangeably with "mindfulness." However, more broadly, the umbrella of "Insight practice" includes meditative practices related to the cultivation of mindfulness (*sati*), concentration (*samadhi*), loving kindness (*metta*), and compassion (*karuna*). Generally, these meditation practices are what Western psychology has adopted from Buddhist psychology, particularly mindfulness meditation and loving kindness meditation.

Meditation practices, specifically mindfulness meditation, have been shown to benefit therapists as well as psychotherapy patients in a number of ways. Even if not directly used or taught in therapy, they have benefits for the therapist, and can impact the therapeutic relationship. We explore this in depth in Chapter 10. For the psychotherapist who intends to use these practices with patients, as we consider in Chapter 11, firsthand knowledge, experience, and understanding of them and their power, impact, and challenges is essential. This chapter provides an overview that also lays the ground for our later exploration.

Mindfulness and Mindfulness Practice

Mindfulness has been incorporated in Western psychotherapeutic approaches, and many benefits have been documented including increased capacity for coping with physical pain, stress reduction, and tolerance for difficult emotions. The Buddhist psychology perspective understands mindfulness meditation to have a different, more encompassing purpose, and sees the benefits more broadly. Mindfulness is at the heart of Insight practice and is embedded in, and an essential part of, the comprehensive Buddhist path. From this viewpoint, we do not practice mindfulness to achieve a particular result or goal, such as symptom relief, although it may also yield these results. Rather, joined with the other elements of the path, the fruits of this practice can include increased awareness, clarity, wisdom, compassion, and ultimately freedom from suffering.

Although we may have aspirations for our mindfulness practice, the only place to begin is right where we are. In mindfulness practice, we do not try to make something of the moment. Rather, we allow the moment to reveal itself as it is. We are not seeking a particular state, like calm or relaxation, but instead the mind is being trained to pay attention to present experience in order to increase awareness of what is. The intention is to come to know the nature of the feelings we have and to connect to them. So when bringing our attention to the actual, present moment experience, anything can be the focus of our mindful attention. Nothing has to be considered a distraction, and nothing is left out. We get to be just exactly as we are, and we get to simply pay attention to what that is. This requires putting aside or being mindful of ideas of what is *supposed* to happen, and instead being present for what *is* happening.

In this practice the attention is not fixed on a single object, instead, the meditator cultivates bare attention to the ongoing stream of experiences that come into present awareness. It is common to start with noticing the breath, sound, or some other easily accessible present moment experience, as an anchor point to bring the attention back to. The practice is to attend to whatever challenges arise in doing this, and to notice what takes the attention away from the breath, or from the present moment. The practice works by either being with the present moment experience, or noticing where one's attention goes, and what makes it difficult to stay present. Attention can also be with any element of the present experience, as these elements come and go. We notice what draws our attention, and we mindfully attend to that bodily sensation, feeling tone, thought process, or emotional experience. This is also a practice of "beginning again." Each time we discover that our attention is no longer with our present experience, this is a moment of mindfulness, allowing us to bring the attention back. So we cannot do it wrong.

The attention is mindful in the sense that rather than being caught in the story of the emotion or sensation, or involved in thoughts about it, we attempt to experience it directly, noticing what is arising and staying present with what is. As we do this, we expand our awareness of the workings and ingrained habits of our own minds, things we might not usually pay attention to, gaining insight into aspects of ourselves, and into the nature of our experience. Cultivating concentration, described in the following section, contributes to the ability to do this. A still, concentrated mind makes it easier to stay with the flow of the mind-body process in successive moments of present perception.

Mindfulness practice involves a directed "bare attention" to what is as we shift from our usual preoccupation with thinking and with mind-made stories toward paying attention to our subjective experience as it unfolds, without attempting to force or change anything. This has been described as the difference between swimming and floating (Fronsdal, 2011). The quality of mindfulness that is cultivated through this practice is defined in various ways. The *Pali* word *sati* is translated as "mindfulness," but the English word does not fully capture its essence. The translation by Buddhist scholars into Chinese yields two characters—one meaning "now/this" and the other meaning "heart/mind." These two characters point to a fuller definition—"being heartfelt in the present moment" (Fronsdal, 2005, p.25).

Mindfulness practice allows for a deeper investigation into the present moment experience as it unfolds, cultivating clear, stable attention and increasing our capacity to see things as they are, freer of our usual filters. Because attention and awareness are not themselves evaluative or reactive—they are not "for" or "against" any aspect of our experience—in this practice we do not even have to try to remove evaluation. Although mindfulness has been defined as including acceptance, pure attention and awareness are themselves neutral processes and so are non-judgmental. And as we will discuss further, "acceptance" is not something that can be coerced or legislated. Rather, we must be aware of our "non-acceptance" as it is. Of course, the thinking process itself can be full of evaluation, commentary, comparison, and judgment of experience, so we learn to distinguish between this running commentary and the non-biased attention to and awareness of experience that is mindful. This practice then enables exploration and understanding of the nature and process of one's own mind and develops the clear seeing that leads to insight. Here we "begin to reveal the *process* of identity building and world construction itself, instead of remaining entirely focused on the *product* of this process" (Olendzki, 2005, p.253).

Mindfulness of our experience also includes noticing how we are relating to it. Suffering is constructed moment-to-moment in ways we are generally unaware of, and mindfulness practice reveals the elements of this construction. This means noticing and learning to discern the difference between primary experience, the feeling tone that accompanies it, and any beliefs, judgments, or resistance to what is occurring in the moment. In this process we can more clearly distinguish the unavoidable pain of our lives from the suffering that results from layering things on top of a primary experience. We see our reactions to wanting pleasant experiences and wanting to avoid unpleasant experiences, recognizing clinging, craving, grasping and aversion, the components of attachment that lead to suffering. We can begin to recognize that although the arising of desire is not problematic as we are mindful of it, our unexamined and out of awareness reactivity to it can create suffering. Clarifying what we construct in this process, we can also discern how we personalize experience, creating the illusion of a solid identity, building the ground of attachment and suffering.

Mindfulness practice trains us to see our own mind processes more clearly. For example, if we are planning for the future, we note that we are "planning," rather than becoming involved in the planning itself and in the content of our thoughts. In this way the particular habitual "themes" of our existence reveal themselves, and we get perspective on them. For example, "I'm always thinking the future is more important than what is happening right now," or "I keep wanting to re-do things that are in the past," or "I'm so impatient to get on to the next thing that I am never fully in my current experience." Deeper investigation can reveal what drives our preoccupations, perhaps longing or fear. Rather than trying to change or get rid of anything, we turn our attention to the planning or worrying itself, recognize and acknowledge it, see it more clearly and name it more precisely, rather than being caught up in it. As recognized in both Buddhist psychology and Gestalt therapy, once we can see reflexive patterns and investigate what drives them, we also have more choices and options in relationship to them.

Four Foundations of Mindfulness

Buddhist psychology describes four foundations of mindfulness. These offer categories to help us clarify the different aspects of experience that arise as we pay attention to what is present. These foundations are: mindfulness of the body, mindfulness of feeling tone, mindfulness of mind/thoughts, and mindfulness of mental objects. While these are often described and worked with separately, in actuality our experience is not compartmentalized and involves all of them. As we attend to one aspect in mindfulness meditation, we see the emergence of the others.

Mindfulness of the Body

Developing and maintaining attention to the experience of the body is an essential beginning foundation of mindfulness practice. Mindfulness of the body requires being in the present moment with one's actual physical experience. Remaining curious about experience, listening to the body, and bringing a sense of inquiry, allows deeper exploration. This can be just noticing sensations, like tingling, tightness, or contraction. If pain or discomfort is present, what is the quality of it? We can notice if it is sharp or dull, consistent or throbbing, whether the sensation remains in one place or moves around. We can experiment with simply softening around and opening to the experience as it is. Then what do we notice? If there is smoothness or relaxation, is it located in a particular area? Is it contained, or does it spread to other areas of the body as we attend to it? The practice supports staying present with and grounded in this bodily experience. As we stay with it, we are likely to notice that the sensations shift and change, rather than remaining constant. In this process we increase awareness of what is actually occurring in our direct experience of the body.

The Buddha instructed that one could be mindful of the body in all postures and physical activities. So, mindfulness of the body can be carried into daily life. This is also an opportunity to notice how we are relating to our primary physical experience, and what we are adding to it that may be creating suffering. For example, we may notice pain in our back, and the feeling tone of unpleasantness. This may lead to aversion, wanting the pain not to be there, or it may lead to fear and jumping into the future, wondering whether we will have to stop running or if we will need surgery. The ability to be mindful of what arises in the body, free of grasping after what is pleasant, or aversion to what is unpleasant, or of mind-created stories about it, can be one gateway to less suffering.

Mindfulness of breathing is a subset of mindfulness of the body. The breath is always present and available for our mindful attention. Focusing on the breath, we can discover if the breathing is long or short, slow or fast, deep or shallow. The idea is to be aware of how the breathing actually is, not to change or control it. Here is another place to notice how we are relating to our experience. What are our preconceived ideas, thoughts, or judgments about the breath? Do we judge that our breathing is too shallow, or constricted, for example? As the capacity to attend to embodied experience develops, the shallowness or constriction comes more clearly into awareness as a direct experience, unmediated by preconception or judgment. Here it is important to recognize the difference between *thinking about* or observing the body or the breath and *feeling* it directly. This process is non-conceptual, with the focus on the actual felt sense of the experience. With practice, we can sense more directly the subtle nuances that make up the physical experience of breathing, and the energy, aliveness, and movement of the body breathing.

Mindfulness of Feeling Tone

Mindfulness of feeling tone involves noticing that every experience and every moment includes a feeling tone that is either pleasant, unpleasant, or neither (neutral). These feeling tones may be associated with sensory and visceral sensation as well as mental experience. As we learn to attend to the body, for example, we can recognize the immediate sense of pleasant, unpleasant, or neutral feeling tones that arise, along with particular physical sensations, like an itch, a sharp pain, or a soft breeze touching the skin. In this process, we notice our inclination to hold onto pleasant experience, to avoid unpleasant experience, or to seek a more interesting experience in the face of neutrality. These feeling tones can lead to reactivity. This automatic reactivity and identification with experience result in the holding on to or pushing away that creates suffering.

The invitation in this practice is to allow the felt sense of any experience and to simply be with it. Noting feeling tone can itself diminish reactivity, and with reactivity diminished we can more deeply explore experience. So, for example, sadness (generally a combination of embodied emotion and thoughts) and the accompanying feeling tone of "unpleasant" can clarify into a direct knowing, as sadness becomes sensation of pain around the heart, or stinging behind the eyes, along with thoughts of something we are longing for that we do not have. Attending to an unpleasant feeling tone that we might label "depression" becomes awareness of heaviness in the limbs, or a sighing quality to the breath on exhalation.

As we attend to the immediacy of direct sensory experience, and have less reactivity in the mind, we might see whether the experience is actually in itself pleasant or unpleasant, or whether we are adding thoughts and stories, creating meaning that results in a particular feeling tone. Aversion itself can be unpleasant, and we often notice relief as we let go of resisting and open to what is actually here. In mindfulness practice we are not trying to fix or change anything, rather we are meeting ourselves just where we are in the moment, allowing the natural unfolding of experience, which we can also discover changes moment to moment.

An aspect of mindfulness practice is the intention to accept whatever emerges. This includes accepting any non-acceptance that is present! The process involves both allowing whatever we feel as fully as possible and becoming aware of any moving away from or cutting off of our experience. Attending to immediate experience can allow emotions that have been in the background of awareness to come to the foreground, and to be more fully felt, along with the related feeling tone. We might notice sadness, or tears welling up, and we might also become aware of an effort to hold them back. It then becomes possible to mindfully attend to the reluctance to experience these strong or painful emotions. The action involved in tamping down, perhaps tightening the throat or distracting ourselves with an unrelated thought, can be more clearly felt. We can also notice the sensation of cutting off—what it feels like to constrict the throat, or tighten the jaw, and the accompanying feeling tone.

Mindfulness of Mind/Thoughts

Mindfulness of mind and thoughts includes all of what is in the mind: the thinking process, an overall "state" of mind, as well as the content of thoughts that are present. Thinking is not a problem in this practice, and mindfulness meditation does not require that we get rid of thoughts. It is the mind's job to generate thoughts, and in the spirit of appreciating the mind, we can value its ability to do this. For the purposes of meditation, however, the practice is not to indulge in the thinking process, or to get caught up in believing that our thoughts are "real," but to notice what we are doing and the process of how thoughts are generated.

Meditation teachers make it clear that for the purposes of meditation, nothing is worth thinking about (Fronsdal, 2009). Thinking, or trying to figure things out, is not meditation. Instead we notice what is here and what it is like. Is the mind peaceful or stirred up? What is in the mind at this moment? We can observe how thoughts come and go, and as we become aware of being caught up in a story line—remembering the past or fantasizing about the future—we are intentional about noting that, which brings our attention back to what we are presently doing—to our breath, to our body. It can also be useful to specifically note "planning," "worrying," "fantasizing."

Permission to simply be mindful of thinking, rather than trying to push thoughts away, paradoxically supports the mind in generating fewer thoughts. Now we can more easily observe it, and our thought processes are more clearly revealed to us. So, as in the above example, when we notice cutting off and constricting of sensation and emotion, we may discover thoughts that are part of this. These may be judgments like, "It's stupid to cry over something that happened so long ago," or "No one will want to be around someone who is sad all the time." Recurring themes in the content of thoughts are seen more clearly. Perhaps worry or planning dominates our thoughts. Perhaps future conversations are constantly rehearsed or past ones rehashed. Thoughts also often have accompanying bodily sensations. For example, when you think about the fight you had with your partner, you may notice tension in your jaw.

We tend to treat thoughts as if they are real and solid. When we pay attention to thoughts and mind processes, the ephemeral nature of thoughts is revealed. Seeing their essential "emptiness" helps release us from their power. From a psychotherapeutic perspective, this aspect of mindfulness allows us as therapists to recognize the importance of thoughts and stories in determining a patient's perspective and experience, and the potential benefit of developing the capacity to hold them more lightly, seeing them more clearly for what they are.

Awareness increases as we are able to stay with this process, and a deeper investigation into how thoughts interact with feeling tone and emotional experience becomes possible. We see that emotional experience is also not static, as its components arise and recede. Tears may well up along with thoughts of a lost loved one, and then subside as the wave of grief washes over and through us. A strong flash of anger at a person who has wronged us may give way to hurt as we recognize the longing for reconnection. Sitting and breathing with a sensation of agitation in the body, we may discover an island of calm at its center.

Mindfulness of Mental Objects

Mindfulness of mental objects or *dharmas*, refers to turning our trained and non-judgmental attention to the reality of our overall situation—the givens and truths of our experience. The lens of a Buddhist view offers a broad perspective. We become more aware of the factors of awakening and the hindrances described below. We discern elements of the aggregates that arise and combine to create present experience. Here there are specific guidelines about how to abandon or investigate the factors that obscure understanding, and how to cultivate factors that enhance understanding.

Mindfulness practice opens up a space in which we glimpse the reality of the "second arrow" of suffering. As we attend to the body breathing, and to our thought processes, are we clinging to what is pleasant and pushing away what is unpleasant? How are we creating a sense of identification with body sensations, or taking self-identity and thoughts as solid, permanent, and real? We start to see how the tendency to criticize, judge, resist, or rid ourselves of any experience does not achieve the desired result. Instead, it actually increases suffering by fueling negative feelings toward and about our experience and ourselves. This tendency can keep an emotion trapped and frozen in place, depriving us of the freedom and relief of fully surrendering to and being with the truth of our own experience.

Sensing the body, feelings, and thoughts as an ever-changing flow of experience allows awareness of whether and how we create solidity and fixity from this flow. As we notice ourselves clinging to a desired experience, or avoiding an undesirable one, we can see that such clinging creates the causes and conditions of suffering. This develops insight into the nature of mind and Buddhist psychology's universal truths. We can sense the space of being that is free of thinking, a more equanimous relationship with experience in which the sense of wanting or not wanting is suspended, and we glimpse the possibility of more peace and freedom.

Mindfulness Meditation

Meditation practice is essential in an experiential deepening of our understanding. This is one example of a meditation practice to experiment with. As with all of the meditation practices, if you have not done this before, you may want to begin with five or ten minutes and gradually work with the practice for longer periods. With this and the other meditations, you may find it helpful to record it and play it back, or to have someone read it to you. Many similar guided meditations can also be found in the resources listed at the back of this book.

Find a quiet place away from interruption. Take a comfortable, upright, seated position and close your eyes or direct your gaze downward. Begin with an intention to bring an attitude of care and compassion for yourself as you practice.

(Pause.)

Taking some long, slow, deep breaths let any surface tension dissolve as much as possible. On the inhalation, see if you can bring more ease to your body from the inside. Allow the exhalation to be a letting go.

(Pause.)

Now allow your breathing to return to what is most easy and natural for you in the moment, not controlling the breath at all. As much as possible, focus your attention on your present experience of sitting and breathing. Starting at the top of your head, allow the attention to travel slowly down the body, as you settle into this posture and into the present moment.

(Pause.)

Pay attention to how it is for you to be sitting and breathing right now, attending to the body ... noticing sensation ... temperature ... or sounds that are present ... and sensing the space around you.

(Pause.)

Feel the weight of the body, the gravity that holds the body to the earth ... surrendering a bit more to this gravitational pull, allowing the body to feel held by it.

(Pause.)

Perhaps you can sense the body as the energy field that it is, the vitality and aliveness of the flow of blood, the movement of the breath at the center of this energy field.

(Pause.)

Allow your attention to come to rest with the breath, wherever in your body it is easiest for you to sense it. This may be the touch of air in and out of the nostrils, or the rising and falling of the chest or abdomen. These sensations of breathing can serve as your anchor point, always available, a place to come home to.

(Pause.)

Now simply remain open to any sensation that arises anywhere in the body, noting the sensation, allowing your attention to be with it. Your attention may leave the breath completely, or you can continue "breathing with" any sensation.

(Pause.)

See if you can allow attention to stay with the actual felt sense of what arises—pain or tightness, ease or relaxation— just opening to whatever is present. When any sensation is no longer compelling, gently allow the attention to return to the sensations of breathing.

(Pause.)

As you attend to the sensations of the movement of breath and to bodily experience, you may notice that thoughts also arise. See if you can notice the quality of your thinking and its impact on your experience. Are there many thoughts or few thoughts? Is the mind agitated or easy?

(Pause.)

When you recognize that you are carried away from your present experience into memory or fantasy, this is a moment of mindfulness. Simply note "thinking," or "fantasizing," allowing the attention to return to present moment experience.

(Pause.)

Paying attention to experience, and creating more space and silence, you may also sense emotion arising. Just open to whatever feeling is present, as much as you can.

(Pause.)

Any bodily experience, thought, or emotion may be experienced as pleasant, unpleasant, or neutral. Bring your mindful attention to this felt sense as you experience it right now. Whether it is an easy moment to be with, or a more difficult one, see if you can stay present with it.

(Pause.)

Notice if there is a desire to hold onto a pleasant experience, or to avoid or ignore something painful. Discover if you welcome your experience, or judge or evaluate it. See if you are rejecting what is and leaning toward some other experience you'd prefer to be having. This is not right or wrong, just notice whatever is here.

(Pause.)

Before you end, take a few moments to just sit and breathe.

(Pause.)

Note how the mind and body are right now and sense any feeling that is present, as you sit and breathe in the middle of your full experience, just as it is.

(Bell.)

Concentration and Concentration Practice

The Pali word *samadhi* is most generally translated into English as "concentration." *Samadhi* describes both the practices and the experienced state of deep concentration that results from these practices. In concentration practices a singular object of attention is taken as a focus. The movement of breath in the body is often used as this focus, as it is always available and brings attention to present moment physical sensation. We begin with settling the attention on the object of concentration. If using the breath as the focus, we may settle our attention on the sensation of the movement of air at the nostrils, the rising and falling of the chest or abdomen, or the whole body resonance to the movement of breath. When we become aware that our attention has shifted (as it will!), we return our attention again to the object of concentration. Other sensations, experience, and thoughts may be noted but are not engaged.

Concentration practice develops the capacity for a relaxed and sustained attention, resulting in more steadiness and stillness of the mind, and a more unified body/mind experience. In strengthening the mind's capacity for this focused attention, concentration also supports mindfulness. With increased mindfulness we also more readily notice when the mind wanders, and in this way the practices support each other. Finely tuned concentration also develops a more refined awareness. As we pay close attention, the details and nuances of experience reveal themselves. When the mind is more still, and the thinking slows or stops, we are able to experience a sense of resting in simply "being," a stillness of body, and spaciousness of mind. This ability for focus and concentration also follows us into daily life, allowing more attunement to the details of experience.

Although this practice and the quality of concentration it strengthens can create pleasant and even blissful states, the value in Insight practice is ultimately considered to be in how concentration and mindfulness work together. Along with the other factors of awakening, concentration and mindfulness allow a deep knowing of the true nature of our minds and phenomena.

Concentration Meditation

Once again, while it is possible to grasp these concepts in a limited way by reading about them, experiential learning is vital;

so you are encouraged to experiment with the practices such as the one offered in this example. Additional concentration meditations can be found through the resources at the end of this book.

Find a quiet place away from interruption. Take a comfortable, seated position and close your eyes or direct your gaze downward. Connect with an intention to include care and compassion for yourself in your practice. Bring your attention to your current experience as you are sitting. Take a moment to notice sound ... to sense the space around you ... to feel the support of what you are sitting on.
(Pause.)
Notice your posture, allowing your body to be upright and alert but relaxed.
(Pause.)
Take several slow, deep breaths, attending to any surface tension that may be possible to let go of. On the inhalation, sense the experience of the body from the inside. On the exhalation, see if you can sense the quality of letting go, surrendering to the out-breath.
(Pause.)
Now, allow the body to return to the natural breath—whatever is natural for your body in this moment. There is no right or wrong way to breathe, just bring attention to the experience, how you sense the breath coming and going in this moment.
(Pause.)
Find where you can most easily sense the movement of breath and allow the attention to rest there ... with just this in-breath ... and just this out-breath. This may be the air moving in and out at the nostrils, or the rising and falling of the chest or abdomen, or the entire movement of the breath in the body.
(Pause.)

You can make a quiet mental note such as "in" on the in-breath and "out" on the out-breath, or "rising" and "falling" coinciding with the rising and falling of the chest or abdomen. If you use this mental noting, allow it to be quiet and in the background, with most of your attention on the felt bodily sensations of breathing.

(Pause.)

If you find yourself "watching" the breath or thinking about the breath, see if it is possible to move into a more direct sensing of the touch of the breath; let yourself be the breath, fully with the sensations of breathing in on the in-breath and breathing out on the out-breath.

(Pause.)

As you do this, you will notice that even as you have the intention to keep your attention with this present process, your attention is drawn away. You may have thoughts, memories, fantasies. You may be worrying or planning. When you notice that your attention has left the breath, you can simply note this and gently bring the attention back. The breath is always available to come home to, a thread of connection to the present moment.

(Pause.)

As much as possible, let go of judgments and effort. It is natural for the mind to wander and to be active, especially as you begin this practice. There is no requirement to do anything perfectly; the practice is simply to notice, to be present as much as possible in the body with the experience of sitting and breathing.

(Pause.)

After your mind has settled a bit, try keeping your attention on the breath for the entire cycle of breath—from the very beginning of the inhalation to the very end of the exhalation. Notice that each inhalation and exhalation has a beginning and an ending.

(Pause.)

(Bell.)

As you open your eyes, take a few moments to be with the experience of sensing, just being present with seeing or hearing before continuing reading or going on to your next activity.

Taking up this practice consistently will develop an increased capacity to stay with the breath longer and to more easily notice when your attention has shifted. The goal of this practice is, again, not to stop your thoughts or to block out other sensations or experiences. It is simply to be aware that the attention has left the breath and to gently allow the attention to return.

Through the development of mindfulness and concentration, the effect of the hindrances (described below) can be reduced, and liberating wisdom can be gained. Although the Buddha described concentration and mindfulness as two qualities of mind developed by meditation that work together and support each other, some practices emphasize one or the other, and sometimes they are taught separately. However, both are necessary for true insight. As Jack Kornfield observed: "When the mind is completely balanced, tranquil, and keenly alert ... comes the deepest insight into the emptiness of all conditioned phenomena, and ... the radiant, natural state of the mind" (Kornfield, 1996, p. 12).

Walking Practice

Walking meditation brings mindfulness and concentration to an everyday activity, offering another posture and modality in which to practice. Ultimately we want to bring the clarity and focus we cultivate in sitting meditation to all of our daily actions, and walking meditation can be a bridge to this. It can also help balance energy and support continuity in practice. Moving through space with our eyes open brings additional sensory stimulation and input that we can attend to mindfully.

Buddhist teacher Thich Naht Hahn's instructions on walking meditation suggest walking as if we are kissing the earth with our feet. This speaks to loving ourselves and the earth we walk on as part of the practice. This is a great practice for therapists since it is a meditation practice we can do without spending more time sitting!

There is no destination in walking meditation. We simply walk back and forth. This helps us notice that we are often focused on trying to get somewhere, rather than on the step we are taking. Walking meditation offers added opportunity to be mindful of things like impatience or being ahead of ourselves. The attention can be on the sensations in the feet and legs, or how the whole body feels throughout the experience of movement. This strengthens concentration as well as mindfulness, as we pay closer attention to something we normally do automatically. You can walk as quickly or slowly as you find helpful in keeping your attention in the movement and the body—remember you are not going anywhere! With practice you will find the right pace. This may also change with your energy level and ability to focus. Limited space is not a problem. If there is room to take fifteen or twenty steps, that is all you need. Again, recording or having the instructions read to you can be helpful.

Delineate a path either indoors or outdoors relatively free of distraction and interruption, with enough space for walking practice. Begin with simply standing. (You can close your eyes for this part, but open them before you begin walking.) Balance your weight equally, with your feet a natural distance apart, and notice your experience of the body standing, settling into this posture. Beginning at the top of your head, let your attention slowly travel down your body, attending to sensation. If you feel tension somewhere, you may want to stretch your back or

roll your shoulders, allowing any surface tension to dissolve.
(Pause.)

Notice how the bones of your legs support you and the rest of your skeleton as you stand. Feel the contact of your feet with the floor. Sense the earth below you, and how gravity holds you to the earth.
(Pause.)

Slowly shift your weight to one foot, allowing the other to maintain contact with the floor. Notice the difference in the sensations of the two feet as one holds your weight and the other maintains contact with the floor more lightly. Feel the sensations in your body as you move. Slowly come back through center, and then place more weight on the other foot. Then return to center.
(Pause.)

Open your eyes to begin walking slowly. You can clasp your hands in front of or behind you or let them be at your sides. Face straight ahead, and allow the gaze to be on the ground out in front of you. As you walk, pay attention to the shifting weight, lifting one foot, moving it forward, and setting it down, with a slight pause before the next step. Do this for each step. Begin a simple silent noting of "left" as the left foot takes a step, and "right" as you step with the right foot, as a way of helping to attend to the step you are taking. Keep your attention with your physical experience, noticing when your attention leaves the body, and gently bringing it back.
(Pause.)

Find the walking pace that feels best to you. You can also refine the noting to "lifting," "forward," "setting" of each foot to help you focus on the particular movement you are making.
(Pause.)

When you reach the end of your "path," mindfully turn (you can note "turning") and walk back to your starting point.

Whenever your attention leaves your bodily experience in the moment, just begin again with the very step you are taking. When you are ready to end this practice session, stand for a moment and simply be with the experience of the body.

Loving Kindness Practice

In a discourse called the *Metta Sutta*, we find the Buddha's teachings on this important practice. *Metta* is variously translated as "loving friendliness," "goodwill," or "loving kindness." The *sutta* begins with: *This is what should be done by one who is skilled in goodness / And who knows the path of peace.* This practice benefits not only those who are "skilled in goodness" and who "know the path of peace," it is also a cultivation of those qualities that lead us toward more goodness and peace. The 9th-century Buddhist sage, Shantideva, taught that all the joy that exists in the world comes from wishing for the happiness of other sentient beings. He emphasized that to the extent that we care only for ourselves, our lives will be filled with suffering. However, the Buddha also said that no one is more deserving of our good wishes than we ourselves are. In *metta* or loving kindness practice, both are included. *Metta* meditation practice is an essential part of Insight practice. Wisdom and compassion have been referred to as the two wings that carry us to enlightenment, and the quality of *metta* is an aspect of both.

As loving kindness practice is generally taught, we begin with ourselves, with the wish that we be happy, healthy, peaceful, and free, that our lives unfold with ease and grace. In this practice, we are creating an opportunity to cultivate these feelings toward others, and ourselves or to open to an *intention* to experience these feelings. Nothing is manufactured or forced. This meditation can also strengthen concentration as we repeatedly bring our attention back to the phrases. This practice can also be an antidote to aversion and self-criticism.

Next, we extend these wishes of well-being to others. We begin with a mentor or benefactor. Bringing to mind someone we feel great caring and gratitude toward without ambivalence helps to open our hearts. From there, we can progress to wishing another loved one well. Then, we make the same wish on behalf of a neutral person in our lives, someone we do not know well. Then, we can send good wishes to someone with whom we have had difficulty. Finally, can we extend these wishes to all sentient beings, known and unknown, without exception.

For most of us, it is a special challenge to extend good wishes to someone with whom we have had or are having difficulty. It can be hard to wish someone well who has hurt or betrayed us. One way to work with this is to focus on an *intention* to let go of anger or resentment, and the aspiration to wish the person well, and to recognize that, like us and like all beings, this person also wants to be happy. This is a place where psychotherapy and Buddhist practices may be used complementarily. When difficult or painful feelings, such as anger and hurt, come up in this practice, they need to be attended to and addressed rather than being papered over, dismissed, or judged as "un-spiritual." If there is unfinished business with a person, psychotherapy can provide a way of working through these feelings. These practices can also be powerful and evocative when used in therapy, and are easily included in Gestalt therapy's experimental method, allowing us to work with whatever emerges as a result of this experimenting. In Chapter 11 we go into more detail as we look at integrating these practices in BPGT.

Some people may find that opening their heart to themselves and wishing themselves well is also a challenge. It can be helpful to hold in mind an image of oneself as an infant or child. It is also powerful to focus attention on the heart center, to feel the energy there, to imagine the heart opening and softening, or to notice if the heart is closed. There may also be people in our lives who we will never wish well, and it is important to recognize that this practice is done so that we can cultivate *metta*, and liberate *ourselves* from the painful experience of holding anger and resentment; it is not "for" the other person in that sense. Therapists may also find benefit in practicing *metta* prior to meeting with patients, particularly someone whom they experience as difficult. We explore this further in Chapter 10.

In *metta* practice, we repeat certain simple phrases silently to ourselves. You may want to use traditional phrases, or make up phrases that resonate for you. It is useful to pick just a few phrases to work with during a meditation period. The intention for using the phrases is to elicit the quality/feeling of *metta*, so that we then take *metta* as the object of meditation. Keep it simple! Some possible phrases are below, and you may also find guided metta meditations through the resources at the back of the book.

May I (you, all beings) be happy.

May I (you, all beings) be healthy in body, mind, and spirit.

May I (you, all beings) be safe and protected from inner and outer harm.

May I (you, all beings) love myself (yourself, themselves) just as I am (you are, they are).

May I (you, all beings) hold myself (yourself, themselves) with tenderness.

May my (your, all beings') life (lives) unfold with ease and grace.

May I (you, all beings) be free of suffering and the source of suffering.

One moving description, that captures an aspect of the essence of *metta* and of the wish for the well-being of others, comes not from Buddhist writings, but from the novel *Gilead* by Marilynne Robinson (2004). The narrator of the novel is a Christian reverend living in a small town. While the focus of his wish is on the well-being of others, this practice clearly brings solace and heart opening as he describes it:

> It was on the nights that I didn't sleep at all ... that I'd walk through town.... In the old days I could walk down every single street, past every house in about an hour. I'd try to remember the people who lived in each one, and whatever I knew about them which was often quite a lot ... and I'd pray for them. And I'd imagine peace they didn't expect and couldn't account for descending on their illness or their quarreling or their dreams. (p. 71)

Buddhist psychology recognizes that some attitudes or mental states create a peaceful mind, and that others create distress, unhappiness, and psychological dis-ease. This emphasis on cultivation differs from Western psychology, which focuses on the contents of consciousness, or *what* our thoughts are. Buddhist psychology steps back to look at these states themselves, teaching us to release (when possible) or investigate the attitudes that bring suffering and to cultivate those that bring joy. From the states of grasping, aversion, and delusion arise envy, rigidity, anxiety, dullness, doubt, and agitation. The healthy factors flow from love, generosity, and mindfulness, which in turn give rise to clarity, joy, adaptability, confidence, and balance (Kornfield, 2008). This practice of *metta* meditation trains the mind toward more loving kindness of self and others.

Compassion Practice

Self-compassion arises organically when we can open to and sit with all of our experience, including pain, loss, or grief. So mindfulness meditation naturally sensitizes and tenderizes us. Compassion is the heart's particular response when we are fully present for pain and suffering, whether our own or another's, when we meet the experience with an open heart and without resistance. Developing self-compassion also opens us to more compassion for others as we recognize that we are interconnected in the universality of human pain and suffering.

Compassion can also be intentionally cultivated the same way as *metta* is, using the repetition of words or phrases to help us access a compassionate response to ourselves and to others. We can offer wishes for others to have more compassion, and this can also be a way to deal with our feelings toward those who perpetrate harm. This helps us open to the reality that those who harm others have also been hurt and acknowledges that the perpetrator of harm may still have the capacity to develop compassion. It also gives us a way to work with our own pain, grief, or guilt for the harm we have caused others or ourselves (Levine, 2011). This practice can offer support for psychotherapy patients to increase self-compassion or compassion toward those who have caused them harm. This is also explored in Chapter 11 as we look at integrating of these practices in BPGT to cultivate beneficial qualities that reside in the background, to increase self-support and well-being. All of the above *metta* meditation instructions can be followed, and these phrases can be substituted for the *metta* phrases:

May my (your, all beings') heart(s) be open to my own (your own, their own) and others' suffering.
May I (you, all beings) be present in the face of pain.
May I (you, all beings) recognize the universality of suffering.

May I (you, all beings) be filled with compassion for others and for myself (yourself, themselves).

May I (you, all beings) meet the suffering and ignorance of others and myself (yourself, themselves) with compassion (Levine, 2011).

Again, it is important in these practices to reference loving kindness and compassion toward ourselves as we do this, not requiring a particular feeling, but opening to what is here and what is possible; what we are trying to nourish within our minds and hearts.

Seven Factors of Awakening

These seven qualities of mind are beneficial in meditation practice. They enhance our ability to see clearly and to make skillful choices and help counteract the obstacles or hindrances described in the next section. These factors can be intentionally cultivated by creating the causes and conditions for their arising. They also arise naturally as a result of mindfulness practice. All of these seven factors are interrelated and work together to support one another. When fully developed, they lead to awakening and freedom.

1. *Mindfulness*

As we have described, mindfulness refers to the capacity to attend to and be present for what is happening as it is happening, and allowing experience to be just as it is. Mindfulness is key in developing all of the other factors.

2. *Investigation*

Investigation involves going deeper into our present subjective experience in a way that supports clearer discrimination and differentiation. This phenomenological investigation furthers understanding and leads to wisdom. Anything can be investigated, including our attitude toward experience.

3. Effort/Energy
Effort/energy refers to the wholehearted engagement, persistence, and continuity we seek to bring to practice. Our best effort will be different at different times and under different circumstances.

4. Joy/Well-being
Joy/well-being often spontaneously arise when we are open to the present moment. Being present with what is, rather than planning the future or rehashing the past, allows us to feel gratitude and appreciate beauty. In these moments the sense of joy and well-being that is inherent in the experience of aliveness can arise, independent of external conditions.

5. Tranquility
Tranquility includes a sense of calm and freedom from agitation. This is easier to access when there is a general sense of well-being. Tranquility also supports mindfulness and concentration. As we become calmer and less reactive, we find it easier to maintain focused attention.

6. Concentration
Concentration refers to a sense of composure, of being "gathered together" so that the mind and body are in the same place at the same time. There is an expansive sense of unity and harmoniousness when we develop the ability to concentrate.

7. Equanimity
Equanimity refers to the ability to remain clear, stable, and accepting of experience without bias. This requires mindfulness of all responses and reactivity.

Five Hindrances

These are the counterforces that hinder the factors of awakening. Each counterforce or hindrance, in its own way, obscures and limits clarity. These hindrances restrict the capacity of the heart and mind to be free, luminous, and present. They keep us lost in preoccupations, impeding our ability to clearly see what benefits others, and us, and what creates suffering.

1. *Sensual Desire*

Sensual desire is craving sense pleasure and wanting something because of the pleasure it provides. It moves us toward clinging, grasping, and craving for more. If we are attached to the desire in a way that inhibits clear seeing, we are unable to be fully present with what is and we are suffering.

2. *Anger/Ill will*

Anger/ill will involve a negative relationship with an object or person. This can include a desire to strike out. If we are caught up in anger/ill will, it keeps us preoccupied and restricted in our thoughts and feelings, predisposed to seeing the negative aspects of the target of our anger.

3. *Apathy/Inertia*

Apathy/inertia results from psychological forces that inhibit our motivation and energy for practice, and make it difficult to be engaged and involved. (This is not simply physical fatigue, which may also be an issue in practice.) The subjective experience is mental lethargy and dullness.

4. *Restlessness/Anxiety*

Restlessness/anxiety describes a mind that is constantly moving, unable to settle or focus. If we are caught in agitation and unfocused energy (rather than mindful of it), we have difficulty being attentive to present moment experience.

5. *Doubt*

Doubt causes lack of trust in the practices, in our ability to practice, or in the teachings. Doubt involves wavering, indecision, and ambivalence that may ultimately lead us to give up. This hindrance is distinguished from questioning teachers or teachings or disagreeing with something which conflicts with our own experience. This kind of questioning can be important and beneficial.

These experiences or shifting states are not necessarily themselves obstacles. They become problematic when we are so caught by them that they interfere with the mind's ability to see clearly. When we become aware of being caught or trapped in a hindrance, we can investigate the experience and come to know it better (Fronsdal, 2006). Hindrances may disappear or decrease with practice or come and go over time. At the very least, our relationship to hindrances will change as we bring our mindful attention to them rather than meeting them with judgment or aversion. In this way mindfulness is the bridge between the hindrances and the factors of awakening.

In the next three chapters, we shift our focus to Gestalt therapy theory and practice. In these chapters we briefly touch on some of the areas of convergence of the two systems, and as you read, other convergences may become apparent. Once we lay out the fundamentals of Gestalt therapy theory and practice, we detail what we see as essential convergences in Chapters 7 and 8.

PART II

Gestalt Therapy Theory & Practice

4

Introduction to Gestalt Therapy

> *The basic endeavor is to assist you to become aware of how you are now functioning as an organism and as a person.*
> —Perls, Hefferline, & Goodman, *Gestalt Therapy: Excitement and Growth in the Human Personality*

EXISTENTIAL, experiential, experimental, holistic, and humanistic all describe Gestalt therapy. At the time it was developed and introduced in the late 1940s and early 1950s, Gestalt therapy was radical in its insistence on the primacy of experience, its focus on a here-and-now process, its authentic patient-therapist relationship, and being with "what is" as an essential precondition for change. It offered a fresh perspective based on healthy functioning, not pathology. Its focus on restoring this optimal functioning and interest in personal growth and human potential meant its benefits were not limited to those seeking mental health treatment and were not limited by the concepts of diagnosis and cure.

The German word *gestalt* has no direct English translation, but it refers to configuration, structure, or whole. The word is used in two ways—to refer to an object or entity that has shape or form, or to refer to a specific property of an object. In English we make reference to the *gestalt* of a situation to refer to the overall sense or combination and interaction of qualities, or sometimes to the "whole *gestalt*," which is a bit redundant. Initially there was consideration of calling Gestalt therapy "concentration therapy," highlighting its understanding of the power of directed attention.

Gestalt therapy work supports emotional growth and self-understanding through increased awareness and connection with authentic experience. This enhances possibilities for contact and interpersonal relatedness, and enriched living. Gestalt therapy is not confined to working with psychological symptoms, although these can certainly be addressed. It encompasses and works with all aspects of functioning, including helping to highlight and draw attention to in-the-moment experience and ways of being in the world and in relationship with others.

The therapeutic relationship is core in Gestalt therapy practice, so the therapist's human engagement is an essential part of the work. The relationship is understood as co-created, with the therapist a full participant in it. Thus the Gestalt therapist seeks to bring an embodied and authentic presence to the therapeutic encounter, relating to the patient in a holistic way that allows for a meeting that in itself has the potential for healing. In this sense, no two Gestalt therapists or Gestalt therapy sessions will look the same, as each interaction is as unique as the people engaged in it. The therapy process includes attending to the patient's experience within this relational field. It involves exploring all that co-emerges with curiosity, and an abiding interest in increasing awareness and understanding rather than trying to fix the patient or solve a problem. The faith is that with increased awareness, the patient can contactfully and creatively take whatever steps come next, opening to the organic change that is part of the human reflex toward growth. This involves a full turning toward and embracing all that emerges—the essence of a relational mindfulness in action!

Like mindfulness meditation, Gestalt therapy's method includes all aspects of human experience, without bias. Gestalt therapy offers methods for working with what is present in the moment, assisting the patient in increasing awareness and allowing therapist and patient to sit in the midst of exactly what is, just as mindfulness meditation methods do. As an existential approach, it helps facilitate increased awareness of the patient's position in the world, enabling a sense of responsibility for the creation and maintenance of this experience, while not ignoring the mutual and reciprocal influence of the person and the environmental field. The focus at any moment may be on emotion, thoughts, or behavior, on the remembered past, or the anticipated future. It is also understood that direct, embodied experience and connection with feelings in the present generally have more potential for a fresh, new, and enlivening experience than intellectual analysis, or "talking about." Of course there are times when telling a story is both compelling and profoundly healing—depending on how it is told and how it is listened to. Gestalt therapy's experimental method offers opportunity for this creative engagement, weaving experiments seamlessly into the therapy session. These are not exercises aiming toward any particular outcome. They rather highlight what is, catching what is alive and enlivening, and expanding possibility. Gestalt therapy is never a one-size-fits-all approach, but an experiential, experimental, and dialogic engagement that is uniquely tailored to each individual patient, therapist style, and context.

History and Roots

Frederick (Fritz) Perls, originally a psychoanalyst, is most identified with the development of Gestalt therapy. Laura Perls also made significant and essential contributions that have not always been recognized. Both were instrumental in its development, its promotion, and in training the first generation of Gestalt therapists. Other significant contributors were Paul Goodman, Paul Weisz, and Isadore From. From is often referred to as the dean of Gestalt therapy. F. Perls laid out many of the basic concepts of Gestalt therapy (although it was not yet called Gestalt therapy) in the book *Ego, Hunger, and Aggression: A Revision of Freud's Theory and Method*, published in 1942. Although L. Perls also contributed to this work (some say she was a co-author), she is again not credited. A number of years later, working with an original manuscript given to him by F. Perls, Goodman created what would become Gestalt therapy's foundational theory. Goodman's essential contribution in synthesizing and developing this eloquent theoretical understanding is also often overlooked, as it is unclear how much was in the original notes of F. Perls, and how much originated with Goodman. Ralph Hefferline developed practical applications of these ideas, inviting the reader to embark on a process of self-exploration and self-awareness, by following the exercises described. This collaboration resulted in *Gestalt Therapy: Excitement and Growth in the Human Personality* (Perls, Hefferline, & Goodman) published in 1951, Gestalt therapy's seminal text.

With this publication came the definitive break with psychoanalysis and the birth of Gestalt therapy. Having evolved out of psychoanalysis, it diverged in significant ways. For example, rather than starting with a focus on the past, Gestalt therapy privileged the present, recognizing that the past is also alive and apparent in current ways of being and experiencing. It also replaced psychoanalytic interpretation with an experimental and experiential methodology, and acknowledged the importance of the current therapist-patient relationship, not simply as a transferential process. In Gestalt therapy, present "transferring" was understood as unfinished business, and an attempt to get needs met, but perhaps in archaic or limited patterns. In this way both disruption and healthy functioning could be recognized. The therapy relationship offered an opportunity to support the innate drive toward growth and novelty, allowing the patient to experiment with a new kind of contact within an authentic relationship.

Gestalt therapy incorporated the work of early 1900s gestalt experimental psychologists like Max Wertheimer. Prior to his work, perceptual processes were studied by breaking them down into smaller component parts. Wertheimer discovered visual, perceptual phenomena that could not be understood this way. He recognized that we do not simply perceive objective, external reality. Instead, we organize perceptions according to specific laws or principles, and perception itself is therefore a subjective phenomenon, interacting with any particular element being perceived. These discoveries contributed to the understanding of wholes as more than the sum of their component parts. Here, more means different from, not greater than.

The discoveries of the early phenomenologists, primarily Edmund Husserl, a contemporary of the early gestalt psychologists, also contributed to Gestalt therapy. Phenomenology's primary directive is to describe phenomena, as they are experienced. This involves bracketing off preconceptions and received ideas in order to describe, not explain. By studying immediate experience and attempting to bracket off biases and preconceptions, Husserl also saw that meaning derives from subjective experience, not an objective, external, physical reality. Edgar Rubin, a Danish phenomenologist, distinguished the *figure* (the appearance of an object) and the *ground* (the homogeneous environment in which the object exists), recognizing that those things that are clearly and sharply perceived form a figure, while everything else remains background. This led to further understanding of how we selectively perceive and organize our visual experience.

Additional significant contributing influences to Gestalt therapy include the dream work of Otto Rank and Wilhelm

Reich's character analysis that understood "body armor" as a manifestation of character. Also influential were Kurt Lewin and his work on field theory and systems dynamics. Kurt Goldstein's work also contributed in his application of the phenomenological method and gestalt psychology's insights about perception to all aspects of human psychological experience. This would be key in translating these concepts to Gestalt therapy theory and method. Laura Perls was instrumental in taking existential philosopher Martin Buber's idea of dialogical relatedness as the model for the psychotherapy relationship in Gestalt therapy.

Both F. Perls and Goodman were familiar with Eastern philosophy and principles of Taoism and Zen Buddhism. These influences are seen in several aspects of Gestalt therapy. One is the recognition that nature, or the flow of natural forces, is what creates healing and that we cannot control or force this process but can only create optimal conditions for it. Other influences are attention to "what is" rather than "what should be," the importance of awareness, the focus on sensing and engaging fully in the here and now, and the both/and dialectic perspective.

While psychoanalysis placed emphasis on meaning, Gestalt therapy shifted attention to direct experience (Polster & Polster, 1999). Gestalt therapy's novel goal and focus was increased awareness, allowing recovery of the lost aliveness and spontaneity of healthy functioning. Gestalt therapy's understanding of the nature of change captured the essence of what makes change possible—the ability to connect with authentic experience directly as it unfolds in the present moment. The intention in therapy was not for the patient to adhere to a set of predetermined expectations—either his own or the therapist's—so this was not an adjustment therapy. Rather, the intention became to aim at a lively present interaction that produced a novel experience from which new meaning emerged, self-regulatory possibilities expanded, and growth and exploration were supported.

The depth and breadth of the synthesis that is Gestalt therapy was sometimes misunderstood and oversimplified. F. Perls himself contributed to this by demonstrating Gestalt therapy in experiential workshops, without speaking to the theoretical underpinnings of the method. Inevitably this led to imitation by those who saw these demonstrations and were captivated by the dramatic results. Because of the creative and experimental aspects of the approach, and the focus on experience instead of analysis and interpretation, Gestalt therapy was mistakenly seen by some as anti-intellectual, or as disavowing the importance of thinking, and only interested in emotional catharsis. Lack of a grounding in theory or a clear understanding of how the methods were used resulted in the mistaken belief that Gestalt therapy practices were cookie-cutter techniques. The idea of a technique that is used to achieve a predetermined outcome is actually antithetical to Gestalt therapy theory and practice. The original emphasis on method was to a great extent in reaction to psychoanalysis and was not meant to suggest a one-dimensional approach but rather a more inclusive one.

Another misunderstanding was the response to Gestalt therapy's focus on the "here and now." Some concluded from this emphasis that Gestalt therapy fails to recognize the benefit of understanding the influence of past experiences and their power to impact the present. Not at all. Gestalt therapy's actual therapeutic grounding is more accurately described as "...an effervescent relationship of figure and ground and the indivisibility of organism and environment and completion of unfinished business" (Polster & Polster, 1999, p. 24). The therapist includes both what is apparent (figure) and what may not be (ground), as well as considering the essential interrelatedness of the person and the wider field, and what is most salient for the patient at the time. Attention to present process also includes the past as it is currently being remembered and related to, and its impact on the present, or the future as it is currently being anticipated (Parlett, 1991). An important perspective that Gestalt therapy brings is that although concern about past and future is central to our human functioning, if we act as if we are actually in the past or the future, it diminishes the lively possibilities of our actual present existence (Polster & Polster, 1973).

Applications

Gestalt therapy is a versatile approach. It has been used successfully in work with adults, as well as with adolescents and children. It has been used in both inpatient and outpatient settings, with numerous diagnoses and levels of functional difficulty, as well as for personal growth, awakening creativity, and increasing self-awareness. It can be beneficial in either a short-term or long-term psychotherapy model in any modality—individual, couple, family, group, or organization. Gestalt therapy has been shown to successfully treat a variety of conditions including anxiety and depression, eating disorders, substance abuse, affective disorders, personality disorders, PTSD, adjustment disorders, relationship issues, and loss and grief. Gestalt therapy is also useful for work with diverse populations. Its field theoretical and phenomenological approach mean that it takes into account context, environment, and culture, and does not impose external meaning nor require adjustment to fixed standards (Frew, 2008).

Contemporary Gestalt Therapy

In the years since its birth, Gestalt therapy has continued to grow and evolve, as its writers, teachers, and practitioners first recognized and clarified misconceptions and later further elucidated and developed theory and method. In the 1970s, a number of Gestalt therapy texts developed and elaborated on the ideas in *Gestalt Therapy* by Perls et al., making Gestalt therapy theory and practice more accessible for clinicians. The groundbreaking *Gestalt Therapy Integrated* (Polster & Polster, 1973) in particular brought Gestalt therapy to a wider audience. Since then there has been ongoing advancement and refinement of the original ideas and methods by practitioners, teachers, writers, and researchers. These have focused on both elements of theory and elements of practice that have contributed great depth and richness to Gestalt therapy.

Gestalt therapy's evolution has not been unidirectional. While there are no formally identified "schools" of Gestalt therapy, different practitioners, training centers, and writers place different emphases. Thinking has evolved and some of the original ideas have been refined and changed in the process. Often this has been done because the original ideas that were holdovers from psychoanalysis needed to be brought more in line with current understanding and Gestalt therapy's philosophical underpinnings. In the process, there has been disagreement about what is a faithful reflection of the original thinking, and what diverges. For example, Gestalt therapy has been seen as lacking a complete developmental theory, and self psychology's perspective has been proposed to fill this gap (Tobin, 1990). Insights from psychoanalytic self psychology and intersubjectivity have been proposed as important for the Gestalt therapist (Jacobs, 1992). A case has also been made for integrating the self psychology/intersubjective developmental perspective into Gestalt therapy (Breshgold & Zahm, 1992). However, not all Gestalt therapists agree that this is a compatible view, or see it as needed. Similarly, some Gestalt therapists now refer to "relational Gestalt therapy," while others view this addition as unnecessary seeing Gestalt therapy as inherently relational.

Gestalt Therapy in the Wider Field

Essential aspects of Gestalt therapy's philosophy, concepts, and methods can now be seen in many approaches to treatment, having found their way into the general psychotherapeutic lexicon. Positive psychology emphasizes strengths and addresses the potential for life satisfaction and personal growth (Seligman, 2002) also articulated by Gestalt therapy. The intersubjective psychoanalytic approach (Stolorow, Brandchaft, & Atwood, 1987) brings contemporary psychoanalytic thought more into the relational and dialogic camp, embracing philosophical and theoretical viewpoints articulated in Gestalt therapy. Intersubjectivity theory has also conceptualized aspects of psychotherapeutic treatment and human functioning in ways similar to that of Gestalt therapy (Breshgold & Zahm, 1992). Contemporary psychoanalytic thought also now recognizes the importance of present moment experience.

The ubiquity of the more widespread incorporation of Gestalt therapy's perspective is revealed in how other therapeutic approaches now support such ideas as "acceptance of what is," the importance of awareness, the value of a focus on the present moment, and the concept of "unfinished business." Mindfulness has influenced the perspective articulated by Steven Hayes (2007) developer of Acceptance and Commitment Therapy (ACT). He points out that over the last decade a number of approaches to therapy have entered the mainstream based on the concept that the more we struggle to change or get away from our experience, the more stuck we can become. Cognitive behaviorists have seen that trying to expunge difficult thoughts or feelings often makes symptoms worse, adding another layer of "shoulds" and self-criticism and leaving the authentic energy of these feelings and experiences unexplored and therefore poorly understood (Hayes, 2007). Hayes notes that Mindfulness Based

Cognitive Therapy (MBCT), Dialectical Behavior Therapy (DBT), and ACT are in agreement that a first step toward fundamental change is to embrace the present moment, even if an experience is painful. While these may be novel ideas for the behavioral tradition, they have always been cornerstones of the Gestalt therapy approach.

Les Greenberg originally developed Emotion Focused Therapy (EFT) from Gestalt therapy principles and methods (Greenberg, 2002). Initially this approach emphasized specific aspects of Gestalt therapy method that could be isolated, quantified, and therefore more easily researched. In *The Practice of Emotionally Focused Couples Therapy* (Johnson, 2004) the author states that the therapist must have a theory of healthy functioning and an understanding of how this functioning becomes disrupted. She says that the therapy attempts to enable increased emotional flexibility as well as identification with disowned emotions and aspects of the self. This describes Gestalt therapy's view. In observing EFT work we also see Gestalt therapy's here-and-now, phenomenological, and experiential methodology. Diana Fosha's Accelerated Experiential Dynamic Psychotherapy (AEDP) (Fosha, 2000) also describes important elements of Gestalt therapy practice, including advocating therapist moment-to-moment tracking of affective and somatic cues, and observation of these in the present, along with recognizing the power of the experiential. She also suggests a focus on assisting the patient to access an authentic, connecting, and genuine experience in the therapy process.

This is not to say that these approaches are the same as Gestalt therapy, as they include and emphasize specific concepts and methodology that are unique to each of them. Still, the number of approaches that have either moved toward the Gestalt therapy perspective independently or have been influenced by it is apparent. Since Gestalt therapy theory and practice derive more from empirical observation than from hypothetical constructs, it is not surprising that other approaches end up "rediscovering the wheel." This movement toward a more unified perspective among various approaches actually appears to be a result of something F. Perls prescribed, that is basing our understanding and methodology on the first-hand observation of human functioning and what actually promotes growth and change (Perls, 1992).

Whether other approaches come to these views independently or draw on Gestalt therapy directly, Gestalt therapy's original articulation of these important contributions to psychotherapy theory and method are often not appreciated or acknowledged. Our hope is that the current influence of mindfulness on Western psychotherapy provides a fresh opportunity for renewed attention to contemporary Gestalt therapy for its richness and unique contribution to the field. Just as Gestalt therapy was once part of the vanguard of the "third wave" of humanistic/existential psychotherapies, it now has the potential to help point the way toward a synthesis of the Eastern wisdom of Buddhist psychology and Western psychotherapy.

The following two chapters outline the basics of Gestalt therapy theory and method. We offer this as a comprehensive overview, though it reflects our particular synthesis, emphasis, and perspective. This perspective is grounded in our assimilation of the original theory, as well as the influence of our teachers, seasoned by decades of our own study, practice, writing, and teaching. The reader is invited to consider these concepts and methods in relationship to what has been covered in the section on Buddhist psychology views and methods. In these chapters we briefly touch on some of the convergences that we then detail in Chapters 7 and 8.

Just as with the chapters on Buddhist psychology, this is a great deal of information to assimilate if you do not already have a working knowledge of Gestalt therapy theory and practice. We encourage an initial reading for a general understanding and then referring back to these chapters as needed. Also, keep in mind that although reading about and studying Gestalt therapy theory and method is essential, just as the Gestalt therapy patient learns experientially, ideally, so does the Gestalt therapist.

5

Gestalt Therapy Theory

*There are indeed theoretical principles that underlie
everything Gestalt therapists do, even though the theory
doesn't precisely say what to do, when to do it, with
whom to do it, or in what proportion to do it.*

—Erving and Miriam Polster, *From the Radical
Center:The Heart of Gestalt Therapy*

FIRST THIS CHAPTER OFFERS an overview of Gestalt therapy's
three philosophical foundations. We also touch on how these
philosophical foundations are an essential part of Gestalt therapy's fundamental convergence with Buddhist psychology and
mindfulness, which we explore in more depth in Part 3. Next,
this chapter outlines Gestalt therapy's basic theory concepts.
These philosophical foundations and theory concepts underlie
all of Gestalt therapy work. In Chapter 6 we show this, as we
describe Gestalt therapy method and offer clinical examples.

Philosophical Foundations or Guiding Principles

We begin with the three philosophical foundations or guiding
principles that distinguish Gestalt therapy. This is not Gestalt
therapy theory per se, but there is general agreement that Gestalt
therapy work requires alignment with these ideas, and that they
are the overarching principles from which both the theory and
method derive (Yontef, 1981). The three foundations or principles are: field theory, phenomenology, and dialogue.

Field Theory

In physics, the field is described as a dynamic, interrelated system in which every part influences every other part, and nothing exists in isolation. Elements of the field are never static but constantly in flux. The essence of this theory as it applies to Gestalt therapy is that a "holistic perspective towards the person extends to include environment, the social world, organizations, culture" (Parlett, 1991, p.70). Any part of the field that we focus on is understood to be a subset of the larger all-inclusive field that also includes the history of the field (Resnick, 1995). Kurt Lewin, a leading proponent of bringing field theory concepts to psychology proposed that this is not a theory in the usual sense. It rather describes a way of understanding and thinking that deeply recognizes interconnectedness (Lewin, 1952).

From this field perspective, in order to understand experience, we must understand the relevant factors in the field. Rather than looking at complex interactive phenomena as separate component parts, we consider the overall picture or total situation as a whole. F. Perls proposed that the individual must be understood in an environmental context, and in fact rather than referring to a person as an individual entity, he described the "organism/environment field." This was a radical departure from the dominant way of thinking of the time.

In Gestalt therapy the relationship between patient and therapist is understood as a co-created field of mutual reciprocal influence. In therapy other relevant field influences may include things like what happened the session before, the current dynamics and nature of the relationship, the interactive process, and the patient and therapist histories as these manifest in their current impact. The relevant patient field factors in therapy may include personal, familial, socioeconomic, political, spiritual, cultural, and historical factors, and how these intersect with emotional and psychological issues.

Keeping in mind that any component of the field affects all others in a complex interactive relationship, the Gestalt therapist is sensitive to the relative importance of field influences and remains open to all elements as a possible focus in therapy. This includes recognizing interaction as dynamic and never static. A field perspective supports the therapist in understanding the potential impact and importance of the therapeutic relationship and interaction; how any relational experience or awareness in therapy may have a profound impact and implications for the patient.

This field perspective corresponds to Buddhist psychology's recognition of impermanence and interconnectedness, encompassing the same understanding that no entities or phenomena exist in isolation, and that everything is constantly in flux. All conditioned things are "field dependent," reliant on those causes and conditions necessary for their existence.

Phenomenology

In Gestalt therapy, phenomenology points to what we focus on and how we focus on it. We are interested in the patient's *subjective experience*. The way we explore it is through the *phenomenological method*.

Subjective Experience

From the phenomenological perspective, there is no objective external reality or truth "out there" to be perceived by the objective observer. Instead, there is only subjective experience, and this subjectivity is an interactive process, in which we reflexively take in, organize, and make meaning of experience based on our own idiosyncratic way of being in the world. Subjectivity is understood as actively created by the interaction of sensory stimuli, how these are perceived, and the created meaning. Sense experiences are not independent of the ways we are already shaping them based on previous experience and current context (Merleau-Ponty, 2014). This perspective also recognizes that it is a human reflex to impose meaning on experience. This viewpoint does not divide the world into subject and object but posits the inseparable unity of the person in the world (Heidegger, 1962).

The implications of this guiding principle in Gestalt therapy are several. The focus in therapy is the patient's subjective experience, and the therapist inquires about and explores the patient's subjectivity in order to understand both the experience and its in-the-moment creation. The therapist also recognizes the patient-therapist relationship as a system of mutual and reciprocal influence, and each encounter as the meeting of two subjectivities in the co-created field. This also means the therapist's viewpoint or experience does not have more validity than the patient's, supporting the non-hierarchical relationship that is the Gestalt therapist's aim. Tracking the intersection of the interacting subjectivities of patient and therapist is one of the Gestalt therapist's tasks.

Phenomenological Method

Gestalt therapy's method is also grounded in and guided by phenomenology. There are three components of this: 1) The therapist brackets off—as much as possible—preconceived beliefs, interpretations, and biases, attending instead to direct sense data. In this way, meaning emerges from experience rather than being imposed upon it; 2) As the therapist attends to what is apparent and observable, she describes what she observes rather than making assumptions, explaining or interpreting; 3) The therapist avoids premature evaluation of what is or is not important, allowing relative importance to reveal itself in the unfolding process. Of course, we recognize that to some extent we are always inevitably assessing and making choices about what is worth attending to, and how to attend to it.

Gestalt therapy's phenomenological perspective aligns with Buddhist psychology's recognition of how experience is created, and that there is no objective, external reality made up of entities and taken in by a passive perceiver. Buddhist psychology breaks this down further with its description of the aggregates that make up experience, as we described in Chapter 2. Mindfulness meditation also takes immediate experience as its focus, prescribing the same phenomenological method as Gestalt therapy's that involves paying attention to direct sense data while bracketing or suspending judgment, evaluation, and interpretation. This is the "bare attention" of mindfulness practice.

Dialogue

Gestalt therapy's model for the patient-therapist relationship is based on Martin Buber's philosophy of dialogue. Buber was an influential existential philosopher in the first part of the 20th century. He differentiated two modes of relating with others and engaging in the world, the "I-It" and the "I-Thou."

The I-It mode involves pragmatic purpose, goal, and judgment. It is necessary for the practical aspects of living and interacting and is more objective and unilateral. Here, others are separate from us, and relating involves a quality of seeing the other as a means to an end. In this mode, the other can be more of a mental representation that is created and sustained by the mind (Buber, 1958).

The I-Thou mode has the qualities of immediacy, directness, presence, and mutuality (Buber, 1958). It is based in mutual co-existence, a complete turning toward the other, that involves a trust in the "between." In this mode we recognize and appreciate our inherent interconnectedness. Buber saw this as necessary for realizing our full humanity. He referred to this way of relating as genuine dialogue, with the potential to be transformative for both participants. Within the I-Thou mode of relating, Buber also described the potential for I-Thou moments. These are rare moments of transcendent and uniquely human connection between two people in which each is fully seen, apprehended, and confirmed by the other. These cannot be aimed for, but rather, according to Buber, occur only through "grace."

Buber's dialogical relationship model guides the Gestalt therapist's attitude and stance. Although patient-therapist contact ranges between I-Thou and I-It modes of relating, an I-Thou (or dialogical) attitude always resides in the therapist's background, as we aspire to hold the patient as a "Thou," even as we may be in I-It mode. This infuses the therapist's way of being and relating with the qualities mentioned above—immediacy, directness, presence, and mutuality. This attitude naturally supports a non-hierarchical stance for the therapist, grounded in the understanding that although the patient and therapist have different roles, they are two human beings meeting. The emphasis is on meeting the patient fully, not aiming for a particular kind of contact or outcome.

There are four qualities or activities identified by Buber that are part of this dialogical relating in Gestalt therapy. The Gestalt therapist holds these in mind and aspires to embody them in the therapy relationship:

Inclusion: This is the therapist understanding the patient's experience as if from the inside and feeling the patient's side of the relationship, as well as his own.

Confirmation: This involves seeing, apprehending, and acknowledging the patient in her complete being, and with all that she has the potential to become. The human need for confirmation is an implicit recognition of our existential interconnectedness (Hycner, 1985).

Presence: The therapist brings all of himself to the relationship, including a willingness to be seen as he genuinely is. This involves the therapist's vulnerability, transparency, honesty, and authenticity. Rather than being limited by a restrictive role, the therapist is available for a real encounter.

Commitment to Dialogue/Surrender to the "Between": In letting go of an "aim" and surrendering to the "between," the therapist lets go of control over what will result from the contact, having full faith in the process of the emergent. This creates a therapeutic relationship that is healing in and of itself—Buber's "healing through meeting." In this meeting, both patient and therapist will be moved, touched, and changed.

Parallels with Buddhist psychology's understanding of human relatedness are seen in this model. Like Buber's confirmation, Buddhist psychology suggests that we can see others and ourselves in our wholeness, with our innate capacity for awakening already in us. The ability to feel another's joy or suffering as one's own, as described in Buddhist psychology, also aligns with Buber's description of inclusion.

Basic Theory Concepts

We now move on to Gestalt therapy theory. These theory concepts are derived from various sources as we described in the previous chapter, including Gestalt psychology's study of visual perception, and an understanding of biological functioning applied to the psychological. Although these are theoretical constructs, they are grounded in what is empirically observable. The rest of this chapter outlines Gestalt therapy's fundamental theoretical perspective.

Figure/Ground Discrimination and Closure

As we pointed out in discussing the roots of Gestalt therapy, some ideas taken from Gestalt psychology's laws of perception were applied more broadly to psychological functioning. One of these is the recognition that we are not passive perceivers of received reality; rather we are active organizers of experience. Two of the specific ways we organize our experience are: 1) a *figure/ground* discrimination, the tendency for something to stand out more brightly against a less differentiated background; and 2) the tendency toward *closure* or completion of figures or *gestalten*.

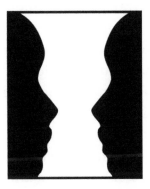

Either the faces or the vase is seen as the figure. Then either the white or black becomes background.

Visual closure occurs as we complete figures even when some information is missing. Here we do not see separate dark regions separated by a continuous expanse of white. What we perceive is a dog.

Gestalt therapy theory applies these laws of perception to psychological functioning, suggesting that psychological processes involve a figure-ground discrimination, and a tendency toward closure. The most salient need or interest becomes figural or foreground, while less salient aspects of the environment or experience remain background. When there is closure on an experience, which involves a need being met or an interest satisfied, it dissolves or recedes, and the next forming figure emerges. To take a physiological example, if you are hungry, you might enter a party and walk right past a beautiful flower arrangement without noticing it, as you make a beeline for the appetizers. Based on your need and interest, food is figural, and the flowers are background. Once you have eaten, that figure recedes for the moment. With hunger and therefore food no longer figural, you may then notice and appreciate the flowers.

Gestalt therapy takes this understanding and applies it to our psychological and emotional functioning described further below. In therapy, we seek to clarify and sharpen what is figural as well as attending to relevant background that may not be available to the patient's immediate awareness. F. Perls posited that unfinished emotional situations are prematurely relegated to the background if they are unresolvable. They then influence current behavior, perception, and functioning, and can demand attention until they are resolved. Background influences can impact the current figure formation process and interfere with forming clear present figures. The now popularized idea of "unfinished business" derives from the understanding of the innate need for closure.

Self-Regulation in the Organism/Environment Field
Gestalt therapy takes its theory of healthy functioning from the biological principle that, in health, an organism interacts with its environment to take in what is needed and to expel what is not. Simple examples of this are taking in food and excreting waste products or taking in oxygen and expelling carbon dioxide.

This is how the organism attempts to maintain homeostasis, adapting in whatever ways are required to maintain balance in changing conditions.

Gestalt therapy's application of this understanding to psychological functioning means humans are seen as naturally regulating, making the best possible adjustment to environmental circumstances and limitations within the relational field. Emotional and psychological wants and needs also organize the field. Given a responsive environment, a person will naturally make contact with others for things like relational connection and social engagement, comfort, or sexual satisfaction.

Figure Formation/Destruction Cycle

Regulating occurs via the figure formation/destruction (FFD) cycle or process, combining the concepts of figure/ground, closure, and the understanding of wants, needs, and interests organizing experience. In Gestalt therapy, this ongoing cycle, also called the cycle of experience, is seen as central to our functioning. In this ongoing process, a figure of interest emerges, and there is an eventual resolution, dissolution, and closure of this figure. Although we describe this in stages, this description actually reflects a flow of awareness, experience, action, and assimilation.

The process begins from a hypothetical zero point. This is hypothetical as there are always background field influences operating. The first stage is a beginning emergent awareness of a need or interest through feelings, thoughts, and perceptions. Then this need or interest is clarified and sharpened. Next, scanning of self/environment determines possible action and mobilization. This energy moves into acting/contacting novelty in which the need or interest may be satisfied. What is novel is then destructured and assimilated, leading to a sense of closure and withdrawal of energy related to this figure. Returning to the hypothetical zero point, this is the ground for the emergence of a new figure. These cycles can extend over a period of time or be as brief as the blink of an eye. This process reflects how a person organizes experience, including field elements, and in this sense it is understood as a process of co-regulation.

**GESTALT FIGURE FORMATION/DESTRUCTION PROCESS
(ORGANISMIC SELF REGULATION)**

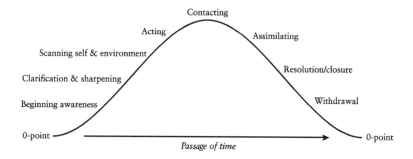

Gestalt Figure Formation/Destruction Cycle. This is also sometimes illustrated as a circle and referred to as the Cycle of Experience.

Here is a basic illustration of this FFD cycle.

Lila, a college student, is at the library on a Friday afternoon, and has just finished studying. Looking up from her text, she notices the almost deserted library and has a vague sense of restlessness (beginning awareness). This sharpens into an interest in and desire for company and connection (need/ interest clarification). She thinks about Andrea, the interesting woman in her Gender Studies class, who had suggested they might get together to study some time. She finds Andrea's number in her phone and feels a rush of excitement (scanning self/ environment). Walking out of the library into the crisp fall air, Lila sits down on the library steps and texts Andrea (action). Andrea immediately calls her back and they talk (contact).

They decide to meet up later at the new restaurant near campus. Lila heads to her apartment, happy that she reached out and relieved that Andrea seemed eager to get together (assimilation). Lila feels her energy ebbing (withdrawal), and she anticipates taking a nap when she gets home to be rested for the evening (beginning of a new cycle).

Of course, all of our needs, interests, feelings, and interactions are not this straightforward. Any FFD process may be more complex in terms of wants and needs, or may end in frustration, lack of satisfaction, disappointment, and lack of or incomplete closure. However, in healthy functioning, and with a responsive enough relational environment, we can make contact in which emotional and psychological needs are met. In this natural regulation, the most salient want, interest, or need becomes figural, and we can act on it.

Completion of a cycle may also occur without contact with another person, as we connect with emergent feelings and awareness. For example, if I have suffered a loss and grief is alive in my background, when I see someone or something that reminds me of the person I have lost, I may move fully into my grief, bring up memories of this person, feel sad, and cry. As I allow these feelings and their full expression, the tears will eventually subside (closure), and the next figure will begin to form. So, closure may occur as a result of contact, or simply by fully engaging a current experience in this organic process. Sometimes this involves assimilating feelings about a need or desire not being met. For example if Andrea had not responded, Lila would have to feel and assimilate any disappointment in order to get a sense of closure.

Contact and Contact Boundary

Gestalt therapy is fundamentally concerned with interpersonal connection and **contact**. Contacting the environment and others is a way of getting needs met, and interpersonal contact is a fundamental way of experiencing and expressing our humanity and interconnection. As Gestalt therapists, we attend to interpersonal contacting processes, including how and when good quality contact occurs, how contacting is organized and experienced, and how it is interrupted or limited. We notice the consequences of these disruptions or limitations, such as a decreased range of experience and restricted living. Gestalt therapy includes methods that attend to these limitations and restrictions, and to restoring better quality contact.

The **contact boundary** is defined as the meeting point of person and other/environment, and where experience occurs. This boundary does not separate person and environment, but limits, contains, and protects the person and touches the environment at the same time (Perls et al., 1951). Contact describes the interaction at this point of meeting. While a physical boundary is easier to understand, this psychological boundary is a construct describing a fluid, shifting, impermanent, and permeable experience of contact and connecting. The interruptions described below occur via co-regulation at this boundary.

From the Gestalt therapy perspective, good quality contact includes awareness, excitement, and the mobilization of energy, free of interruption. Interference with awareness of a strong figure of interest, blocking of excitement, or avoiding direct expression can interfere with good quality contact. In natural functioning, given a relatively supportive environment, a person will be aware of, identify with, and choose whether to express and/or act on interests and desires, making satisfying contact with the other if the other is available for this contact.

Contacting occurs within the FFD cycle and can also be broken down into stages: fore-contact, contact, final contact, and post-contact. In therapy, fore-contact might be the initial comments the patient makes about traffic or the weather, before moving into the reasons she is there. Therapeutic contact involves engaging with the therapist in a substantive interaction from which novelty and meaning may emerge. Final therapeutic contact has been described as the patient connecting with previously unaware affect or anxiety (Isadore From, personal communication, 1983). It can be instructive to notice patient difficulties at particular stages, for example, difficulty surrendering fully to powerful emotion (final contact) or difficulty leaving at the end of a session (post-contact).

Disruption of Natural Regulation

Gestalt therapy's understanding of development involves how the natural process of self-regulation is subject to disruption based on environmental, field, and relational influences interacting with developmental needs. Interruptions in this process (as described below) can diminish awareness, interfere with development of a strong and clear figure, and limit possibilities for action and interpersonal contact. These interruptions can impact the ability to maintain the necessary energy and motivation to support action, or they can create difficulty with assimilation and withdrawal. If any early stage is disrupted, it will impact the subsequent stages and, therefore, the potential for assimilation and closure. When there is no interference, what becomes figural is the most pressing need or interest, and acting/contacting is unimpeded.

Creative Adjustment in Early Development

In order to understand how the natural FFD process becomes disrupted and limits contact possibilities, we start with the concept of creative adjustment. In natural functioning within a supportive environment, the FFD cycle proceeds as described. There is a natural expression and flow of interaction with the other and/or the environment. This is easy to observe in infants and children, and in the child–caregiver interaction. The hungry child cries, and the responsive caregiver attempts to understand what the need is and meet it. If the mother knows that the child is hungry, she offers the breast. As the child begins nursing, he quiets. However, this natural self-regulation/co-regulation process can easily go awry.

When infants and children experience a disjuncture between what they want or need and what is available, they make the best possible adaptation based on their perceptions, experience, creativity, and resources. An infant or child's natural response is to cry when hungry or distressed, seek physical contact or comfort, and express frustration if he cannot get his need met. But what if the mother wants to feed her child on a schedule, and does not respond when the infant is hungry? What if the infant is ignored by caregivers when crying, or pushed away when seeking comfort, or punished for expressing frustration? The child then learns to tamp down awareness as well as these natural responses. So, perhaps the mother who wants to feed her child on a schedule leaves the room if he cries. This child may learn to ignore hunger signals, and to suppress crying. If a child is rejected or humiliated for expressing needs, or receives an inadequate response, he creatively adjusts by avoiding awareness of feelings and needs. Or, if the child remains aware of them, he learns to avoid expressing them, concealing them from others, and attempting to meet needs in other ways. The basic principle underlying these adjustments is an environmental requirement that the child be what he is not. These are spontaneous, in-the-moment, creative adjustments—the best adaptations available at the time.

Creative adjustments can be a way of seeking safety and protection, as in the case of a child who learns to hide feelings, or to stay quiet with a parent who has angry, violent, or shaming responses. They can be attempts to seek love, attention, and approval, as in the case where a child learns to ignore her own interests in order to pursue what will make the parent happy or proud. They can be a way to avoid being abandoned, if the child molds her behavior so as not to trigger the parent's emotional or physical withdrawal. The most important need is generally the attachment/relational one—to stay connected to the caregiving other upon whom emotional and physical survival depends. When this is threatened, or must constantly be monitored and adjusted to, the child's other needs, like connection to and expression of her own authentic feelings and experience, may be sacrificed.

Over time, creative adjustments that were spontaneous, adaptive, and essential when developed can become habitual; the original reason for them now relegated to the background, so these adjustments are maintained out of awareness. In order to accomplish this, aspects of the self and self-experience must be ignored, dis-identified with, or disowned completely. The child learns not to identify with these needs and aspects of self, and may reject them just as the caregivers have, developing enduring internal conflicts and a judgmental stance toward her own feelings, experience, or needs. What were once survival adaptations become the limitations in behavioral and emotional flexibility we see in adults. These are generally out of awareness, or if in awareness they can be experienced as essential to emotional safety and self-preservation. They become habitual ways of being and relating, and the lens through which we see others, the world, and ourselves.

These adjustments, the current manifestations of them, and how they intersect with a current situation often bring people into therapy. The ability to connect with one's experience and to make aware contact with others is self-supporting and leads to growth and life satisfaction. Alienating or disowning emerging experience results in psychological conflicts, symptoms, and a lack of wholeness. Examples include having difficulty acknowledging one's vulnerability, not wanting to depend on anyone, not allowing one's anger, always deferring to others, and experiencing symptoms like anxiety if unwelcome feelings threaten to emerge. Although aspects of these enduring traits and ways of being can be understood as strengths, they may also condemn a person to a lifetime of internal conflict, inauthenticity, and interpersonal and relationship problems, including difficulty expressing emotion, standing one's ground, or being close and vulnerable with an intimate partner. These may also make an individual prone to psychological symptoms such as anxiety, depression, or low self-esteem, and contribute to a general sense of dissatisfaction in living.

We continue to creatively adjust over the course of our lives in response to the ever-changing environmental field. However, those creative adjustments that were required in early development and that have rigidified to form the entrenched aspects of our character, and enduring relational themes (Jacobs, 2017) generally become the focus of therapeutic intervention as they emerge in the present. Additionally, in adult life, we may encounter situations that echo the early experiences that required us to make these adjustments. Familiar situations may re-ignite these reliable but limited ways of coping and experiencing. Or, as we view things through the current lens shaped by our early experiences, we may be more likely to see the commonalities than to notice the ways we as adults, and our current situation, actually differ from the past. In Chapter 6 we detail how Gestalt therapy works with these processes.

Self-Regulating Processes at the Contact Boundary

The following six processes are the "how" of any disruption of contact; they are: introjecting, projecting, retroflecting, confluence, deflecting, and egotism. These are the rigidified, creative adjustments that are observable in present contacting.

In the original Gestalt therapy literature, these processes were referred to as "contact boundary disturbances." As contemporary Gestalt therapy has moved toward non-pathologizing and more experience-near language, these processes have been described as "self-regulating activity at the contact boundary" (Miriam Polster, personal communication, 1992) or "modifications to contact" (Joyce & Sills, 2010). Each of these processes may also be used in adaptive and beneficial ways, and even those that appear detrimental or limiting, can be understood as necessary and protective from the patient's perspective. In psychotherapy we are generally addressing the unaware, habitual, and enduring aspects of these processes that contribute to symptoms, diminish self-experience, inhibit the capacity for lively and satisfying contact, and limit interpersonal relating. Nevertheless, we work with them from a perspective that is grounded in our phenomenological and dialogical method, focused on the patient's experienced perspective, as we show in the clinical examples in the next chapter.

Introjecting is experiencing something from the environment as if it were part of the self. This can be thought of as "swallowing whole" without the "chewing" necessary to tailor, assimilate, and make something one's own. The content of early introjects generally consists of parental, cultural, and institutional messages. These messages can be directly stated and/or how one is treated can result in introjected self-concepts. A child might be told directly, "Big boys don't cry." Or a child might pick up the message that showing anger is not acceptable when she is sent to her room after an angry outburst. The child who is hit may take this in as "I am bad." A child whose parents do not show emotion, may "swallow" this as a model and develop her own stoic stance. Introjects involve rules and "shoulds" that come to regulate and control behavior, for example, "I should think of others; my own needs don't matter."

Introjecting can become a primary way of responding to situations and relationships, so that one consistently looks outside of oneself for rules on how to be and what is required. This can include striving to live up to perceived expectations, ignoring one's own wants and needs, and operating primarily from these "shoulds." In therapy we see introjected ideas and beliefs that conflict with a person's actual wants, interests, and needs. For example, a patient is angry, but restricts expressing it because of an introject that makes anger unacceptable and because of an expectation, based on past experience, that expressing anger results in abandonment or rejection. Early introjected relational experiences mold our sense of self, impacting how we see ourselves in a world with others. The content of introjects, as well as how and why this early introjecting process was required, are addressed in Gestalt therapy. The introjecting process itself must ultimately be tackled, so that the patient determines and clarifies his own views, values, and behavior, restoring connection with disowned aspects of authentic experience. This results in less dependence on externally imposed rules, or others' opinions or positions.

On the positive side, introjecting is required for some types of learning, and is often an initial stage of the learning process. Current research on how children take in the world reveals the importance of watching and imitating. Ideally, when introjecting is no longer required, the developmental and learning processes do not stop there, and what is learned in this way is subsequently individually tailored, assimilated, or rejected in favor of understanding based on one's own experience.

Projecting is disowning a feeling, behavior, attitude, or trait of one's own and attributing it to another. The person can then experience it as being directed toward him. For example, a person who is unable to be aware of his anger (due to an introject) may see the person he is angry at as angry. Projection also occurs when a person does not identify with, or is not aware of, his own traits and can only see them in others. For example, a patient may say, "My father is always so critical," without being aware of how critical he is of his father.

Contemporary Gestalt therapists have suggested that the concept of projection does not align well with Gestalt therapy's phenomenological and dialogical tenets, in that it can shift us toward an objective assessment of the "accuracy" of a patient's perspective, rather than an interest in understanding the patient. The danger here is that the therapist might see the patient as "distorting," rather than the therapist maintaining an experience-near and phenomenological stance about the patient's experience (Jacobs, 2012).

There are also many instances of misunderstanding or differing experience between two people that do not result from projection. Because we are imperfect at interpreting others' facial expressions, words, or body language, we may "read" a different experience than the other is having (for example you may be confused, and I may read your facial expression as a lack of interest or as criticalness). This is not necessarily projecting my disowned feelings, but an inaccurate reading of your experience through my perceptual lens. Also, there may be both projection *and* a kernel of truth in how the patient perceives the therapist or others. In Gestalt therapy work, the guiding principle is to explore the patient's experience fully versus making assumptions. The Gestalt therapist strives to maintain the relational and phenomenological stance, with a focus on understanding the patient, as opposed to assessing the "truth" of any perception.

On the beneficial side, projecting is an aspect of empathy, as well as an element of the creative process. For example, writing a novel requires "projecting" from one's own experience onto the characters one is developing, and creating physical art requires projecting aspects of self-experience onto the clay or canvas.

Retroflecting is a process in which energy that would naturally move into contactful action or expression is held back. To retroflect means "to turn sharply back against." The impulse toward outward action or expression is contained, and the energy is directed back toward the self. "When a person retroflects behavior, he stops directing various energies outward in attempts to ... bring about change in the environment that will satisfy his needs; instead he redirects activity inward and substitutes himself ... as the target. To the extent that a person does this, he divides himself "into 'doer' and 'done to'" (Perls et al., 1951, p. 146.)

Gestalt therapy identifies two types of retroflecting. One type is doing to oneself what one wants to do to another. This can also be seen more generally as holding back energy that wants outward expression. This can manifest as anger at oneself, guilt, self-criticalness, or self-harm. Habitual retroflecting in this way can result in tension and physical symptoms such as headaches, from the muscular contractions required to contain the impulse or energy. It can also be connected to depression and anxiety symptoms.

The second type of retroflecting involves trying to meet one's own needs, rather than having them met in relationship. This involves doing to or for oneself what one may actually need or want someone else to do. When others are seen as unreliable, hurtful, or disappointing, we may try to solve our own problems rather than asking for help or support. We may turn to food, alcohol, or drugs as a way to get needs met without relying on anyone else. Self-soothing behaviors in children, like rocking and thumb sucking, can be examples of this type of retroflecting.

Retroflecting was originally a creative adjustment in response to repeated unsuccessful attempts to get needs met by others. It can be in reaction to being hurt, shamed, or criticized for showing needs or feelings, or perhaps being punished for expressing oneself. For example, the original creative adjustment may have helped a child avoid exposing vulnerability in the face of unresponsive caregivers. Or it might have been an attempt to prevent the punishment or rejection that followed expressing unacceptable feelings or affect. Retroflecting might have been required to maintain the relational connection or required for emotional or physical survival. One example is a child who is made fun of for crying and learns to hold back tears or to only cry alone. Another example is a child who is punished for "talking back" and learns to keep opinions or disagreement to himself, withdrawing and becoming self-critical. A child may criticize herself for being "too needy" rather than seeing her parents as unavailable or withholding, and feeling or expressing anger or disappointment toward them. As these energies or expressions cannot be directed outward but still need an outlet, the child becomes the target of her own aggression or the source of her own comfort.

In psychotherapy, awareness of this process is increased, leading to recovery of the original blocked impulse or affect and clarification of the original creative adjustment. An advantage of working with retroflecting is that it is typically within reach of awareness, and can be readily observed by the therapist. With focused attention, the patient can become aware of and directly experience it. Retroflecting can be seen and heard in gestures, language, behavior, and how the patient engages with the therapist, as we show in the next chapter.

Recognizing the importance of retroflected aggression in disruption of self-regulation is a major contribution of Gestalt therapy, and a core theoretical concept. It influences how the Gestalt therapist understands functioning, how we work with this process, and how we see the therapy relationship. Often this involves working through or "undoing" this retroflective process, including facilitating awareness and expression of healthy aggression, disagreement, and the ability to say "no" clearly to the therapist and others.

One of the challenges of reversing the retroflective process is that reconnecting with these original feelings can be accompanied by the fear, shame, or guilt that originally required or supported the retroflecting. Reconnecting with these aggressive energies is essential, however, and it is important to remember that doing this work is not "creating" the aggression but is rather bringing this aggression that has been directed toward the self into awareness and rediscovering its original focus. Of course, aggression can be harmful or destructive when directed toward others, but this is also true when it is directed toward ourselves! In any case, working through these feelings offers the possibility of non-harmful, contactful, and appropriate direction of these energies.

We do not act on all of our impulses, of course, and this is necessary in living in a world with others. For example, rather than lashing out at his three-year-old child, a father tightens his body and speaks in low, controlled tones. This is a choice, made with awareness. An audience member refrains from blurting out a comment in the middle of a theater performance. Exhibiting self-control when appropriate is sometimes called "aware retroflection." This aware choice would not be the focus of therapeutic intervention however; whereas reflexive, habitual containment *without* choice or discernment would be. This distinction is also field dependent and culturally determined. Additionally, it is useful and adaptive for a child to develop resiliency and self-reliance, when needs cannot be met by others or the environment. And for adults, self-reliance and resourcefulness are essential and beneficial skills when they do not preclude the capacity for connection, for being able to ask for help when needed, or for companionship and intimacy with others.

Confluence is the attempt to deny the existence of the self-other boundary. This requires a lack of discrimination and articulation of points of difference and otherness. A person who has a confluent style may talk excessively in terms of "we," habitually agree and go along with others, and rarely express opinions of his own. This results in a diminished sense of self and autonomy and does not allow for healthy conflict or disagreement. The original creative adjustment may have resulted from a parent requiring this type of confluence, due to his or her own needs, or intojects like, "Don't make waves," or "Be seen and not heard."

The capacity for confluence is beneficial and important in allowing an experience of complete merging with another. This is a temporary confluence in which two people feel so joined that the boundary between them momentarily dissolves (such as at the moment of orgasm). A capacity for confluence may also allow one to participate in a family or group and to experience belonging without undue need to differentiate oneself. When one is "confluence phobic," it may result in an inability to get along with others or to be part of a group consensus. There are also cultural differences in relation to confluence, in that some cultures emphasize the cohesiveness of the group or family and a lack of differentiation between members, or, conversely, some cultures focus more on differentiated individual experience and needs.

Deflecting is behavior that dilutes or reduces the intensity of contact. Examples are avoiding eye contact, laughing off what one says, circumlocution, or understating one's true feelings. Gestalt therapy theorists differ on whether this is a distinct self-regulatory process, or whether it is a behavioral manifestation of the others—that is, a result of introjects and their consequent retroflection, projection, or attempt to maintain confluence.

Egotism is a boundary process that has been less central and less discussed in Gestalt therapy than the others. It involves going to the edge of contact with novelty, but not going all the way. This reflects an inability to let go of control or surveillance, which prevents surrendering to actions that would lead to growth, even though the grounds for final contact are adequate (Perls et al., 1951). Spontaneity is interrupted and replaced by further deliberate introspection designed to avoid risk or surprise. This is called egotism, as it is an overarching concern with one's boundaries and identity rather than what might be contacted. Although this can interfere with the experience of surrender to spontaneity, novelty, or surprise, this capacity also supports calm deliberateness and may guard against impulsive actions. We revisit this concept in Chapter 11 in considering an expanded view of natural regulation.

Originally, Gestalt therapy theory conceptualized these boundary processes as *obsolete creative adjustments*, that unnecessarily limited a person's potential for satisfaction and growth. However, a more contemporary experience-near viewpoint recognizes that they are best understood and explored through the lens of the patient's perspective. As awareness of these processes increases, patients may in fact discover them to be obsolete and no longer serving them. Or, they may continue to see them as necessary for emotional safety or to maintain a particular self view, even if limiting. This is importantly the patient's, and not the therapist's, determination. As the work evolves and awareness increases, along with self-support and therapist support, patients generally move toward more flexibility, choice, and expanded possibility.

The Gestalt therapist observes and works with all of these self-regulating boundary processes. Attending to them points to psychotherapeutic themes and psychological issues to be addressed, as we illustrate with the clinical examples in the next chapter. In this work, the how and why of the original creative adjustment are clarified. Relevant memories emerge, enabling the patient to understand their influence and explore them in a way that is fresh and relevant; often allowing previously unavailable closure.

Self in Gestalt Therapy

Along with increased awareness, the goal in Gestalt therapy is transformation of self-experience (Isadore From, personal communication, 1982). In Gestalt therapy, self is understood as the system of present contact-making and withdrawal, and the agent of growth. This is seen as a fluid process, not static or reified, the function of contacting the actual transient present. The self-activity is viewed as a temporal process, the FFD cycle in action, with a resulting self-sense, or "I" in the process of each cycle. Selfing does not exist in a vacuum but exists as a co-emergent process. "Self" is not independent of "other" but rather comes into existence in contact and relationship within a field of interconnection.

Although Gestalt therapy understands self-as-process as described, it also recognizes the human reflex to categorize, cluster together, and reify the experience of self. In A Population of Selves, Erving Polster (1995) describes various aspects of self, or self-concepts, that arise as a result of contact conditions of the field. These senses of self serve an orienting function. We may experience ourselves as altruistic in one moment and as withholding in another, passive in one situation and dominant in another. Gestalt therapy facilitates development of more flexibility and responsiveness in this system. The resulting growth expands the repertoire of self-experience, allowing richer and more varied interpersonal interactions. Whatever spontaneously arises is then fresh and novel, promoting a sense of energy and adequacy for contactful meeting in any particular moment.

Ruth Wolfert, in writing about Gestalt therapy and Buddhist psychology, observes that, from a Gestalt therapy perspective, the continuity of our self-sense "provides a stable structure as

ground for quick responses in complex situations: the identifications and alienations of the ego function. This can give us
the idea that we *are* our self-concepts. But that is impossible,
for we cannot *be* an abstraction. We always *are* self as process" (Wolfert, 2000, p. 80). This is another important place of
convergence between the two systems in that Gestalt therapy's
self-as-process perspective aligns with Buddhist psychology's
understanding of not-self. We describe this further in Chapter 7.

Self-Regulating Processes and Ego Functioning

Both the natural functioning described by the FFD cycle, and
good quality contact, require being able to connect with experience and to identify with what is "me" or "for me," as well
as to know what is "not me" or "not for me." In Gestalt therapy, this is referred to as the yes/no, or identification/alienation
of ego functioning. Loss of this ego functioning manifests in
one or more of the self-regulating processes described above.
Introjecting, projecting, retroflecting, confluence, deflecting, and
egotism all reflect this loss of functioning, resulting in self-alienation and interruption of what could be more satisfying contact.

With loss of ego functioning we can see lack of awareness of
or inability to identify with wants and needs in the beginning
part of the FFD cycle, which will interfere with the completion
of the cycle. If I do not have access to how I feel or what I
want, I am not only disconnected from my own experience, I
am missing needed information for taking action or interacting
in a satisfying way. In therapy, increasing awareness of and restoring connection with feeling and sensation leads to renewed
self-awareness and increases contact possibilities later in the
cycle. Sometimes, although a person is aware of and able to
connect with feelings, wants, and needs, we see inhibition at
the action/contacting stage of the FFD cycle. Here, although
I may know I am sad, and even be aware that I want to be

comforted, I restrict crying or asking for comfort, or perhaps only cry alone. In this case the work in therapy can focus on contact and expression. At any time with a particular patient, the focus may be on the *awareness* or the *contact* dimension, or how they are essentially interrelated.

The following is an example of how these theoretical concepts can be seen in a patient and some ways that they might be explored in the therapy process.*

Anna, thirty-six, takes care of her two young sons, is active in her church, and does volunteer work. She comes to therapy because she wants to stop being so dissatisfied, angry and frustrated in her relationship with her husband, Marc. She says that if she were a "better person," she wouldn't be angry, and instead would be kinder, more appreciative and loving to him, not distant and withdrawn. Anna describes some generally negative feelings about herself as a wife and mother, and says she feels depressed, disappointed, and hopeless when she is not able to change her outlook and actions.

Growing up, Anna was told by her parents that she should "always be kind" and "never show anger." She introjected these messages as she was criticized and shamed for any outward indication of "meanness" or resentment, something she often felt toward her younger brother, Barry. She had a vivid memory of one particular time when she was spanked and sent to her room for getting mad at Barry for breaking a doll that was special to her. Anna ended up with a sense of herself as bad and

---

* Names have been changed and identifying information fictionalized in the clinical examples throughout this book to protect patient confidentiality. All vignettes are based on our clinical experiences, and they have been chosen and tailored to illustrate the particular concepts and processes described.

selfish for feeling angry or having her own needs. She learned to withdraw and hold in her anger, directing any negative feelings only toward herself (retroflecting).

This process is observed in therapy in Anna's minimizing of her own experience and being critical of herself for having any negative thoughts or feelings toward her husband. Even when Marc hurts or disappoints her by "forgetting" to do something he has agreed to do, or by not appreciating her, she does not directly express hurt, anger, or disappointment to him, or about him in therapy. Minimizing her feelings and self-blame (deflecting and retroflecting) are observable boundary processes that are manifestations of her early creative adjustments. These creative adjustments were needed to maintain her parents' approval and to avoid their rejection, as well as to maintain her own sense of herself as "a good person."

Several months into therapy, Anna talks through tightened lips and sounds angry as she describes an incident with Marc. Reluctantly acknowledging that she does feel some anger toward Marc, she says it is like there is a "mad little girl having a temper tantrum" inside her and that she "just hates" that part of her. She describes the little girl as "about seven, sitting in the corner, facing the wall, being punished." Experimenting with talking directly to this part of her, Anna tells the little girl that she is "mean and selfish" and that she "should just stay in that corner and shut up!" As Anna does this, she becomes aware of the strength in this position, and how she can use it to silence this young part of her that is mad. She also discovers that although she can keep her contained, she cannot get rid of her. The little girl in the corner may be silent, but she is still there.

As Anna stays with this awareness, her attitude toward this young, angry part of herself begins to shift. She describes feeling "a little sorry for her, too," and that "she might be sad."

Identifying with and moving fully into "hating" this part of her allowed some closure with that aspect of her experience, resulting in this newly emergent figure. It is novel for Anna to feel anything about her anger other than wanting to be rid of it. She now identifies with this young, angry part of herself for the first time. Reconnecting with this disowned aspect of herself, rather than only trying to distance from and stifle it, Anna can now feel some of the pain that has always been there.

In subsequent sessions, Anna sees the bind that she was in as a child when there was no acceptable expression for any of these feelings, and she was shamed, rejected and alone. She is now freer to question the introject that if she has certain feelings, she is "bad and selfish." She recognizes how she now does to herself what her parents did to her by rejecting and disowning her own experience, resulting in this familiar pattern of trying to comply with perceived external demands and blaming herself when she doesn't. Undoing this retroflective process also allows Anna to connect with her anger toward others. She recognizes that she was (and still is) hurt by and angry with her parents for their lack of caring about her needs and feelings, and for shaming and rejecting her when she did not meet their expectations. This begins a therapeutic process of working through these feelings.

In her current life and relationship, Anna begins to identify more with her own wants and needs, and what she really feels toward Marc, rather than trying to live up to an idealized version of herself. This increased awareness supports expressing these feelings, and she can now make contact with Marc in a way that is fresh and novel for both of them, instead of withdrawing. She becomes more engaged in the actual relationship with her husband rather than silencing herself and replicating the withdrawn, "alone in the corner" position of her childhood.

The philosophical principles and theory concepts described in this chapter are the ground of all Gestalt therapy work, informing the method and therapeutic choices. In the next chapter we look at, and illustrate with clinical examples, how these principles and concepts translate into Gestalt therapy method.

6

Theory into Practice:
Gestalt Therapy Method

> *Logic can be contradicted, but experience cannot.*
> —Erving and Miriam Polster, *From the Radical Center:*
> *The Heart of Gestalt Therapy*

GESTALT THERAPY'S METHOD and interventions are derived from the philosophical principles and theoretical concepts described in the previous chapter. The influence of field theory, phenomenology, and dialogue are always guiding the therapist's stance, the therapeutic process, and the relational perspective, creating the ground for Gestalt therapy's spontaneous improvisational interventions. Although Gestalt therapy is improvisation, just as in improvisational theater, there are orienting procedures and guidelines. While the theory offers an in-depth understanding of the complexities of human development and dynamics, in the clinical examples we attempt to show the relational and organic unfolding of the work itself. Importantly, Gestalt therapy methods are not techniques to achieve a particular outcome. Instead they encompass the broad possibilities for therapeutic intervention aimed at increasing awareness.

Psychotherapy is a complex interpersonal interaction. There are far too many facets and subtleties to be able to completely deconstruct or describe all that is happening at a particular moment, over the course of a session, or over the duration of this intimate and multifaceted relationship. Nevertheless here we lay out what we see as essential elements of this healing, multi-faceted and intimate relational process.

The Gestalt therapist's perspective includes an appreciation for the ongoing mutual and reciprocal nature of the patient-therapist encounter. This includes recognizing that the healing potential in therapy relies to a great extent on the quality of the patient-therapist relationship and contact. The therapist's intention is to create a relationship conducive to the patient's growth and welcoming of whatever emerges. This includes highlighting aspects of the patient-therapist dynamic that can clarify the patient's characteristic ways of relating, and looking at how this may impact other relationships in the patient's life. Considering and experimenting with new ways of being within the therapeutic encounter support the expansion of self-experience and relational possibility.

The Gestalt therapist helps clarify and sharpen the patient's here-and-now experience. This includes attending to emotional and embodied responses. We notice the shifting flow of the patient's affect and energy, as well as our own. Possibilities for therapeutic focus include the relational, interpersonal process, as well as the patient's particular way of organizing and interruptions to contact. Attending to interruptions in the figure formation/destruction (FFD) cycle reveals how self-experience is restricted and how lively engagement and present contact is limited. By attending to what is observable at the contact boundary, Gestalt therapy method addresses the essence of a person's existential position in the world, which impacts all of their experience. The therapist both observes these processes and helps the patient explore them experientially.

In this chapter we look at key aspects of Gestalt therapy practice: The importance of awareness and the present moment, the power of process, the paradoxical nature of change, therapy without resistance, the experimental method, functional diagnosis, therapist self-disclosure, and self and environmental support.

Awareness and the Present Moment

The overarching goal in Gestalt therapy is increased awareness, along with transformation of self-experience. Awareness is seen as key to all growth and change. The therapist's interventions support the patient paying attention to experience in ways that lead to increased awareness. The increased awareness aimed at in both meditation practice and in Gestalt therapy is different from intellectual understanding or insight. It is an experiential and embodied knowing, an immediate and present felt sense. Focusing on increasing awareness generally leads the Gestalt therapist to attend to the "what" is happening and "how" the patient is doing what she is doing. Although "why" is not ultimately excluded, it is only part of a fuller understanding.

Awareness is important for conscious activity, creative pursuit, self-regulation, contact, and growth. We can be aware of what is happening inside our skin, like sensations of hunger or a headache. We can be aware of embodied emotion, like sadness or anger, along with their physical manifestations of tears or tightness in the jaw. We can also be aware of what we take in through the senses: seeing, hearing, tasting, smelling, and touching. These two zones of awareness—sensation inside the skin and what we take in via our senses—encompass all of our immediate present reality as we directly experience it (Stevens, 1971). In addition we can be aware of the processes of thinking, like fantasizing, remembering, or planning. However, when we become embedded in thinking and "lost in thought," awareness of our actual here-and-now experience is diminished.

Awareness is always available to us—we are always aware of something, no matter how subtle. The capacity for awareness of inner sensation and feeling, as well as the ability to make aware contact with what is lively and engaging, are essential in the recovery of self-regulation. With increased awareness, choice also expands. Charlotte Joko Beck, a Zen Buddhist teacher, describes the increased awareness that comes with meditation practice, and this is what happens in the Gestalt therapy process as well. "There is a richness of sensory input, which is just our natural state if we are not blocking out experience with our ... minds" (Beck, 1993 p. 87). Both Gestalt therapy and meditation contribute to this brightening of awareness in which sensory inputs become sharper and clearer, as there is less mental "static" interfering with direct experience.

Awareness is different from attention. Although attention is volitional and can be directed, awareness is what emerges organically. For example, if we say, "Pay attention to the sensation in your hands right now," you can intentionally shift your attention and focus on your hands. However, what you become aware of as you do this—the particular sensations that you notice—will then emerge organically, unique to you in this moment. You might notice how the sensations of the top of your hand are different than those of your palm. You may become aware of warmth or coolness, tingling, or the sensation created by this book meeting the skin. We can direct attention, but we cannot legislate what comes into awareness.

When we direct attention to a specific aspect of experience, however, we are more likely to become aware of something related to it. Likewise, avoiding paying attention to an aspect of experience can help keep something out of awareness. Often, we avoid paying attention to an aspect of experience because we want to avoid what this attention may bring into our awareness. This avoidance and the motivation for it may itself be out of our awareness, and based in early creative adjustments that have become habitual. In Gestalt therapy, directed attention can be used to both increase awareness, and to work with this avoidance. For example, the therapist may call the patient's attention to how quickly she moves away from a feeling. The focus may remain on the moving away to increase awareness of this process and what drives it, or the patient can come back to the feeling to discover more about what is being avoided.

Awareness is always in the present, and often present experience is the focus in Gestalt therapy. Attention to the here-and-now also supports the organic emergence of memories of relevant past experiences, leading naturally to the origins of creative adjustments, and revealing how these connect to what brings the patient to therapy. Attention to here-and-now functioning can capture and increase the patient's awareness of how the past is alive in present contacting, and in the organizing of self-experience and relationship.

Increased awareness is always available to us. At any given moment we can dip into this ongoing stream by simply making the choice to do so through directing our attention. You can try this yourself in just a few minutes of exploration with this awareness exercise.

Sit quietly in a relaxed and comfortable but alert position. You can do this experiment with your eyes either open or closed. Take a few deep breaths, and then allow your breathing to return to what is natural. Notice what you are feeling in your body as you sit and breathe. Now, try starting several sentences with, "Right now I am aware of ..." and allow the sentence to complete itself with whatever comes to you as a direct experience. Continue this process for several minutes.

You may discover that you are mostly aware of internal sensations, such as tightness in your stomach, or your heart beating. Or, you may be mostly aware of external sensory experience, such as sound. You may find that you are primarily involved with fantasies, or plans for the future, or thoughts about the past, with less attention to immediate experience.

Next, experiment with intentionally focusing your attention on a sound, or on a sensation in a particular part of your body. Notice how this focused attention changes what you become aware of. If your eyes have been open, you can experiment with closing them, and notice what happens. If your eyes have been closed, see how (or if) your awareness shifts when you open them. Stay with the exercise for as long as you wish. When you decide to stop, notice why you are stopping.

Attending to and experimenting with your own awareness process can expand your capacity to recognize the value and importance of this in working with patients. A focus on increasing awareness is also one of the important intersections of mindfulness meditation and Gestalt therapy.

The Power of Process

Attending to content in therapy involves dealing with the subject matter being talked about, and attending to process involves noticing and exploring what is happening in the moment, in the room. Important aspects of process include patient behaviors, contact boundary phenomena, and the interactional patterns between patient and therapist. For example, if the patient is telling a story, the content is the story itself, and the process is *how* it is being told. The patient may be muted or enthusiastic. She may look for the therapist's reaction, or seem to be telling her story to an unseen audience. Processes we can observe include a way of speaking, language usage, posture, gestures, movement or stillness, tone of voice, and eye contact or lack of it. We may also notice that with us the patient is argumentative, compliant, vulnerable, self-protective, demanding, diffident, self-revealing, or withholding— all aspects of the patient's process.

The interactional patterns are the dynamic interpersonal processes between patient and therapist. These are understood as co-emergent and co-created in the therapy relationship, influenced by the histories of both patient and therapist and other field factors. For example, a patient might be naturally reticent, and the therapist may respond by being more hesitant in interventions. This may increase the patient's reticence, as the therapist does not instill confidence. If a patient presents herself as helpless, the therapist may find himself wanting to come to the rescue. Or, if the patient wants to avoid painful affect, the therapist may either cooperate in this avoidance or push the patient to move into deeper feelings. When the therapist is aware of an interactional process, patient and therapist can attend to this rather than remaining caught in it. The Gestalt therapist both participates in and tracks the unfolding of the relational process in each interactional moment, neither minimizing the importance of the impact of historical relational dynamics, nor overlooking the potential for novel contact in the current patient-therapist relationship.

Gestalt therapy method is often described as process-oriented, but it is more accurately understood as a seamless interweaving of focus on content and process, which are indivisible facets of experience (Polster & Polster, 1999). The Gestalt therapist highlights process or content at any particular moment, depending on what is most relevant, with each one lubricating and informing the other. At times story and content are most compelling, contributing essential elements to the therapist's understanding of the patient and enriching the background for the patient-therapist interaction. The Gestalt therapist can also see content through a process lens, always open to noticing and being informed by process observation.

Actively engaging in the moment-to-moment unfolding process in therapy, the Gestalt therapist can sharpen what is figural, deepening the work. The therapist might notice the patient's constricted breathing or a laugh that ends a serious sentence. Bringing the patient's attention to an emerging emotion, a gesture, or physical experience at the right moment can allow enlivening, new awareness. Perhaps a patient talks about a recent, discouraging event in her life, yet sounds upbeat as she describes it. Rather than only focusing on the content being presented, the therapist notices *how* the patient talks about what happened and can draw her attention to this. This may increase the patient's awareness that she is avoiding feeling or revealing her sadness or discouragement, help her see how she does this, and allow her to explore what makes this avoidance important. The therapist's process observations can lead to more contactful engagement, bringing a fresh outlook.

While content level interventions may be limited to what is already in awareness, process level interventions can facilitate deeper awareness, illuminating character as it is reflected in patterns of process. As we attend to the process in therapy, the patient's way of experiencing himself in the world and in relationship are revealed. Therapeutic themes emerge, and the building blocks of these—the self-regulating contact boundary processes—are clarified.

Focusing on present moment process can increase the patient's awareness of aspects of his behavior and experience that need to be addressed in therapy, as the following example shows.

Max is in his early fifties. He sought therapy because of symptoms of severe anxiety after a number of health crises left him exhausted and unable to work at his graphic design job or to pursue his other, normal activities. He had gradually become more dysfunctional. He suffered from physical pain, gastrointestinal problems, and tension headaches. This session is many months into therapy. Max is talking about the way his husband, Ted, expresses anger toward Max when Ted has been drinking. Max has a slight build and sits slightly hunched forward. As he talks, he twists his legs around each other and holds both hands under his legs.

Max: *This is such a pattern with Ted. He'll go along for a while, and things will be good. Sometimes he won't drink at all, or he controls it. Then, I don't know ... he gets stressed about work, or his kids, or something happens with his mother, and he just loses it.*

Steve: *Without changing your posture, just notice how you're sitting, what you're doing with your legs and arms as you tell me this.*

Max: *I ... well. (Pause.) I ... it's like I'm tying myself up in a knot ... and my hands are held down. They're trapped. (Pause.) I'm trapped. Everything feels really tight, like I'm in a vice.*

Steve: *Are you willing to stay with this?*

Max: *(Nods.)*

Steve: *Just keep paying attention to your physical experience right now.*

Max: *(Does this for several seconds.) It's hard to sit this way. It really takes a lot of effort. (Lets out a deep sighing breath he had been holding in, and unwraps his arms and legs.) I have to work so hard to hold everything in ... to try not to feel anything. (Sits back and sighs again.)*

Steve: *You've shifted your posture, and you've stopped holding your breath. (Pause.) What are you aware of now?*

Max: *(Quietly.) I guess I'm a little ... maybe ... angry with Ted.*

Steve: *See what happens if you say that to me again, without* *the qualifiers, "I guess, "a little," "maybe."*

Max: (Pause, then stronger voice.) OK. (Pause.) I am angry with Ted. And it hurts, the way he treats me....

In this example, Steve's initial process intervention directs Max's attention to what he is doing in the moment. Focusing on his body, Max becomes more aware of both the experience of what he is doing physically and the function it serves. As he loosens this hold on himself, the body's energies and emotion, previously blocked from awareness, become figural. The observation of his deflective language and the suggestion to experiment with dropping the qualifiers also helps Max move more into the truth of his experience. This later becomes a springboard for exploring how it is for him to take a stronger stand and to express his feelings more directly. Had he been unable or unwilling to go with this direct expression, another possible experiment would have been to emphasize the qualifiers, in order for Max to more clearly experience this impact.

These interventions bring Max's attention to his experience in a way that focusing on content could miss. This increased awareness is both connecting and empowering. At the end of this session, Max is less restricted in his own awareness and in his physicality. With more self-support he considers new possibilities. For example, Max decides he will return to Al Anon, feeling more empowered to deal with Ted's disapproval about that choice. In subsequent sessions, Max is able to further explore the contrast between tying himself in knots—a retroflective process that was based in his early, creative adjustments—and allowing his fuller connection with what is true for him, even when this truth involves difficult or painful feelings.

Paradoxical Nature of Change

Gestalt therapy's understanding of change has been described as paradoxical in the sense that change occurs when we become what we *are* rather than attempting to become what we are not (Beisser, 1970). Although this understanding is referred to as a *theory* of change, it is more accurately a principle—an empirically observed phenomenon. We include it in this section on method because it informs all interventions and every aspect of Gestalt therapy work. In Gestalt therapy we are guided by the understanding that change occurs not through our attempts to change but rather by our stepping fully into what and who we actually are and the truth of our experience. When a person identifies with his authentic experience and enters wholeheartedly into it, the awareness and acceptance that follow allow the unfolding of natural self-regulating. Change occurs naturally when we allow and embrace what is, as this creates the solid ground for stepping off into a new direction.

The more we deny any aspect of ourselves or of our experience in order to force a change, the more internal conflict we create and the more likely we will stay stuck where we are. In trying to change, we are often attached to an idea of what the change should look like, or how we should be different, rather than trusting the process of allowing ourselves to be with what is and to discover what comes next. The more we bring acceptance to any experience (even if it is acceptance of a lack of acceptance!) the more we are grounded in our authenticity, fully inhabiting who we are, rather than striving for an artificial ideal of who we "should" be. The change that occurs in this process is organic rather than imposed.

Although not specifically articulated by Beisser, *closure*, as described in Chapter 5, is part of this organic process. Difficulty connecting and identifying with one's actual experience interferes with the movement of the natural regulating process and the completion of the FFD cycle, just as controlling one's breath and restricting a full exhalation will limit the depth of the next inhalation. When the natural movement toward closure is prevented, figures or *gestalten* remain fixed. Being with what is, and accepting it, is *in itself* change, shifting our relationship to ourselves and to our experience. Not every unfinished situation will have closure. But as we let go of trying to change, or of trying to get rid of feelings or some aspect of ourselves, we step into the flow of movement that is always happening; and an experience may then be held or understood differently.

Gestalt therapy has always been grounded in this fundamental truth about change—that change is made possible as we become what we truly *are*—and the belief that increased awareness, acceptance, and closure underlie it. As other approaches have been influenced by mindfulness, there is a more widespread understanding that "change follows acceptance," and that trying to surmount resistance or to talk people out of feelings or beliefs in order to get them to change is not beneficial. Of course, a patient may want to bring resolve and intention to specific changes, for example, deciding to get more exercise and setting up a structure to support this. Or, perhaps therapist and patient recognize a need for a particular skill, like assertiveness, that would allow desired behavior, and different experience. These may also be explored in Gestalt therapy work.

Often, people seek therapy because they want to "let go of" something. They may want to get rid of certain feelings, aspects of themselves, or ways of experiencing. The thing they want to let go of may be old pain from childhood, current anger, or grief about a failed relationship. This expressed wish to let go is often a disguised desire to avoid feeling something painful, and a drive for premature closure, to avoid this pain. This also reflects the mistaken belief that "letting go" can be accomplished by an act of will rather than recognizing it as an organic and derivative process that is a *consequence* of attending to, working though, and getting closure on unfinished feelings or experience. When we have done the needed work, whatever has been holding on can let go of us.

The following example shows how this process, consistent with this understanding of change, can be addressed in Gestalt therapy. It also illustrates directing attention to present moment experience, focusing on increasing awareness, and working with introjecting, retroflecting, and projecting.

Nicole is twenty-seven-years-old and single. She presents as very composed, with an every-hair-in-place professional dress and demeanor. Her mother died ten months ago, and she comes to therapy with me (Eva) wondering why she is not yet "over" her mother's death. She says that she did not cry at the funeral because she did not want her younger siblings to see her in tears, afraid that it would make them feel worse. Also, she says that she had to "be strong" for her father. Since her mother's death, she has been "going through the motions" of her life, but she feels isolated and takes little pleasure in relationships, leisure activities, or her job. She works for a non-profit and had previously felt passionate about the agency and her role in it. Nicole has come to therapy to figure out how to "get through" the stages of grief, so she can "move on."

Nicole's grief is, of course, a natural response to her mother's death. Grieving is a way of acknowledging the depth and importance of a relationship and a process for integrating and assimilating loss. In therapy it becomes clear that Nicole's objections to experiencing her grief and to showing her sadness are a result of the need to "be strong for others" (introject). Maintaining this position also requires retroflecting. She prevents the outward expression of grief and the contact she might make with others, and forces herself to comply with perceived expectations. Doing this, she cuts off awareness of her actual feelings and substitutes ideas of how she is supposed to be. Then she is critical of herself for not "getting over" her loss.

Nicole's interruption of what would be natural regulating (for example crying when sad) and how this interruption limits contact possibilities can be readily seen. Being cut off from her experience and keeping herself alone with her grief likely contributes to the depression symptoms she describes. Also her sense of dullness appears to be a result of this shutting down, muting her overall experience. This interaction took place in a session about six weeks into therapy.

Nicole: So it's going on a year since my mom died ... and well ... I don't know why I still haven't gone through all those stages of grief. But Ginny (younger sister) is actually doing better than I am. She's in a grief group and I guess that's helped her.

Eva: Would you like help with your grief?

Nicole: (Nods.) Well ... I'd like to be stronger, and I'd like to get over it, and not feel so blah about everything.

Eva: So, not help with your grief, but help to be stronger, and to get over it. Tell me more about "being stronger."

Nicole: Just—you know—back to normal, my old energy level. Not feeling so bad or like crying all the time.

Eva: Of course, it's understandable you'd want to feel better, and that you'd wish you could get back to how you felt before your mom died. (Pause. I notice her eyes welling.) What's coming up for you right now?

Nicole: Well, I feel like crying just hearing you say that.

Eva: Yes. (Softly.) I see your tears. (Pause.) Are you willing to stay with what you're feeling?

Nicole: I guess, but I hate being sad and weepy. (Impatiently wipes tears.)

Eva: So ... you are sad and weepy, and you also hate it.

Nicole: Yeah. It just hurts so much. *(Chokes back tears.)* And I hate feeling so weak.

Eva: I see the two parts struggling right now—the sadness and how much it hurts, and also hating those feelings and what you see as weakness...

Nicole: *(Nods.)*

Eva: Just feel how it is right now to be in the middle of those.

Nicole: *(Closes eyes, pauses, then opens eyes; looks at me, crying.)* I really want to just let my sadness out. I'm tired of having to be so strong all the time...

Eva: So right now you're more with the sadness, wanting to come out with it.

Nicole: *(Nods, crying.)*

Eva: OK, so see if you can stay with your sadness and that want...

Nicole: *(Crying)* It's ... a lot.

Eva: Yes, I see that. *(Long pause.)* And is there something your tears want to say to the part that hates these feelings and wants you to "be strong"? *(Gestures toward chair.)*

Nicole: Uh huh, there is. *(Turning to empty chair, talking through tears.)* I'm so sick of trying to be strong! You're always trying to push me down. I'm not strong. *(Crying.)* I'm sad ... and I miss her so much. *(Pause.)* I don't think that's so bad. *(Sobbing, looks at me.)*

Eva: So much feeling comes up as you give this part a voice.

Nicole: *(Nods, wipes tears. Long pause.)* I feel ... good actually. It's a relief. *(Pause.)* She's still here, though. *(Points at chair.)* Thinking I shouldn't cry, should be stronger. *(Tears subside.)*

Eva: Yes, she's still here. Do you want to see what she has to say now? *(Indicates switching chairs.)*

Nicole: *(Gets up and goes to the other chair.)*

Eva: Take your time. See if you can connect with the "be strong" part. (Pause.) And if there is something you want to say from there to your sadness.

Nicole: (Pause.) Hmm ... I'm surprised this side doesn't seem to have that much to say right now. I guess ... well. (Speaking from "be strong" part.) I do try to keep you pushed down, but right now I feel some relief too, like maybe it's OK. And I don't have to keep such a tight lid on all the time.

As the work continues over the next several months, Nicole becomes more aware of her lifelong pattern of pushing herself to "get over" things. Growing up, taking responsibility for younger siblings, and ignoring her own feelings and needs was a creative adjustment to fit her parent's expectations. Showing feelings or expressing needs of her own was met with lectures about how she "should" be as the responsible, oldest of four stair-step siblings. These "shoulds" were introjected. As Nicole understands and works through these introjects and the retroflections they require, she feels a deeper longing to connect with her authentic experience. She discovers that the pain of never getting the nurturing and comfort she deeply longed for from her mother makes her grief more complicated. Nicole begins to feel anger toward her mother about the ways she was distant and how it hurt and deprived Nicole in not having these longed-for experiences. She connects with her actuality rather than with a version of herself that her parents required, questioning the introject that says it is weak for her to have her own feelings and needs.

In this process Nicole also discovers more satisfying ways of making contact with me, and she begins opening up more with her siblings. They grieve together rather than Nicole "being strong" for them. She sees that her idea that her siblings needed her to be stoic for them has been her own projection of this "be strong" part of herself, and that what they actually want is to connect emotionally with her. With these processes of Nicole's character illuminated and explored, her depression symptoms resolve, and her grieving process proceeds at its own pace rather than being obstructed by an artificial timetable, introjects, projections, and retroflected needs and feelings.

As this example shows, when we are attempting to become something we are not, we can become captive to this fixed, rigid view. Pushed into a corner, aspects of experience remain unexplored, and can create symptoms as well as interfering with meaningful contact and connection. Connecting with our authentic experience opens up new possibilities.

Therapy without Resistance

When Gestalt therapy was originally developed, the concept of resistance was included. This was a holdover from psychoanalysis in which analyst interpretations enabled the patient to gain understanding of the unconscious. A patient's lack of acceptance of an interpretation was likely to be construed as resistance. Although Gestalt therapy kept the concept of resistance, it was looked at differently. Gestalt therapy eliminated the idea of "the unconscious," simply recognizing that some aspects of experience were readily accessible to awareness while others were out of awareness. In the Gestalt therapy model, however, what was out of awareness was not seen as inaccessible to the patient. Rather it could be accessed with focused attention to current experiencing and behavior. This did not require therapist interpretation; in fact it was quite the opposite. It was the therapist directing the patient's attention to present experience that allowed the patient's access to what was out of awareness. So, Gestalt therapy did not require overcoming a patient's resistance to interpretation, but still saw patient resistance to a particular subject matter, or resistance to particular ways of contacting as something to be clarified, made more explicit, and directly expressed and explored. Later, it was proposed that the concept of resistance itself is unnecessary in Gestalt therapy (Polster & Polster, 1976). Subsequently this was built on, making the case that the concept of resistance is actually antithetical to the tenets of Gestalt therapy theory and practice (Breshgold, 1989).

Here is why. In Gestalt therapy, the therapist takes an empirical focus and attends to what is most important for the patient. As work with each emerging figure progresses, the natural process that leads to closure of that figure is facilitated. The therapist trusts the process and that the next important figural development will naturally emerge as the patient and therapist focus on what is. As shown in the work with Nicole, as we work with each emerging figure, that figure is clarified. Then the therapist, in collaboration with the patient, facilitates the natural unfolding that allows organic movement toward whatever closure is possible. So in this example, the therapist notices that Nicole has tears welling up, while at the same time she is objecting to moving into sadness or allowing her tears. The therapist's role is not to persuade her to give in to her sadness, but to help her to simply stay with and explore the lively figure of the affect, along with her objection to feeling it, supporting both. This could be seen as "supporting the resistance," but this would still imply something is being resisted, as opposed to simply seeing this as what the patient is currently experiencing and doing. From a Gestalt therapy perspective, if the patient is avoiding something, this avoidance is for good reason, and this avoiding process is just as important as what is being avoided. Even if currently limiting, these processes were originally essential creative adjustments, as we described. In this sense the patient may experience so-called "resistances" as actually helpful "assistances." The therapeutic task is to bring this entire process into awareness. We are not trying to get the patient somewhere else, but rather we seek to help clarify the patient's experience.

Appreciating the "yes/no" of ego functioning, as described in Chapter 5, also means that the Gestalt therapist assists the patient's connection with and assertion of what she does or does not want, or want to do, as opposed to encouraging compliance or acceptance of the therapist's perspective or suggestion. If the therapist senses even subtle reluctance or disagreement, this is most usefully sharpened. This might be supporting the "no" function by suggesting that the patient experiment with expressing any disagreement or saying "no" more directly. The consistent message to the patient is that the therapist welcomes contact around and expression of disagreement, dissatisfactions, or reluctance. Introjecting the therapist's ideas or suggestions, or "going along with" is neither expected nor required. So again, what could be seen as "resistance" is not something to do battle with or overcome. It is rather something to clarify, make overt, and support.

The Gestalt therapist also remains free of investment in any particular outcome. Going back to the above example, why is it important for Nicole to avoid certain feelings? How were her tears or sadness received—or rejected—when she was a child? And how does that influence her current experience of herself? How does she continue to identify with an ideal of how she is supposed to be that alienates aspects of her own authentic experience? Can she become aware of what it was like to be on the receiving end of this treatment as a child and notice the ways she may now reject aspects of herself and of her own feelings? As clarity of these processes is facilitated, and as the therapeutic relationship provides needed support for emerging affect, and for her opposition to it, Nicole regains choice as to how she relates to this affect and her experience.

When it is not the therapist's job to fix or change the patient, or to make something happen, this frees the therapist to be more fully available for contact, to be more present and spontaneous. It further allows for putting aside any expectations and biases and trusting the "wisdom of the organism." In the therapy process, this wisdom emerges in ever-increasing increments, as awareness and therefore self-experience are expanded, because our natural tendency—when conditions support it—is toward contact, healing, and growth.

Experimental Method

The Gestalt therapy experiment provides an opportunity to try something and to see what happens. The therapist is not aiming at any particular outcome in proposing the experiment, but remains interested in whatever emerges. The most fruitful experiments develop organically from the present process and content, and are collaborative. Gestalt therapy's experimental method is based in the understanding that meaning emerges most powerfully from experience. Experiments maintain this focus on the experiential present moment. "The experiments are not fixed constellations of technical steps, but invented *ad hoc* to facilitate awareness of *what is*" (Perls, L., 1992, p.139). Experiments can explore automatic patterns by bringing them into the foreground, where they can be experienced with more intention and awareness, assisting the patient to take responsibility for them. Experiments allow meaning and insight to derive from what the patient feels and discovers, rather than from intellectual analysis or the therapist's ideas. They can also help diagnose and clarify aspects of the person's character and functioning, opening up possibilities for expansion of self-experience and contact. The experiment shifts the focus from "talking about" to an engaged, active exploration, creating opportunity for experiential learning and growth.

The therapist always attends to the patient's response to any proposed experiment, and, if needed, this is explored before moving on to the experiment itself. The goal is not to get the patient to do the experiment; that is up to the patient. At times the patient may need more support in order to engage in an experiment, or it may be collaboratively modified. Tailoring of experiments can make them more or less challenging, staying at the patient's growing edge without going beyond it. For example, suppose a patient implies that he is disappointed with the therapist. The therapist might suggest that the patient say directly, "I am disappointed in you." If the patient indicates reluctance or difficulty with this, the experiment can then be scaled back; for example, the patient could close his eyes and just imagine saying this to the therapist, noticing what comes up. This allows continued exploration.

Gestalt therapy's experimental method is broad and inclusive, involving all modes of functioning—visual, auditory, feeling, thought, and bodily sensation. Experiments can include anything the patient says, does, sees, hears, feels, or thinks. For example, an experiment can attend to language, like asking the patient to either exaggerate or eliminate the use of qualifiers such as "probably," "maybe," or "I guess." Or, the patient might repeat a word or phrase, or add, "I really mean that," after a sentence to feel what it is like to take a stronger stand. An experiment can attend to, highlight, and increase awareness of physical posture, gestures, or movement. This might be minimizing or exaggerating this physical language for emphasis, or freeze-framing it to stay with and notice how it feels. It is sometimes useful to mix modalities, or to shift to a different one. If a person says, "I'm tied up in knots," an experiment might suggest expressing this metaphor physically. Other examples are: "Is there a posture that expresses your despair?" or "Can you make as sound that captures your joy?" At times we might shift from a physical expression to words, for example, "Give your tears a voice." Experiments can be woven into the therapy in an organic way at any time. Examples of this are suggesting the patient attend to his constrained breathing, or notice his difficulty exhaling completely. Frequently used experiments involve asking the patient to stay with a sensation or emotion, or to attend more fully to any aspect of experience.

Only the therapist and patient's creativity and the patient's interest, willingness and capacity limit experimental possibilities. They can be an opportunity for the patient to try something she has never done before and to see what happens. Potentially, there are as many different types of experiments as there are idiosyncratic differences in people and situations. They are an ongoing opportunity for improvisational, creative, and spontaneous exploration; always relevant to the current moment and unlimited in variety and breadth.

The following example shows an experiment clarifying and revealing a central therapy theme. This experimental exploration provides an inroad to recognizing an important way of limiting awareness and contact.

Bill is a gruff, fifty-eight-year-old delivery truck driver. He sought therapy for depression that was interfering with his ability to function in his time-pressured job, after going through a painful divorce from his wife of over thirty years. In this session I (Steve) notice that Bill's voice gets noticeably quieter as he tells me about how it is for him to live alone since his divorce. I point this out and suggest he try exaggerating it, and speaking even more softly. He does try this, and then he says, "It's like I'm hiding or something." Bill reports that this sense of hiding feels familiar to him. I ask if he wants to continue hiding, and we can look at what he is hiding or hiding from, or if he wants to experiment with speaking louder.

Bill does move into speaking more loudly with rising energy, and also with some trepidation. As his voice gets louder, he feels more power and strength in what he is saying. He also discovers that anger toward his ex-wife is bubbling up. As he begins to feel the anger, he reflexively gets quieter again. This process leads to exploring his reluctance to connect with his anger. In subsequent sessions Bill recognizes that he is cut off, not just from anger but also from feelings in general, including grief over the end of his marriage. Slowly over time and with continued attention to this process, Bill reports his depression symptoms subsiding as he connects more with his emotional experience. He also feels less isolated as he is able to share this with me in therapy.

Homework Experiments

Homework experiments are an opportunity for continued exploration outside of the therapy session. They offer more surface area for continued attention to the therapy themes, and extend the work into the patient's life. This also allows patients to continue work on their own, and to have more agency in their own growth. Developed in collaboration with the patient, these experiments can take many forms. The patient might try out a particular way of being, or pay attention to and notice in more detail an aspect of experience. She may want to practice or challenge herself to be more assertive, or to speak up in meetings, but again and importantly these are not therapist-driven agendas. If the patient does not do the homework, the "not doing" is the outcome of the experiment, and can be explored.

Working with Dreams

In Gestalt therapy, dreams offer the opportunity for experiments designed to bring the dream to life in the therapy room. For example, experimenting with the patient telling the dream in the first person present tense creates more immediacy and may help the patient clarify what is most interesting or compelling about the dream. This also gives the therapist an opportunity to attend to *how* the patient presents and tells the dream, for example, with reticence or with enthusiasm. The therapist may notice minimizing or distancing from aspects of the dream, or discounting its impact. In the dream itself, images or content may be vague and confusing, or in sharp detail. As with all of Gestalt therapy, the therapist is attentive to the relational aspect of the patient bringing the dream to the therapist. How the patient makes contact with the therapist in the process of telling and working on the dream can be as important as, or more important than, the process and content of the dream itself.

Depending on what initially becomes figural or where the energy is, experiments may include the patient playing out different people or other parts of the dream, such as being the haunted house or the speeding car, and telling the dream in the first person from this perspective. This is based on Fritz Perls' insight that all parts of the dream represent aspects of the dreamer (Perls, F., 1969). Often, a dialogue between different characters in the dream can be revealing. Dreams can be a pointer to something unfinished for the patient that needs attention. They can be a reflection of the patient's overall existence and position in the world, for example, a patient's recurring dream of being "lost" on campus, and "late to" or "unprepared for" an exam in a class he has not attended all semester.

Dreams can be understood and experimented with as communication from patient to therapist. Isadore From (personal communication, 1980) suggested that a dream the patient has on the night *after* a therapy session might be a communication of something retroflected and unspoken from that session. For example, if the patient reports a confusing dream the night after the previous session, From might ask, "How did *I* confuse you in our last session?" He considered that a dream the night *before* a therapy session might point to what needed to be worked on next. From maintained the importance of keeping in mind that the patient "produced" the dream and chose to bring it to the therapist, also clarifying the patient's responsibility in this process.

Working with Polarities

Nagarjuna, an ancient Buddhist philosopher, put forth the idea that with polarities, each pole's existence depends on the existence of its opposite. Gestalt therapy's dialectic embraces this perspective. Carl Jung's views influenced Gestalt therapy's understanding of polarities, in that Jung "articulated the polar quality of human life ... (in which) aspects of the overt personality by their very prominence cast into shadow a counterpart aspect" (Polster & Polster, 1973, p. 312). Jung proposed that integration of disowned or unrecognized aspects of character was needed for a person to be whole. Gestalt therapy's view of polarities is more all-encompassing, not limited to specific archetypes, but "springing into life as the opposite of any part, or even any quality of the self" (Polster & Polster, 1973, p. 312). For each aspect or characteristic of ourselves that is emergent, implicitly residing in the background we may find its opposite.

Experiments can clarify the polarities when two opposing forces within the person pull in different directions. With the experimental method, we can explore internal conflict, self-criticalness, or difficulty with a decision. This can develop into a dialogue between the different poles, for example, the daredevil part of the person talking to the cautious part. The two parts can engage in a dialogue in which the patient alternately identifies with and speaks from each side, allowing a fuller, more direct experience of each perspective than can be achieved by simply talking about the conflict. A deeper more holistic understanding of the issues in which these dynamics are embedded also emerges.

This embodiment and articulation of each position frequently results in a synthesis, and sometimes the development of a novel third perspective. So, when the daredevil and cautious parts actively engage, allowing the patient to step fully into each aspect, the patient may discover that each has value and come to a third novel perspective that integrates the two. In conflicts about decisions, the patient can also experiment with alternately taking both sides. For example, the part of a person that wants to leave a relationship can make a case to the part that wants to stay. This process increases awareness as well as a sense of personal responsibility. Polarities may initially appear as indecision in life choices but may actually reflect polar aspects of the person. For example, the woman trying to decide whether to go to medical school or pursue her dream of an acting career may recognize not only the pulls of each choice but the aspects of herself that they represent, such as the responsible caregiver and the creative free spirit.

Experiments with polarities can look into aspects of self-experience that are in the background, and not being represented. This requires that the therapist recognize that important qualities of a person can be residing in the background, unacknowledged. Small clues can lead to their uncovering, and when attended to experimentally these may take on more power or have a voice for the first time. For example, a person who presents himself as humble might experiment with arrogance. The self-sacrificing martyr might experiment with how she wants to be more self-serving.

A classic polarity, identified in Gestalt therapy, is the top-dog/

underdog split (Perls, F., 1970). In this dynamic, one part of the person criticizes, commands, and berates, while the other part passively resists or halfheartedly attempts to comply with the ongoing requirements and demands. Often the person identifies strongly with the top-dog and is not aware of the existence of the underdog, although that part may control much of behavior. The top-dog is often the internalized voice of a critical parent.

The following example illustrates working experimentally, with a top-dog/underdog polarity.

Teri, thirty-eight, has a successful and challenging career as a nursing instructor. She is often harried-looking and generally arrives to her sessions a few minutes late, rushed and breathless. Teri is divorced, and the single parent of two young children. She came to therapy because of a long history of depression, and with a desire to lose weight. She had periodically tried anti-depressants that did not help and contributed to weight gain. Teri had been on many diets, but she did not stick to them; and she was frustrated by this cycle. Wanting to exercise more, eat less junk food, and prepare healthier meals, she was discouraged that she never stuck to those plans. She was quite critical of herself, referring to herself as a "lazy pig." In initial sessions, it was apparent she did not have much awareness of this automatic self-criticism.

In this session, several months into therapy, Eva suggests that Teri imagine the "lazy pig" part of herself in the empty chair and speak to that part, fully identifying with the "critic," berating the "lazy pig" for her slothful ways. Teri initially moves into this experiment with enthusiasm, enjoying letting loose with her critique. When she is finished, Eva suggests switching to the other chair, seeing if she can feel what it is like to be on the receiving end of this. For the first time, Teri connects with what it is like to have this barrage of criticism directed at her.

Teri: (Speaking to critic.) I can't stand it when you talk to me that way. (Slumps down and looks away into the distance.) I want to just hide in my room with a bag of Cheetos.

Eva: See if you can say more about what you're feeling.

Teri: You make me feel horrible about myself. (Pause.) And I'm pissed at you, too. You sound just like Dad—always telling me how worthless I am.

Eva: OK. How it for you to say this?

Teri: (Turns and talks to me.) I'm ... so mad ... that this is what I've always gotten. (Pause.) And now here I am doing it to myself.

Eva: Yes. (Pause.) Sounds like you have more to say to the part that is doing this—that's always criticizing?

Teri: (More energy.) Leave me alone! I'm so pissed at you. You just make everything worse. (Pause.)

Eva: So, do you want to see what the critic says back? (Indicates switching chairs.)

Teri: (Changes chairs and shifts to more upright posture.) No way I can leave you alone! Without me keeping you in line you'd be a blimp, and you'd never get anything done. You would be in your room all day eating Cheetos—you'd be a total mess if it weren't for me.

Teri: (Spontaneously switches chairs.) You think you're help-ing? If you really want to help me, you'd stop calling me names! You think I'm lazy? I have two kids and a full-time job. I'm NOT lazy, I'm tired. And you're such a taskmaster, nothing ever satisfies you.

This experiment opens up a window into important as-pects of Teri's character, allowing the work to go beyond what is presented as a desire for behavior change. Teri's lifelong pattern of self-criticism and its impact is revealed. Identifying with the "top-dog" critic and unaware of and therefore not able to give voice to the "underdog" has kept her stuck in a pattern of passive resistance, with the two sides constantly engaged in an unawares tug-of-war. This results in a self-defeating pattern, difficult or impossible to change without a clear awareness of what and how it is created and maintained.

As we explore this in subsequent sessions, the "lazy pig" morphs into Teri's desire for less restriction, and more spontaneity and enjoyment in her life. Unaware of these needs, she had been trying to meet them by not going along with the "top-dog's" demands, even if she actually agreed with the benefits of healthier eating or exercise. She also starts to see the criticism that she has always directed against herself as the unexpressed anger toward her father (retroflected aggression). Ultimately, Teri recognizes that she feels deeply hurt by him, both wanting his love and approval and conflicted about having to prove her worthiness to him—the top-dog/ underdog dynamic that she was now engaged in with herself. As this is seen more clearly, the critic's important function is also recognized. Teri sees that this part originally attempted to help in both trying to get her to comply with expectations in order to get love and approval from her father, and keeping her anger and criticism at herself instead of at him, which might lead him to reject her.

Functional Diagnosis

Functional and process oriented, diagnosis in Gestalt therapy is qualitatively different than traditional clinical diagnosis, which generally involves labeling, as well as categorizing symptoms. Traditional diagnosis is based in a different paradigm, one that aligns with a medical model, potentially pathologizing the patient and putting the therapist in a position of assessing what is wrong and knowing how to fix it. Although useful for Gestalt therapists in a limited way, for example, as a short-hand way of considering symptoms and communicating to other professionals or insurance companies, traditional diagnosis offers minimal information about the person's whole being, unique functioning and interaction in the world, and does little to orient interventions.

Gestalt therapy's functional diagnosis, on the other hand, is an alive and ongoing assessment of the "how" of functioning. It is not geared toward labeling an individual, but toward understanding the whole person by identifying relevant processes and relational patterns. How does a person organize experience and self-regulate? How is this natural flow of self-regulation interrupted and contact inhibited? Where and how in the FFD cycle does this happen? Generally the processes that we observe are an important feature or example of the person's character and interactive patterns. Gestalt therapy diagnoses limitations and also importantly diagnoses strengths within the context of field and relational influences.

A functional diagnosis orients the therapy interventions, as they naturally flow from this ongoing assessment. This becomes part of the collaborative patient-therapist interaction, as contact boundary phenomena and therapy themes are freshly understood within the co-created field, and patient input is actively sought regarding the relationship and therapy experience. Experiments are part of this process, adding new and more nuanced information to where difficulties occur and where expansion is possible. Functional diagnosis is simple, clear, and descriptive, and requires no interpretation. It is a clarification for both therapist and patient of what is most apparent in the patient's experience and overall functioning.

The following is an example of ongoing collaborative functional diagnosis.

Kalesha, a single, thirty-three-year-old physician, came into therapy to deal with her lack of ease in connecting with people, and generally missing passion in her life. Kalesha appears self-assured but reserved. This reserve contrasts with her fashionable and colorful way of dressing. In this session she is reporting on a recent first date. She tells me (Steve) that she likes this man better than anyone she's met in a long time. "I'm definitely interested in him," she says.

As Kalesha talks, her affect does not match her words. She sits quite still, with little facial expression, and her tone of voice is subdued. My process comment takes the form of a question: "Do you feel as neutral on the inside as you appear on the outside right now?" In response to this question, Kalesha becomes aware of dampening excitement, keeping her face neutral and her body still. Exploring this, she discovers not only how constrained she is, but how this results in more muted, less satisfying contact with me.

Intervening at this process level helps shed light on a particular emotional and behavioral pattern directly related to Kalesha's reasons for seeking therapy. This creates an important opening for exploration of both a habitual process and what is happening in the therapy relationship. As the session continues, Kalesha's reluctance to show her feelings and how she manages this is explored. She feels more of what it is like to be muted, and her difficulty moving into more energy or excitement, and connects with some fear about showing feelings in general and in the session. She relates this to her teenage experiences of being unmercifully teased by her older sister if she showed excitement about something, especially boys. Her family members often related by teasing, and Kalesha's reticence helped her guard against being embarrassed or shamed. This muting is what she now does with me in therapy, and in relationships in general.

Steve: So, it makes sense that it's hard for you to really let on about your excitement.

Kalesha: Yeah, it is hard.

Steve: But you know I'm not your sister...

Kalesha: I know, and I'm not a teenager! (Laughs.)

Steve: OK, so are you interested in talking to me with the energy or excitement you actually feel?

Kalesha: I am. (Pause.) And I'm not sure how to go about it.

Steve: OK, well, how about just starting to connect with your excitement, as you feel it right now. Experiment with closing your eyes and focusing in on the feeling.

Kalesha: OK. (Pause.)

Steve: What's coming up?

Kalesha: A fluttery feeling in my chest, light and ... happy.

Steve: Fantastic! See if you'd like to speak to me from that light, fluttery, happy place in you.

Kalesha begins talking in a livelier, more energized way about her date. Then, as she continues, she gradually goes back to being more muted. We label this her "mute function" and look at what is required to accomplish this—tightening of muscles and shallower breathing along with a felt sense of diminishing and constricting herself. With this clarity, she begins to play with moving back and forth between the experience of expansion into fluttery, light, and happy that feels risky, and the experience of constriction when she engages the "mute function" and feels more protected but shut down.

This example shows how patient and therapist collaborate on "diagnosing" what is happening in the moment and in the interaction. Although it did not emerge as figural in this session, looking at the therapist's contribution, or the co-created dynamic interaction, can always be part of this ongoing functional diagnosis.

Therapist Self-Disclosure

The Gestalt therapy approach is contact based. Along with our dialogical perspective, this encourages the therapist's authentic engagement. This has at times resulted in a misconception that anything the therapist feels or is aware of in the session will be therapeutically useful, regardless of the relevance or impact, and that complete therapist transparency is required. Contemporary Gestalt therapists have clarified this issue and developed some general guidelines for therapist self-disclosure (Zahm, 1998). Laura Perls (1992) suggested that she would share only as much of her own life as offered support for the patient taking a risk, or a needed next step. Another clarification was that if withholding something diminished the therapist's ability to be present and engaged, this must be judiciously revealed as needed (Kempler, 1973). The current prevailing view is that the Gestalt therapist is "asked to be genuine and selectively transparent where it serves the growth of the client" (Melnick & Nevis, 2005, p.110).

In Gestalt therapy, there are no rigid rules regarding self-disclosure. Like all other therapeutic choices, this choice is based on the specifics of the patient, the situation, the therapist's experience, the relationship, and the moment. Self-disclosure can serve a variety of functions in Gestalt therapy. It is an aspect of the genuine unreserved communication prescribed by the dialogical relationship, potentially furthering intimacy and enlivening contact. At times, a heartfelt therapist disclosure at the right moment, a surrender to the "between," can spark a deeply felt connection, that rare "I-Thou" moment. Other functions of therapist self-disclosure are validation or support, counteracting potential hierarchy in the relationship, and letting the patient know how he is impacting the therapist (Zahm, 1998).

Broadly there are two types of therapist self-disclosure. The first is the therapist sharing a life experience or personal situation. This may be in response to a direct question like, "Have you ever gone through a divorce?" Or, it can be a spontaneous response from the therapist, "I understand. I felt that way when my father died." The second type is a disclosure of the therapist's immediate current experience, such as, "What you're saying touches me." The therapist uses what she knows about the patient and the relationship to assess the possible impact of either type of self-disclosure. Individual patients can also have very different responses to self-disclosure depending on their history and how they organize experience. And different patients can extract different meanings from the same type of intervention. For example, a patient whose parent used her as a confidant may feel imposed upon by the therapist's revelation of a personal experience. Another patient who felt left out and disconnected from her parent's life may feel more connection, trust, and closeness as a result of the very same disclosure. Of course, we cannot always predict the impact of self-revealing or any intervention, so we also track spoken and unspoken responses, observing or inquiring about the impact on the patient if it is not already clear from the patient's response.

Self and Environmental Support

In Gestalt therapy, support is understood to be an essential aspect of therapeutic exploration, assimilation, and growth. There are two potential sources of support for the patient in therapy—self-support and support from the therapist. Both allow the patient to take the risks that lead to increased awareness and open up new possibilities for contact. In an effective therapeutic relationship, the relationship with the therapist and the therapy process itself enhance self-support as patients identify with their own experience, connect with the therapist, and tap into their internal resources. In the example above, Kalesha needed both support from Steve and self-support to more fully feel and show her excitement. In any therapeutic interaction, no matter what the therapy theme or figure is, the support function is always operating. At times support itself is the focus, as patient and therapist look at what the patient might need to do to support herself, or what she might need from the therapist. Even when in the background, therapist support is always an essential element of the relational connection.

In therapy, patients may become more aware of how their posture, gestures, voice, or breathing are not supporting them. For example, constricted breathing, frequently seen in emotionally charged experiences, makes it difficult to "let go" into a complete exhalation, resulting in the inability to take in enough air on the inhalation. This shutting down restricts physiological support for building excitement and emotional expression, often resulting in anxiety. Patients may also discover how they scare, criticize, or otherwise undermine themselves. These discoveries then allow experimenting with new possibilities. In the example with Teri, she developed more self-support in the form of self-compassion as she identified with the part of herself on the receiving end of her criticism. In the example with Max, self-support involved a change in both physical posture and language. This shifted his experience and allowed him to connect with a wish for more support from others, and the decision to seek this through Al Anon. Both self-support and environmental support were needed to help him feel sturdier in dealing with his husband's reactions.

In Gestalt therapy it is vital for the therapist to recognize when support is needed, and to offer it judiciously. Support never means false reassurance, disingenuous agreement, or skipping over necessary and painful steps for the patient. These are anti-therapeutic and undermine the patient's autonomy and agency, interfering with growth. Ultimately, skillful functioning in the world requires a balance of the ability to access self-support and the ability to develop and make use of support from others and the environment. The therapeutic interaction offers practice and experience with both. In Chapter 11 we also explore meditation practices as an aspect of enhancing patient self-support.

Now that we have outlined Buddhist psychology views and methods and Gestalt therapy theory and practice, we move to the next step. Where do we find the essential convergences of this Eastern wisdom tradition and this Western psychotherapy system?

PART III

Convergences & Clinical Implications

7

Convergence of Views

*If we do not focus on human limits and pathology, what
is the alternative? It is the belief that human freedom
is possible under any circumstances.*

—Jack Kornfield, *The Wise Heart:
A Guide to the Universal Teachings
of Buddhist Psychology*

EXPLORING THE COMMON GROUND of Buddhist psychology and
Gestalt therapy has been a continuous process of discovery for
us. Each time we come upon a new and unexpected connection,
there is the satisfaction of finding yet another valuable nugget.
The challenge of exploring and clarifying these connections
has often yielded even greater treasure in the form of deeper
understanding. The four chapters in this section of the book are
the result of this process of exploration, discovery, clarification,
and synthesis. Some of these areas of convergence have been
touched on in the preceding chapters. In this chapter and the
next three we offer a more detailed look at what we see as the
essential common ground, as well as the clinical implications
of this. This chapter's focus is on the convergences of Buddhist
psychology and Gestalt therapy views. In Chapter 8 we look at
the convergences of mindfulness and Gestalt therapy method.
Then in Chapters 9 and 10 we explore the clinical implications
that emerge from this ground of convergence.

This chapter's consideration of convergences of views includes the two systems' views of human nature, relationship and interconnectedness, self, suffering, and what is understood as curative. We also look at the convergences in the understanding of impermanence, and the recognition of the universal/relative perspective. In addition, we point out some important differences between these two systems' views.

View of Human Nature

Buddhist psychology recognizes the essential dignity and goodness in every person. It views humans as fundamentally whole and complete as we are and possessing the potential for growth and awakening. This is referred to as "basic goodness" and sometimes as "buddha nature". From this perspective, everyone has the possibility of realizing the innate potential to transform greed, hatred, and delusion—the causes of suffering. The transformation occurs via the clear seeing that leads to insight and develops wisdom and compassion. This has been likened to the bud's natural blossoming into a flower, given adequate conditions of sunlight, water, and nutrients. Buddhist practice, therefore does not add something to us, but rather cultivates what is already in us.

According to Buddhist teacher Jack Kornfield, we have forgotten our essential nature and operate instead from a protective layer that we have developed. He says that the primary aim of Buddhist psychology and its practices is to enable us to learn about and experience what is beneath this armor, allowing us to restore this original nature (Kornfield, 2008). Although we have the capacity for both beneficial and harmful ways of being, the negative or harmful can be seen as transient, like clouds that temporarily obscure the blue sky. From this perspective, the feelings, thoughts, and behavior that are harmful to others or ourselves are understood as unskillful, the result of incomplete understanding. Following the Buddhist path helps dissolve these obscurations, letting us see through them to what is more true and essential in ourselves. As we do the practices, qualities like wisdom and compassion are naturally nourished, and our ways of being in the world become more skillful. Recent brain research lends support to this Buddhist psychology view in that we appear to be "hardwired" for qualities like empathy and compassion.

The Buddhist psychology view also suggests that more than normal levels of happiness are available to us. We are capable of greater joy and clarity than we ordinarily experience, and we have the capacity to be more fully present and awake in our lives. We are seen as having the potential for ever-expanding awareness, and the path is understood to develop this capacity, helping us to see through the effects of our conditioning and to access an essential purity of mind and heart.

Gestalt therapy recognizes that people naturally make the best possible adjustment in any situation, given their needs, limitations, and current field conditions. Gestalt therapy operates from the faith that we have a natural tendency toward growth, and that the factors that narrow experience and reduce behavioral flexibility can be brought into awareness and understood. From this perspective, what could be viewed as restricted or even pathological functioning is rather seen as a limitation resulting from disrupted healthy self-regulation. So difficulties in contact with others and psychological dysfunction or symptoms are not fundamental to the individual. Rather, they are viewed as resulting from creative adjustments. These have rigidified and are often maintained outside of awareness in the service of what is (or was) felt as necessary for emotional and psychological protection or survival. In therapy, as support and optimal conditions for increased awareness are available, the innate human potential for expansion, wholeness, and natural healthy functioning is restored.

Both Gestalt therapy and Buddhist psychology see each person's fundamental wholeness, recognizing the possibility for growth and the innate capacity to connect more deeply with our authentic nature. Each sees the opportunity for optimal functioning and expanded potential as a result of increased awareness. In neither system is a person defined by limitations. Both systems also recognize that the protective layer from which we function was developed for a reason. They both also emphasize increasing awareness as essential to working with obstacles to more fully realizing our human potential.

View of Relationship and Interconnectedness

In Buddhist psychology, all humans are seen as inherently having buddha nature; therefore any meeting between two people can be seen as two buddhas meeting. This imbues our contact with a quality of sacredness. A related essential understanding of relationship is Buddhist psychology's recognition of interconnectedness. Consistent with this understanding, actions are seen as skillful or unskillful based on their consequences for us, others, and our entire essentially interconnected world. As we follow the path and engage in Buddhist practices, we come to recognize that another's joy or pain can also be ours, and we are moved to care for others as we care for ourselves. Generosity toward and compassion for our fellow humans is also a natural extension of the understanding that by harming another or carrying anger and hatred, we are inevitably harming ourselves.

Gestalt therapy's dialogical stance supports a non-hierarchical relationship in which we hold the other as a Thou. This dialogical attitude recognizes our shared humanity, our capacity to deeply apprehend the other, and to feel the other's experience as if from the inside. It allows us to see the potential for sacredness in each encounter, always open to those I-Thou moments in which our interconnectedness and shared humanity is recognized and deeply felt. The value of relationship is seen in recognizing the power of "healing through meeting" as well. Seeing our essential interconnectedness is also within Gestalt therapy's field theoretical view. Gestalt therapy's emphasis on the indivisibility of the person/environment and the mutual, reciprocal influence of patient and therapist also reflect this field understanding.

In both Buddhist psychology and Gestalt therapy there is a foundational value placed on non-hierarchical human connection and relationship and an aspiration to treat others, the relationship, and our interactions as sacred. Both systems are also grounded in the truth of our essential interconnectedness and interdependence. We do not exist in isolation but rather in relatedness, which includes the potential for shared understanding, compassion, and healing connection. The two systems also align in recognizing individual flourishing as possible only within a relationally interconnected field.

View of Self
Buddhist psychology's understanding of not-self refers to the absence of any essential, separate, and enduring self-entity. "Selfing" is seen as a dynamic experience of always-changing process that is mistakenly reified. "When we inquire carefully into the question of identity, the creation of self is discovered to be a moment to moment process" (Kornfield, 2008, p. 76). As previously pointed out, this understanding of not-self does not deny that we have a sense of personal continuity of experience over a lifetime. It only points to the error of reification of this self-experience. Although some mistakenly believe it is the goal of Buddhism to "dissolve" the self, this is not the case. To paraphrase Buddhist teacher Thich Nhat Hanh, why try to dissolve something that does not exist? Rather, he explains, Buddhist practice seeks to dissolve mistaken views of the self

(Nhat Hahn, 1998) and emphasizes the importance of seeing how we create and identify with our reified self-sense.

In Gestalt therapy, self is also not seen as a static or reified entity. It is rather understood as the system of present contact-making and withdrawal. This is a dynamic, relational, and fluid process, the function of contacting the actual transient present. At the same time Gestalt therapy recognizes the human reflex toward categorization and reification. As Erving Polster observes: "Reification is an innate function of the mind." There is a "metaphorical agency that is carried out by the psychological clustering. Once we name these clusters, like the altruistic self ... they are indeed reified" (Polster, 2010, p. 47). For each figure formation/destruction (FFD) cycle, there is a corresponding self-sense; this self-experience is transitory, a field interactive effect. From this perspective the activity of selfing is viewed as a temporal process. In Gestalt therapy the experienced self-sense is expanded, allowing identification with emergent feelings, interests, and wants, enlarging the possibilities for novel contact.

Buddhist psychology and Gestalt therapy each see self-experience as an ever-changing, experiential, field-dependent phenomenon. They both describe in process language what can be mistakenly perceived as a solid, reified entity, thus challenging inaccurate and limited self-views, while also recognizing the reflex toward self-reification. In both systems, rather than the idea of a separate essential self, self-experience is understood as a more relational and contingent subjectivity that is created and dependent on field influences.

Gestalt therapy and Buddhist psychology do converge in recognizing self-as-process, along with acknowledging the human reflex to create and identify with a reified self. However, the way that the two systems address this understanding is different. In Buddhist psychology, the focus is on recognizing created self-identification as a misunderstanding that leads to suffering. In Gestalt therapy identification with self-experience is seen as essential to healthy ego functioning. At the same time, a fixed or rigid self-sense is understood to restrict awareness and limit the capacity for responsiveness and interpersonal contact. In Chapter 11, we consider how these two perspectives can be reconciled in the Buddhist psychology informed Gestalt therapy (BPGT) approach.

View of Suffering

From Buddhist psychology's universal perspective, failing to see the truth of impermanence, unsatisfactoriness, and not-self is the root cause of suffering. Ignorance of these truths leads to attachment in the form of craving and aversion, being opposed to the truth of our experience. In avoiding the truth of a painful experience, for example, we reject what is and crave what is not, as if there were something "out there" that could make us happy. But from this universal perspective, there is no inherent or essential substance to what we are grasping for. The first step of the eightfold path points us toward recognizing this and seeing through this delusion.

Gestalt therapy, too, recognizes that symptoms or suffering result from being in opposition to the truth of our experience, from objecting to what is. Gestalt therapy's focus is, of course, on the relative level, where suffering is understood to reside in our individual history and personal experience rather than in relationship to larger universal understanding. In therapy we pay attention to all the ways experience is disowned or denied, derailing natural self-regulation. Gestalt therapy unpacks these psychological elements of what the Buddha described as "second arrow" suffering, working with them in the individual form they take for each person.

Buddhist psychology and Gestalt therapy both understand

suffering to be in *how* we relate to experience, situations, and ourselves. They each recognize the need to fully move into and be with what is, and they both see the consequences of a lack of ability to do this. They each offer methods that bring heightened awareness to this process, recognizing that pain in life is inevitable and that it is the attempt to avoid this pain that leads to suffering. The two systems are aligned in the recognition that pain and difficult feelings are not problems that require solving; they are part of life. If there is a chance of healing what is painful, we must first experience it fully (Beisser, 1970).

On a relative level, the essential convergence in the two systems is clear. It is in denying or avoiding pain that we create more difficulty or suffering. A fundamental difference is that Buddhist psychology also involves the universal level and sees the recognition of the truths of existence as key in achieving liberation from suffering. Although Gestalt therapy does not include this view, in Chapter 11 we consider how a BPGT approach can integrate this perspective as well.

View of What Is Curative

Buddhist psychology's prescribed remedy for suffering is the eightfold path. The first step on the path is recognizing the truths of existence. Clarifying intention and recognizing skillful action in life choices follow from this clarity of view and point us toward cultivating mindfulness and concentration through meditation. In meditation we can then directly experience impermanence, unsatisfactoriness, and the lack of a solid self. This experiential understanding includes recognizing the difference between pain and suffering, as described in Chapter 2. The cure for suffering then lies in both seeing reality as it is and the ability to mindfully meet all aspects of ourselves—our physical, psychological, and emotional experience. Understanding what can release us from suffering is essential. The fruits of this path are increased capacity for joy, wisdom, compassion, and love, the ability to be more present and awake, and ultimately liberation from suffering.

In Gestalt therapy, opening to and embracing the totality of all of who we are and all of our experience is at the heart of what is curative. Through increased awareness, and within the healing relational field of therapist and patient, self-experience is expanded and interpersonal contact possibilities are enlarged. The Gestalt therapy patient sees more clearly that avoiding feelings or disowning aspects of experience—although once necessary maneuvers for psychological survival—are limiting and contribute to symptoms and self-alienation. As support for embracing authentic experience increases, fixed or rigid processes no longer impede the capacity to feel, express, and make contact, and natural self-regulation is restored. Emotional and relational expansiveness, creativity, spontaneity, and meaningful living are enhanced, with greater capacity for satisfaction and growth.

The ultimate awakening that is the promise of dedication to the eightfold path is, of course, different than Gestalt therapy's aim of increased awareness in the service of restored natural regulation. Yet the essential common denominator that connects the two systems' views of what is curative is the emphasis on the capacity to be with things as they are, and ourselves as we are. Both systems are grounded in the understanding that as we increase awareness of obstacles to connecting with our fundamental wholeness, healing and growth naturally unfold. In both systems "cure" is not an aimed for, permanent state of being or an end result but a living process. It is also not relief or escape from life's inevitable pain and disappointment. It is a deepening understanding of and connection with one's actual experience and the ability to embrace all of what is, as it is.

Recognition of Impermanence

In Buddhist psychology the truth of impermanence is one of the three universal givens. This truth also underlies the other truths of unsatisfactoriness and not-self, as everything in existence only arises from causes and conditions that are by their nature constantly changing. As the aggregates cycle, so do all aspects of experience arise, exist, and vanish.

Gestalt therapy's grounding in field theory, places it clearly in the Buddhist psychology camp, seeing everything that exists as within an interconnected field that is constantly in flux. In addition, recognizing the FFD cycle as the basic unit of experience— and how functioning is understood—means that in Gestalt therapy work, we are oriented by this ongoing process of movement and change. Each cycle has its beginning, middle, and end, and one cycle follows another in a continuous arising and resolution. In attending to the FFD process, we see that there is no fixed "now" and that experience is never static. As soon as we think we have captured the "now," it has already passed and something new has emerged, as each closed figure becomes part of the ground for the next emergent figure. At any point in the cycle, fixity or a sense of "stuckness" can be created, but as we come back to present moment experience in the work, we see that one thing always follows another and that experience is never static. It is a field interactive phenomenon in which movement and change are constants.

Universal and Relative Perspective

As previously described, Buddhist psychology recognizes two complementary aspects of existence, the universal and the relative. Buddhist psychology's view and meditation practices help us directly apprehend the universal reality of interconnectedness, and the truths of impermanence, unsatisfactoriness, and lack of an independent, essential, enduring self. From this vantage point we can also see our reflexive creation of solidity and fixity, the relative level of form and meaning making, which is how we orient to the practicalities of living.

Although "universal" and "relative" are Buddhist psychology concepts, we can see parallels in Gestalt therapy views. Gestalt therapy is field theoretical, based in this essential recognition of interconnectedness. As described above, Gestalt therapy's understanding of the importance of the FFD cycle, and attention to it, aligns with the universal truth of impermanence, even while the work itself focuses on the experienced fixity at the relative level. In addition, Gestalt therapy's perspective on self as process, along with the recognition of the human reflex toward reification, can also be seen as paralleling Buddhist psychology's universal/relative perspective.

These parallel views reflect fundamental convergences in these two systems' paradigms, and support our proposed integration. Their differences point to the benefit we envision in an integration of the two, as we explore in Chapter 11. In the next chapter we revisit Gestalt therapy method through the lens of its convergences with mindfulness meditation method.

8

Convergence of Methods

You have at your disposal everything you need to undertake this journey. There is only one prerequisite: the willingness to do the work, to follow the path through the darkest recesses of your mind and heart... and continue in the direction of freedom.

—Noah Levine, *Against the Stream: A Buddhist Manual for Spiritual Revolutionaries*

THE ORIGINAL TEXT that laid out the foundations of Gestalt therapy (Perls et al., 1951) offers a series of experiments for the reader. The first set of experiments is "Feeling the Actual." Here the authors describe the common experience of being only "half there," of wandering off from the present into fantasy, daydreams, or planning. They describe our tendency to use these processes as a kind of emotional painkiller, of which we are mostly unaware. They go on to prescribe methods of directed attention that can increase awareness, uncovering this self-defeating behavior, and gradually changing it. The first experiment suggests beginning sentences by "stating what you are at this moment aware of" (p. 31) The instructions further suggest beginning each sentence with "now" or "at this moment" or "here and now." The questions posed include, "What is your actuality? Can you genuinely feel it?" (p. 36).

The authors point out that what we are likely to discover as we attend to feeling the actual is that, what is actual—*and thus all that one can actually be aware of--is always in the present.* They go on to say that remembering and anticipating, when they occur, are also occurring in the present. A second point is that the feeling of actuality in the present *does not stay static but constantly changes.* The authors liken this to the view from a train window where the scenery is always shifting. A third point is the contention that *if actuality seems permanent and fixed, this is a created actuality that we are continually building anew because it is serving some present purpose to preserve this solid, unchanging sense of actuality.* Here we clearly see essential Buddhist psychology view--and a description of what is revealed in mindfulness practice--as foundational in Gestalt therapy.

A follow-up experiment suggests noticing *if and when you leave the present experience, and where your mind tends to go.* The instruction is *not to try to change this process, but simply to notice it in as great a degree of detail as possible.* The aim of these experiments is to "expand or heighten awareness of what you are doing and how you are doing it" (Perls et al., 1951, p. 39). The instruction continues:

> In this experiment on actuality, what present grudge, gratitude, remorse or excuse makes you anticipate the future? Our method is not to suppress that grudge or that ambition but simply for you to become aware that, in terms of the way you are now... *structured,* this is how you behave! With awareness this structure will change in line with changes in your functioning, and your escapes into past and future will diminish. Do not moralize to yourself about escapist tendencies, but simply *describe* them in terms of the actuality—that is as behavior that is going on (p. 39).

It is likely as clear to the reader as it is to us that this is instruction in mindfulness. Both mindfulness practice and Gestalt therapy method involve opening to all aspects of our subjective experience, without either rigidly identifying these as who we are or resisting them. Both help us distinguish between actual present experience and the ways we move away from it. Gestalt therapy's attention to the actual gives us perspective on how we can be caught in a rigid pattern of experiencing. Similarly, mindfulness meditation allows us to observe the mind's process rather than being caught in routine thought patterns that are out of awareness. In both Gestalt therapy and mindfulness meditation, all aspects of experience—cognition, behavior, emotion, bodily sensation, and the awareness process itself—are equally worthy of attention and exploration. Both approaches lead to a richer more nuanced and embodied connection with our actuality.

Gestalt therapy method and mindfulness both involve bringing attention to current experience, and opening to present awareness. In doing this, we gain insight into elements of the field and the shifting flow of experience. Both processes recognize the essential difference between thinking or talking about something and a direct and embodied knowing. As we notice this difference and move into our actual felt sense in the present moment, we discover that this is where awareness increases, insight develops, and transformation occurs. This involves an experiential understanding of the difference between intellectualizing or mind-made stories, and an embodied exploration that allows meaning to unfold. A basic experiment in Gestalt therapy—staying with what one is aware of and attending to what emerges as figural—is also the essence of mindfulness.

In mindfulness meditation we do not seek a particular state, like serenity or calm. Instead we bring attention to what *is* happening—our experience in the moment and how we are relating to it. The Gestalt therapist is similarly oriented. We do not try to change the patient or to get the patient to do or feel something. Rather, the therapist's function is to facilitate the patient's attention to, and full embodiment of, the current experience, or to clarify any objections to doing so; in other words how the patient is relating to her experience. While facilitating the patient's awareness process and welcoming whatever emerges, the therapist also remains present for and attentive to her own experience. This interpersonal mindfulness process involves the capacity for a fluid shifting attention guided by what emerges as figural.

To further explore how these two systems converge, we consider in detail four specific areas of intersection: phenomenology, attention to the present, being with what is, and embodiment. These are interwoven, each supporting and necessary for all of the others in both mindfulness meditation and in Gestalt therapy method.

Phenomenology

One of the insights of Buddhist psychology that has been validated by science is that while the "outside world" appears as substantial and solid, there are no "objects" separate from the mind's interpretation of what is perceived by the senses. Experience is subjective not objective, although we tend to understand reality as existing "out there," and we are generally unaware of how we shape and actively create our own experience. The Buddha was perhaps the first phenomenologist, recognizing our active role in this process. Gestalt therapy is also grounded in this understanding of the creation of subjective experience, and for both systems our subjectivity is the focus of attention.

Mindfulness meditation practice suggests a method of bare attention that focuses on what we actually experience in the successive moments of perception. In this process we discover the difference between our concepts and our direct experience. This is also part of Gestalt therapy's phenomenological method. The therapist attempts, as much as possible, to bracket off preconceived concepts and biases and to attend to sensory data.

The therapist facilitates the patient's process in doing this too, exploring the patient's phenomenology so that the patient can attend to what is experienced directly, as distinguished from analysis, evaluation, or judgment.

In both mindfulness meditation and Gestalt therapy method, phenomenological investigation is supported by curiosity, interest in what is, and noticing or suspending evaluation, preconceptions, and beliefs. Bare attention widens and expands awareness, not by trying to change anything but by allowing us to stay present with what is. This process—whether in meditation or psychotherapy—cultivates the capacity to be present for things as they are, as they arise in the moment. This process requires trust that healing occurs as we learn to move from the realm of concepts to the world of direct experience.

Attention to the Present

In both mindfulness meditation and Gestalt therapy, present experience is the focus of the phenomenological investigation described above. In each system, directed attention creates conditions for increased awareness. Because this can only occur in the present, immediate experience is central. Mindfulness practice emphasizes the benefit of staying with or returning to present experience. This also means noticing when we are remembering the past or fantasizing about the future, and in this moment of mindfulness we can return to "the now." Sometimes we may think we are in the moment and not realize that we are actually thinking about what is happening rather than experiencing it. Even the intention to focus on the breath can become thinking about breathing, evaluation, or judgment, as opposed to feeling the actual present sensations of breathing in and breathing out.

The Gestalt therapist's energy and attention are also directed toward being perceptive about and attentive to present process.

This includes noticing the quality of contact, what is emerging as figural, and what the patient is currently aware of. Immediate experience, behavior, and feelings are highlighted. The Gestalt experiment sets up an action system in the present that counters "about-isms," allowing the patient to have an experience and to connect with immediate feeling and sensation in the action (Polster & Polster, 1973). The experiment is here and now, and the primacy of the moment is central. In following the awareness continuum, immediate experience is what is investigated. The present moment is ever changing, as one thing follows another, and the Gestalt therapist tracks this process in an ongoing way. A relevant question, and something the Gestalt therapist generally holds in his background, is "What is happening now?"

Being with What Is
Both mindfulness meditation and Gestalt therapy recognize the value of attending to and being with what is. Both understand that change does not occur through attempting to force or coerce change. Because emotional and physical experience is always in a state of flux, as we attend to what we feel, embrace our actuality, and stay present, we are in this process as it unfolds. If we can do this rather than trying to get somewhere, get rid of feelings, or make something happen, we experience flow versus fixity. When anything is either resisted or held onto rigidly, we interfere with this flow.

In both systems, acceptance of experience is aimed for, but it is also understood that this cannot be imposed. While mindfulness meditation and Gestalt therapy method are both based on the recognition that accepting and being with experience is a prerequisite for transformation, both also recognize that "non-acceptance" (for example not wanting to feel sadness or anger) must be attended to, understood, and embodied. At times what is figural is a person's objection to "what is." If, for example a person is sad or angry and reluctant to experience this, the reluctance itself is the "what is." In both Gestalt therapy and mindfulness practice the focus of attention is then on the experiential unpacking of this reluctance or objection. In Gestalt therapy what is key is the understanding that, as we have closure on an aspect of experience, the next figure will naturally emerge. Mindfulness meditation practice relies on this same process, as we simply note the arising and passing away of thoughts or feelings, although the concept of closure is not specifically articulated.

Embodiment

Mindfulness of the body is the first of the four foundations of mindfulness. Mindfulness practice helps us become more aware of and attuned to bodily experience and sensation, allowing us to touch the essence of our actual physical existence. Mindfulness practice also directs attention to the embodied nature of emotion and the intimate interconnection of body and mind. This attention brings us more fully into the present, connecting us with immediate experience. As we move from evaluating experience, pushing it away, or clinging to it, we can open to and soften into our embodied consciousness.

In Gestalt therapy we also pay attention to embodied experience. The "wisdom of the organism" is essential to the work. In this process, the "feel of oneself" that has been lost can be regained through focused attention to felt experience and sensation (Perls et al., 1951). Gestalt therapy methods focus on the body by exploring posture, gestures, movement, voice tone, breathing, and physical sensation. Often experiments direct the patient's attention to bodily experience. This exercise (Perls et al., 1951) is an example of Gestalt therapy's understanding of attention to the body.

While lying down, but not deliberately relaxing, get the feel of your body. Notice where you have an ache ... realize where you are tense. Do not "give in" to the tension, nor do anything about it. Become aware of the tensions in your eyes, neck, around the mouth. Let your attention wander systematically ... through your legs, lower trunk, arms, chest, neck, and head. Should you find you are lying in a crooked position, adjust it accordingly. Do not move jerkily, but let the self-sense develop softly. Notice the tendency of your organism to regulate itself—the tendency to pull back into a better position in one place, to stretch out in another. Do not fool yourself that you are feeling your body when you are merely visualizing or theorizing it ... you are working with a concept of yourself, not yourself. But this concept is imposed by your "I" ... it is not self-regulating and spontaneous. It does not come from the felt-awareness of the organism. By waiting, refusing to be put off by visualizations and theories, can you get the glow of awareness which arises directly from the parts attended to? (p. 164).

The above Gestalt therapy exercise could as easily be an instruction in mindfulness of the body or of the body scan commonly suggested in meditation practice. It includes an emphasis on awareness rather than doing, and recognizes that the imposing of an "I" in this process interferes with organismic felt awareness. In Gestalt therapy, the body is recognized as an access point to authenticity, a "truth button," helping us to connect with present moment experience. Here the convergence of Gestalt therapy method and mindfulness method are again apparent in the distinction between theorizing or concepts, and attention to direct bodily experience.

Examples of these Processes

The following examples of a mindfulness meditation process and of a Gestalt therapy process show how these four convergent components—phenomenology, attention to the present, being with what is, and embodiment—are involved in each. In both examples we see staying with subjectivity in the present moment, suspending preconceptions and judgments as much as possible, and connecting directly with an embodied felt sense. These examples also illustrate how, in entering the flow of what is, we open to the natural, organic process of change and transformation.

This example shows a mindfulness meditation process:

One morning, while sitting in meditation before work, Karin, a forty-six-year-old married attorney with two teenagers, notices she is thinking about all the things she has to do that day. She becomes aware of how the thoughts crowd in on top of each other in a big jumble, and she has a vague sense of being overwhelmed by them and what she labels as being depressed. She is able to bring attention to her actual present experience, noticing that her body feels heavy and that there is a sense of a weight pressing down on her, especially on her shoulders. She notes this as unpleasant and recognizes the familiar impulse to avoid this experience or to change it. As an experienced meditator, she catches this and chooses to stay with her experience as it is. Again Karin's attention is pulled back to thoughts of all her obligations and responsibilities, and she observes how her mind goes from problem to problem; she sees the connection between this process and "being overwhelmed" or "being depressed."

Bringing a more focused attention to her body, Karin senses directly how these thoughts manifest in the physical experience of heaviness or burden, noticing a sensation of tightness in her shoulders, along with constriction in her chest. Karin continues to allow the details of her physical experience to emerge, noting the sensations and breathing with them. As she does, her mind begins to slow and quiet. There is an opening to and softening into her experience, as she does not resist it. She notices that the sensation of weight pressing down has shifted and what takes its place is more spaciousness and freer breathing. Her body feels lighter. With this recognition comes increased awareness of the impact of her thoughts on her well-being. This is an experiential reminder to her of the impermanence of feeling states, the relative insubstantiality of thoughts, and that what she tends to experience as fixed is actually not.

Karin may choose to explore changes in her life in order to ease some of her burden; however, in this process she recognizes the power and impact of her part in creating the particulars of her experience in each moment. Importantly, the initial awareness of her evaluation of her experience as unpleasant, and the impulse to change or avoid it, offered the possibility of choosing instead to stay present with it. Staying mindfully in the present allowed Karin increased awareness of her own process, as well as insight into the givens of experience.

This example shows how a similar process might unfold in a Gestalt therapy session:

Karin sought therapy because she was overwhelmed and wanted to feel "more control" over her life. She came into this session and described herself as "depressed." She talked about her experience with a muted affect and in a general and abstract way.

Steve: *Are you feeling depressed right now?*

Karin: *I don't know—I think I'm always depressed lately.*

Steve: *How about checking in with yourself--see how you experience your depression right now as you sit here with me.*

Karin: *You mean like right now?*

Steve: Yes, just notice what your experience is right now.

Karin: OK. (Pause.) I feel ... well kind of heavy. Like there is a ... um ... almost a weight coming down on my shoulders.

Steve: Good--just stay with that. See if you can focus on your shoulders ... feel the weight.

Karin: (Pause.) Wow, I didn't realize how weighted down I feel. (Pause.) So heavy, like I can't even move.

Steve: How is it for you to realize it now?

Karin: (Shoulders droop, more curled in on herself.) Well ... it feels ... bad, I guess.

Steve: Instead of guessing, see if you can pay attention to your posture ... what you're feeling, noticing what you're doing.

Karin: I'm curling up, or... I don't know ... weighted down. Everything feels like—it's just too much. Like I'm ... stuck, trapped ... it feels bad, and I want to just get away...

Steve: OK, see if you're willing to stay with that stuck-trapped feeling, or notice how you move away from it.

Karin: (Nods, sighs, and continues same posture.)

Steve: (Pause.) Without changing anything, try speaking to me from your posture right now- I'd like to get more of a feel for how this is for you.

Karin: (Looks at me.) So much is piled on me. (Tearfully.) It feels ... so oppressive ... just all the responsibilities.

Steve: Yes, so there is a lot on you, and some feeling comes up as you tell me about it.

Karin: (Nods.) I feel sad ... angry, too. (Sits more upright, gestures with arms.) My job, the kids, the house—it's just work, work, and more work. (Stronger voice.) It's like there's a ton of bricks on top of me! (Gestures with arms.)

Steve: Your energy has shifted. Try doing that movement with your arms again, and pay attention to what it feels like to do that.

Karin: (Does gesture again, even bigger, like she is throwing

something off.)
  Steve: What do you notice?
  Karin: (Gestures again, grunts.) I'm trying to throw off all this … It's way too heavy … I want to be able to breathe, and to move.
  Steve: Right now it looks like you are breathing and moving!
  Karin: (Brightens, laughs.) Yes!
  Like the mindfulness meditation process, the therapy work also involved moving out of abstraction and connecting more directly with embodied and emotional experience. Sharpening and resolution of what was initially figural allowed an organic emergence of new energy, including Karin's spontaneous movement and wanting to throw off her experienced burden. This therapy experience and the new awareness that resulted could become a springboard for moving out of a lifelong pattern of avoidance. This pattern in which Karin is vague and abstract about her own needs and feelings, keeping them out of awareness, contributes to her ending up feeling "stuck."

These examples show how the methods of the two systems correspond. There is also a difference in emphasis, with mindfulness practice leading to a broader perspective, and the Gestalt therapy session highlighting individual psychological issues. In Chapter 11 we explore an integration that encompasses both of these.

Based on the convergences we have outlined, in the next chapter we consider how Gestalt therapy can be seen as a clinical application of aspects of mindfulness and Buddhist psychology.

9

The Clinical Application of Mindfulness and Buddhist Psychology

> *The therapist needs this moment by moment awareness to see the client just as they are and to appreciate their world as it is revealed. The therapist notices the client's bodily movements, mental states ... not directly trying to change the client.*
>
> —David Brazier, *Zen Therapy*

MANY WESTERN PSYCHOTHERAPISTS have been deeply impacted by personal experience with Buddhist psychology and its meditation practices. Directly experiencing the power of these views and practices has led to an interest in bringing them into our work with patients. To this end Western psychotherapists have taken up the challenge of how to bring aspects of Buddhist psychology and its practices, especially mindfulness, into the work of psychotherapy. Although Buddhist psychology addresses human suffering, it is not a psychotherapy system. Psychotherapy requires an understanding of individual psychological development and psychodynamics that includes the relational. It requires a methodology, consistent with this understanding, which informs therapist interventions, to directly address the patient's enduring patterns that create internal conflict, relational difficulties, distress, and symptoms. Since Buddhist psychology and mindfulness do not offer this way of conceptualizing or addressing individual psychological issues, psychotherapists have bridged this gap by creatively exploring and developing ways to bring both a Buddhist psychology perspective and meditation methods, particularly mindfulness, into psychotherapy practice.

To this end, mindfulness informed therapy has incorporated insights from mindfulness and Buddhist psychology to guide the therapist's understanding and interventions. A variant of this is mindfulness based psychotherapy that includes teaching mindfulness to patients (Germer, 2005). Other systems have also been developed to specifically incorporate mindfulness, such as Mindfulness Based Cognitive Therapy (MBCT) and Mindfulness Based Stress Reduction (MBSR). Dialectical Behavior Therapy (DBT) teaches mindfulness to assist with emotional management and regulation. Compassion focused therapy (Gilbert, 2010) includes teaching the self-compassion cultivated in mindfulness and other Buddhist practices as a skill in therapy. Many clinical applications of mindfulness have been researched (Davis & Hayes, 2011) and the preliminary results, which show their benefits in clinical practice, have supported more interest in this exploration

There are also relational mindfulness approaches that integrate mindfulness, along with compassionate awareness and inquiry, into psychodynamic and other systems. The interface of Buddhist psychology and psychoanalytic psychotherapy has been explored in depth (Epstein, 2013). Recently the relationship between Buddhist psychology and cognitive behavioral therapy has been more broadly considered (Tirch, Silberstein, and Kolts, 2017). Approaches like Zen therapy (Brazier, 1995) take Buddhist psychology concepts and suggest ways to apply them in psychotherapy. Mindful therapy (Bien, 2006) and contemplative therapy (Wegela, 2014) have done the same, emphasizing therapist qualities of mindfulness, presence, and a healing attitude more than any particular therapy method. Buddhist teacher and psychologist Jack Kornfield (2008) offers a broad perspective on Buddhist psychology useful for psychotherapists, along with examples of interventions that can be used clinically. All of these perspectives have contributed to this richly diverse and evolving exploration.

Gestalt therapy's contribution to this exploration is based in the theoretical and methodological convergences described in the preceding two chapters. Given this fundamental alignment, Gestalt therapy offers the clinician a compatible, holistic framework that can translate essential aspects of mindfulness and Buddhist psychology into the "how to" of a relational psychotherapy process. Gestalt therapy method offers the therapist guidance as to what to pay attention to and how to pay attention to it, highlighting and illuminating key patient and interpersonal dynamics, in a relational mindful process. Now, building on the convergences laid out in the previous two chapters, we look at the ways Gestalt therapy translates some of the fundamental aspects of mindfulness and of the Buddhist psychology perspective into psychotherapy.

Gestalt Therapy as Relational Mindfulness

In the sections below, we describe how essential aspects of Gestalt therapy offer the clinician the "how to" of a relational mindful process in action. This involves the therapist's way of being, as well as therapeutic focus and interventions that contribute to a co-created field in which the patient can attend to and connect with present experience in a way that leads to increased awareness.

Contact, Awareness, and Present Focus

In mindfulness meditation we discover the value of paying attention to present experience, and also the challenges in doing this. We can become so involved in thoughts, or focused on past or future, that our present moment experience does not register, and we miss the moment. This can easily happen in therapy too. The therapist caught up in thinking, trying to make something happen, or in figuring something out, may overlook the obvious and important process unfolding right in front of him, rich with therapeutic possibility. Gestalt therapy's phenomenological method supports the therapist's present focus, directing attention to immediate sense data and to making descriptive observations rather than interpreting or explaining. Focusing on current experiencing, attention to what is figural, interpersonal contacting, and the interest in increasing awareness, all train the Gestalt therapist's attention on what is happening *now*.

Interventions that help clarify and allow sharpening of what is figural require that the therapist be on top of the moment. The therapist has to pay attention to what is happening as it is happening (process) in addition to what is being talked about (content), as shown in previous clinical examples. This discernment and tracking both supports and requires bringing mindful attention to the therapeutic engagement. Then when present process becomes figural, Gestalt therapy interventions give the therapist ways to highlight and work directly with what is available in the present therapeutic moment. These interventions may include making an observation, such as, "I notice your fist clenching as you're talking," or inquiring about the patient's experience, for example "What are you aware of as you are telling me this right now?"

The Gestalt therapist's attention to contact also brings us right into the moment. We can note, comment on, ask questions about, and draw the patient's attention to how contact is being made, avoided, or diluted, and where and how contact is interrupted in the here and now. For example, the therapist might say, "It sounds like you're angry about what I just said. Are you willing to tell me that directly?" Or, "What prevents you from telling me that directly?" Recognizing the importance of the mutual and reciprocal influence of patient and therapist in the co-creation of experience, the therapist also attends to moment-to-moment shifts as they occur. In order to do this, the therapist must not only be tracking the patient, but must also track her own experience in this relational mindful process.

For example, Steve had noticed a pattern with his patient Marco that when Steve expressed enthusiasm or excitement about something, Marco would back away or fade out, and sometimes just change the topic. Steve had developed his own response to recognizing this process by moderating his own energy or enthusiasm. In one session, he comments: "It seems that this pattern we've talked about is happening right now. I got excited as you were expressing this new sense of confidence in yourself. And as soon as I showed my enthusiasm, you seemed to fade out. Now I'm noticing myself wanting to mute my excitement so that you can re-find your own."

The therapist's perceptiveness about and description of observable details of current behavior and interaction also invites patients to observe, describe, and connect with themselves in the moment. As new awareness and meaning emerge, this supports patients' mindfulness of what they are doing as they are doing it. An example of this is the clinical vignette in the previous chapter. Steve invited Karin to pay attention to the details of her current experience, increasing awareness of this, rather than staying with the more abstract concept of "depression."

Being with What Is
The mindfulness meditation practitioner learns to notice and connect with what is, rather than trying to change or improve on experience. Doing this, we discover that acceptance

of experience can arise organically out of this neutral attention and awareness. Gestalt therapy also orients the therapist toward staying with what is, rather than trying to change the patient or aiming for a predetermined outcome. This freedom to be with what is empowers the therapist to explore and help increase the patient's awareness of actual experience, as we have described. This requires taking the patient and ourselves just as we are, including being with our patients in those difficult places of pain, confusion, or frustration. Recognizing that the path to healing requires moving fully into the truth of the moment, we trust that this is the ground out of which new possibilities emerge. Gestalt therapy interventions that meet patients where they are enhance and support the patient's capacity to do this as well.

Of course, patients come to therapy with goals and a desire for change, and therapists want their patients to get maximum benefit from therapy, and to actualize their potential. To this end, the Gestalt therapist actively engages with and supports patients in taking novel risks, learning new interpersonal skills, making desired changes, or letting go of ways of being that are not serving them well. However, Gestalt therapy's perspective reminds us that in order for patients to do this, they generally need to start right where they are. Just as in mindfulness meditation, the acceptance that comes as we are able to be with what is provides the firm footing that transforms self-experience, and leads to real transformation.

The Challenge of Acceptance

As therapists we do have our own feelings about, reactions to, or wishes for those we work with. At times these may include wanting the patient to be different, discouragement that the patient is not moving in the direction we think he should, or feeling frustrated in our desire to be effective. As

Gestalt therapists if we notice that we are not accepting where the patient is, we know we have lost our bearings. This is an opportunity to look at and investigate more deeply what is being evoked in us and what is happening in the relationship. Remaining attentive to the possible impact of these responses, the therapist might also choose, at times, to bring these to the interaction. In other words, this is a chance to bring mindful attention to our own judgments, agendas, preconceptions, and reactivity! This self-awareness is then an essential step in regaining our footing and our ability to be present with our patient, and to be with what is, just as it is.

When therapists practice mindfulness and experience the transformative potential of acceptance for themselves, they also naturally see the benefit of helping their patients move toward more self-acceptance. This can misdirect therapist energy and attention toward trying to "get" patients to be more accepting. Gestalt therapy's perspective reminds us that acceptance, like any other feeling or aspect of experience, cannot be imposed or legislated, and that an agenda to get the patient to be more accepting means the therapist is ironically no longer being with and accepting the patient's actual experience. This recognition helps us avoid getting caught up in trying to get the patient to do something different, or to be somewhere they are not—including to be more accepting.

Instead, Gestalt therapy's perspective and interventions guide us in working directly with our patients' "non-acceptance"—of themselves, their situation, their feelings, and their experience. The experiential and experimental framework allows us to focus directly on helping patients identify, clarify, and express any and all objections to aspects of themselves or what they think or feel. These interventions also offer ways to look at how and why aspects of self and experience are rejected. In this work we avoid imposing another set of "shoulds" that result from aligning ourselves with the idea that the patient be accepting. Instead we explore and inquire into any "non-accepting" attitude—the objection to what is—an important focus of psychotherapeutic exploration. For example, an intervention might be, "Tell me what makes it important for you to stay away from your sadness," or "What scares you the most about connecting with your anger?" or "A part of you really misses your boyfriend and wants him back, and you're also critical of yourself for not getting over him." This opens up and expands possibilities for working with internal conflict and polarities.

As the patient's self-judgment, self-criticism, avoidance, and any other aspect of non-acceptance becomes figural, Gestalt therapy gives us the perspective and tools to work with these directly. As each figural development is illuminated, obstacles to desired change can also be addressed. This helps the therapist remain free of bias that these responses are a problem to be solved; they are instead seen as processes to be illuminated and understood. This perspective and these interventions support the therapist in embracing all of the patient's experience, translating the accepting, open, and curious inquiry of mindfulness practice into the psychotherapy process.

Therapist Mindful Presence

Mindfulness meditation opens new channels of awareness in us, sensitizing us to both our own embodied experience and to the world around us. This kind of mindful presence is ineffable, a quality not easily quantified or defined. However, we immediately recognize it when we sense it in ourselves or experience it in another. Therapist presence has always been an important element in humanistic psychotherapies, and more recently mindfulness has brought added emphasis to therapeutic presence as a vital component of a healing relationship. Although presence is more a quality of being than anything specific that we do, Gestalt therapy's perspective and method allow and support bringing the quality of presence cultivated in meditation into the therapeutic encounter. In both meditation and in therapy, presence requires connection with our actuality; the truth of our own embodied and lived experience. For the Gestalt therapist, presence is not conceptual, or something we "try" to do. Rather, every aspect of the therapy approach itself supports bringing ourselves to the meeting with our patients in a way that invites them to connect more fully with us, and with themselves.

Focus on contact and awareness, attention to the present, being with and accepting the patient's and our own embodied experience all support therapist presence. Gestalt therapy's phenomenological method encourages this as well. Observing and describing what is, bracketing off preconceived ideas, and attention and receptivity to sensory experience all require and also enhance this capacity for presence. In addition the dialogical stance supports therapist presence in its attention to deeply understanding the patient's experience as if from the inside. It points us toward willingness to be seen as we are, letting go of aims, and surrendering to "the between." This requires full engagement and availability that includes receptivity, curiosity, and willingness to be deeply touched by the other, all of which lead us into a deeper presence.

Just as the tennis player is not simply "present," but is rather present *with* the tennis ball's trajectory over the net, and with the timing and movement of her entire body as she brings the racket to meet the ball, so is the therapist always present *with something*. Just as we support our patients to be with their actual experience, our own embodied mindful presence requires willingness to be with *our* actual experience. For the Gestalt therapist, presence means we are not trying to feign interest if we are not interested. We are not pressuring ourselves to feel compassion or connection with our patient if what we are experiencing is distance or disconnection. Presence requires willingness to be with and feel what is actual, what is true for us—whatever it is.

For example, the therapist might be curious, pursuing his curiosity and interest in knowing the patient's experience more deeply. Or the therapist might be bored when the patient repeats a story she has told him before. The therapist might be connected with his own bodily sensation—how his breathing constricts as a patient relates a traumatic experience. Or he might sense his stillness, as he is riveted by the patient's emotional account of an event. As we described in the section on therapist self-disclosure, the therapist may also judiciously bring aspects of her experience of being with the patient into the interaction. This is an essential component of our presence and willingness to make contact in a way that is meaningful and healing.

Compassion and Recognition of Interconnectedness in Gestalt Therapy's Dialogical Stance

Sitting with pain and suffering in mindfulness meditation develops self-compassion as well as greater compassion for others, as we recognize the commonality of our human pain and struggle. As we have pointed out, the Gestalt therapist's dialogical stance includes the aspiration to feel the patient's experience as if from the inside, a direct apprehending of the other made possible by our shared humanity. Compassion and a sense of interconnectedness are necessarily at the heart of this work, as we attend to contact and the mutual and reciprocal influence of patient and therapist—the unique "between" that is created at the point of meeting. The capacity to be fully with another more naturally arises when we are free from a role, the need to be seen in a particular way, a concept of hierarchy, or a need to change the patient. These components of the dialogical stance support the therapist's ability to open to compassion and to recognize interconnectedness in this relational mindful process.

The following example reflects what we have described in this chapter so far. This part of the session highlights attending to and working with patient and therapist mutual and reciprocal influence in the interconnected field.

Samantha is a college student in her early twenties. She came to therapy because of longstanding difficulty with anxiety and depression, along with social discomfort that was sometimes disabling. Over the course of therapy, Samantha has developed more self-awareness and understanding of what contributes to these difficulties. She experiences less anxiety and more comfort in social situations.

In this session she tells me (Eva) about a difficult situation with her roommate. As I begin to respond, I notice that she looks down, her long hair hiding her face, and physically withdraws. I stop and inquire about her experience. She responds quietly into her hair, "I know what you're saying is right, but I feel like ... like I'm being lectured."

This is a big step for Samantha. I support her telling me this and encourage her to see if there is more she wants to say to me. She describes how as a child she was forced to listen silently while her mother lectured her, and she was not allowed to speak or respond. Her mother's feelings and opinions were important, not hers. She learned to shut down feelings, and to discount her opinions as stupid or not important.

I let Samantha know that I appreciate her clarity and courage in speaking up. I also check in with myself, discovering and letting Samantha in on an aspect of my own experience with her. That is, when I see her vulnerability and difficulty in asserting herself with others, I feel protective and am more inclined to make suggestions or to give her advice. I recognize that I want her to be more empowered so that she isn't hurt or disregarded. And I now see that in "lecturing" her, I am contributing to diminishing her sense of power and agency here with me. This also echoes the relationship with her mother. "Yes, exactly!" she responds. Samantha comes out from behind her curtain of hair and looks at me directly, letting out the breath she had been holding.

The moment is ripe for further experimenting. I support Samantha staying with her experience and seeing what comes up next for her. She spontaneously says, "I don't care what you think—even if you are right!" Delighted by this, we both laugh out loud as Samantha acknowledges, accepts, and expresses her authentic feeling, fully embracing the truth of her experience in the moment. Growing up, she had learned to always contain this kind of expression with her mother for fear of being rejected or punished. My joining in her delighted laughter and enjoying her contactful expression is a moment of celebratory connection between us, and a novel way of making contact for her.

Over the next several sessions, Samantha discovers that she can care what I think, without feeling silenced or small, if she also has a voice. She begins to see that my maternal or protective feelings toward her do not necessarily have to diminish her, and that I am not her mother. Our relationship and interaction clarify, allowing a new quality of contact, as Samantha begins to feel less like a child with me. I pay attention to eliciting her opinion and any disagreement with me, even if minor, encouraging her to tell me how she feels and what she thinks. As Samantha finds her voice, both with me and in her other relationships, I feel less protective. If this does come up, Samantha now has fun experimenting with lecturing me about "sounding like a parent," and I discover more about myself in this process too.

This work shows a focus on contact and awareness, as the therapist stays with what is and attends to present process. Throughout, therapist mindful presence is seen in the therapist's attentiveness to and observations of the patient, as well as attention to her own experience, and to the reciprocal mutual influence in the interaction. We see the patient step more fully into and identify with previously disowned aspects of self, as the therapist embraces what is, in both the patient's experience and her own.

Experimental Approach

In mindfulness meditation, attending carefully to the details of experience allows processes that have been out of awareness to be seen more clearly as physical sensation, sensory experience, and our thoughts come into sharper focus. Experiments are one way that Gestalt therapy translates this mindful attention to the details of present experience into the "how to" of psychotherapy. Experiments can slow things down, offer immediacy and focus, and direct the patient's attention to nuances of experience. They can highlight emotion, bodily sensations, thoughts, behavior, or content. This focused attention increases awareness of what is happening as it is happening, revealing and sharpening what is figural. Experiments allow the patient to move from the conceptual to an embodied felt sense. They offer the opportunity to explore anything in more detail, and can illuminate experience like a focused spotlight beam. Experimental interventions support experiential learning, allowing the therapist to facilitate this mindful attentional process in therapy.

In mindfulness meditation we face ourselves directly and see our patterns, allowing us to take more responsibility for our lived experience. For example, we may notice things such as "I am constantly pulled to focusing on a problem and trying to solve it," or "I am often imagining what others are thinking of me." Along with this awareness comes expanded possibility, and more choice. The Gestalt therapy experiment can do this as well. It clarifies and emphasizes responsibility in the sense of "This is *what* I am doing right now; this is *how* I am doing it; this is *what* I am feeling." Thus the Gestalt experiment brings this aspect of mindfulness into the therapy room.

As described in Chapter 6, Gestalt therapy's experimental repertoire is extensive and varied. Experiments can range from elaborate and expansive improvisational exploration to simple suggestions woven seamlessly into the therapeutic dialogue. A variety of experiments have been shown in the previous clinical examples. The following are examples of the particular type of experiment that aligns with and reflects a mindfulness perspective, in that it focuses on the simple highlighting of immediate experience.

These experiments direct the patient's attention to what he is doing/experiencing in the moment:

"Notice what you are aware of as you tell me this."

"See if you can stay with the feeling."

"Pay attention to (or stay with) the sensation in your chest."

"Allow the fear to be as big as it is right now."

"See if you can make space for all the sadness you're feeling."

"Where in your body do you sense anxiety right now?"

"See if you can just let the sensation of anxiety in your belly be there, without trying to change or get rid of it."

"Notice how it is for you right now to sit in the middle of your 'want' and your 'should.'"

"Feel your clenched fist."

These experiments suggest an action to highlight what the patient is doing/experiencing in the moment:

"Try looking at me and notice what happens."

"Now experiment with looking away again."
"Tell me directly 'I don't want to feel this.'"
"Do that gesture again more slowly."
"Allow your voice to become even quieter as you talk."
"Try saying that again, and say it louder."
"Put both feet on the floor and say that."
"Give your tears a voice."
"What does your shaking say to me?"
"Squeeze this pillow in the way you are squeezing in on yourself."
"Imagine your posture could speak. What does it say to me?"

Working with Suffering

Buddhist psychology's universal view, as we have pointed out, recognizes suffering as based in ignorance of the truths of existence. On a relative level, suffering is understood as in the created relationship to experience, often in our opposition to experience that is painful, as we attempt to avoid or deny this. In mindfulness meditation we can deconstruct this process, bringing attention back to elemental experience and also noticing our avoidance tactics. We can then see more clearly how we try to get rid of aspects of experience that we do not want, grasp for what is out of reach, or try to change ourselves through self-criticalness, self-coercion, or detachment. We can also more deeply investigate what is driving our striving and the attendant feelings; for example, a fear of humiliation driving perfectionism. We also discover that when we can hold something in awareness non-reactively, including painful experience, we avoid creating added, "second arrow" suffering.

Although Gestalt therapy does not include the "bigger picture" of Buddhist psychology's perspective on suffering, it attends to the subset of suffering that involves the psychological opposition to what is. The overlap between the two is in this psychological domain. Gestalt therapy attends directly to the ways patients may be divided against themselves, or avoiding aspects of experience, the relative-level suffering that is based in individual psychological issues that patients seek therapy to address. In therapy, patients can develop more awareness of how they may be rejecting, avoiding, or denying feelings, or disowning parts of themselves. In this process, they can connect with, give voice to, and embody their objection to aspects of themselves or their experience. This creates the potential for closure, opening the possibility for whatever the next emergent figure in this transformational process may be.

This way of working directly with this aspect of suffering, is Gestalt therapy's psychotherapeutic "how to" of exploring the same processes that we explore in mindfulness meditation. In this work, patients can discover the suffering created by rejecting their authentic experience, or parts of themselves, and they can also directly experience the relief of surrendering to what is. Although this process may result in new awareness of and connection with pain, this is the unavoidable pain of the "first arrow," not the created suffering of self-alienation or of rejecting aspects of experience. As Ruth Wolfert (2000) suggests, when we can stand out of the way, allowing the truth of pain and loss to touch us, we can assimilate what has previously been unbearable; and figures complete themselves and resolve.

Impermanence and Not-Self in Gestalt Therapy

Two of Buddhist psychology's universal truths, impermanence and not-self, are implicit in Gestalt therapy method. Gestalt therapy work directs the therapist's attention to tracking the flow of moment-to-moment experience. The therapist is oriented by the understanding that one thing always follows another, as each completed figure becomes the ground for the next in a continuous process of movement and change.

Also, seeing all emergent senses of self and self-identifications as fluid and field dependent orients the work to exploring expansion and flexibility of self-experience. Although our patients may appear caught in ingrained self-concepts and patterns, the Gestalt therapist recognizes that any unchanging self-view is antithetical to the actuality of a never static field. Rigid self-identifications limit how patients relate to others and to their own experience, and we can explore this fixity or attachment to any self-view as it is revealed in the present interaction. This aligns Gestalt therapy work with Buddhist psychology's recognition of self as impermanent, and not a fixed entity. Grounding in Gestalt therapy perspective and method translates the Buddhist psychology understanding of these ultimate truths into the work that unfolds in psychotherapy.

The following example illustrates what we have described in this chapter. This work shows a relational mindfulness process and how impermanence and not-self are revealed in it as well.

Pete, thirty-nine and single, is a successful entrepreneur who prides himself on his stoic independence. He learned this early, as his mother was often hospitalized for psychotic episodes and his father was withdrawn and emotionally unavailable. Reluctant to acknowledge emotional needs, he finds himself with no close friends and in a pattern of romantic relationships that fizzle out. He sought therapy with me (Eva) as a "last resort" to deal with periods of overwhelming depression and loneliness, but he struggled with admitting he might need help, and was skeptical that another person could help him. Over many months in therapy, he has started to understand that his strong, independent exterior protects a soft, vulnerable inner core. In this session we explore this.

Pete: I can feel it there right now in my gut ... small and scared feeling. (Pause.) I really don't want anybody to know it's there either. It's like who I really am—young and weak—is behind this strong shell.

Eva: So you don't want anyone to know this part is there ... and right now you're also telling me it's there, behind the shell.

Pete: (Looking at me more directly, his face softening. He looks younger, more vulnerable.) I do ... and I don't want you to know. I'm scared for you to see it, but I need ... I just.... (Chokes up.)

Eva: So, "I'm scared for you to see me and I also need...." Just stay with the feeling that's coming up. (Pause.) And see if you want to let me in on it.

Pete: (Pauses. Then nods.) I want to at least try...

Eva: OK. (Pause.) How about talking to me from your gut?

Pete: I don't know ... that's really hard.... I've never done that.

Eva: I know. (Nods.) So just feel into the difficulty.

Pete: (Long pause. Takes a deep breath.) It's scary, too ... vulnerable. I don't think I want to.

Eva: OK, you're getting clearer. Try saying that to me directly. "Eva, I don't want to let you in."

Pete: (Looks at me.) I won't let you in. (Strongly.)

Eva: (Nods.) You sound firm, like the shell. How is it right now to say that to me 'I won't let you in'?

Pete: Good, true. I feel more ... safer. But it's only partly ... it's not the whole story.... In my gut (puts his hand on his stomach) I do need ... I want someone ... (becomes tearful) to see that I am hurting ... (Looks down.)

Eva: So, in your gut you do want me to see you, to know you're hurting?

Pete: (Nods, crying. Looks back up at me.)

Eva: And right now you are showing me, and I do see you ... both your need ... and your fear. The vulnerability in letting me see that you're hurting, letting me see your tears ...

Pete continues to meet my eyes, and I have a sense of seeing into the depth of his pain and longing, allowing me a more dimensional sense of him than I have had before. This sense of connection is deepened, as he sees the tears in my eyes and knows that he has touched me.

In this example we see the therapist's presence in a relational mindful process, how experiments are used to highlight what is, in the moment, and the patient and therapist's interconnectedness in the co-created field. The fluidity of self-experience is also revealed in the unfolding of Pete's awareness, and the shifting contact between Pete and Eva. We see how the patient's disowning his need, and fixed ideas about how he must be to protect himself, interrupt natural regulation and create suffering. Pete's avoidance of the pain associated with feeling unmet emotional needs leads to the suffering inherent in rejecting a part of his self-experience.

The therapy process reveals the way out of this suffering. Rather than trying to be different, Pete becomes more aware of and steps fully into what and who he is in the moment, allowing organic acceptance, and restoration of self-regulation. Initially this involves recognizing, accepting, and fully owning the part of him that does not want to let Eva in. This allows the closure of that figure and the emergence of the need to be seen. The work reveals how the therapist embraces each emergent figural development, orienting to the ever-shifting nature of the co-created experience. The process also reveals self-identifications as fluid, as we see the creation and re-creation of these in the patient's self-and-other experience in the session.

In this chapter we have considered how Gestalt therapy can be seen as a psychotherapeutic translation of aspects of mindfulness and Buddhist psychology. Psychotherapists of any orientation can also integrate the elements of practice highlighted here to align their work more closely with this perspective. In the next chapter we consider the ways that Buddhist psychology and meditation practices can make us better Gestalt therapists. Looking through this additional lens further illustrates the complementarity of the two systems, another part of the foundation for the integration we propose in Chapter 11.

10

How Meditation Practices and Buddhist Psychology can Make Us Better Gestalt Therapists

> *The intimacy that arises in listening and speaking truth is only possible if we open to the vulnerability of our own hearts. Once we have held ourselves with kindness, we can touch others in a vital and healing way.*
>
> —Tara Brach, *True Refuge: Finding Peace and Freedom in Your Own Awakened Heart*

AS PSYCHOTHERAPISTS, our own self-awareness and personal development impact the work we do. Who the therapist is as a person enhances or limits what can be brought to the therapeutic engagement. Meditative practices can be an important part of therapist personal development; they can increase self-awareness, contribute to the therapist's well-being, and expand the therapist's capacity to be emotionally available and present. Mindfulness practice particularly can also support therapy skills by enhancing the ability to attune to the patient, to pay attention, and to stay with difficult emotions. Mindfulness practice may increase the capacity for empathy, compassion, acceptance, and equanimity, as well as support the therapist in being less bound by theories and concepts (Fulton, 2005). These are skills and capacities that positively affect the therapeutic alliance, and they relate directly to the "common factors" that have been shown to impact treatment outcomes across therapy orientations. Although psychotherapists of any orientation can reap these benefits, in this chapter we look at specific ways that mindfulness practice can help the Gestalt therapist.

Mindfulness is only one component of the Buddhist path, and we are not advocating practicing it divorced from the system in which it is embedded. Nor are we suggesting that we practice for a particular result or as a means to an end. We do not take up these practices to improve our therapy skills, but the path and its practices inevitably have far-reaching effects on all aspects of our lives. This includes our experience of and how we relate to others and ourselves, and this will naturally affect the work we do as therapists.

In this chapter we highlight the particular ways that mindfulness meditation can benefit the Gestalt therapist. We also consider the benefits of other practices such as cultivation of qualities like compassion and loving kindness. And we look at how Buddhist psychology views support Gestalt therapy work.

How Mindfulness Meditation can Enhance Gestalt Therapist Qualities and Skills

Mindfulness practice, as part of the Buddhist psychology path, has the potential to profoundly transform us. Here, we look specifically at the Gestalt therapist qualities and skills that mindfulness practice can enhance. All of these are interconnected, supporting and reinforcing each other as they are interwoven in Gestalt therapy work, and each is strengthened in mindfulness meditation.

Attunement and Attention to Present Experience

Noticing what is obvious seems simple, but it is not always easy. Mindfulness meditation offers practice in seeing the obvious more clearly, as we pay attention to present moment experience and see what is actually here. Mindfulness meditation also refines our attention as we learn to notice the details of present experience and small movements of the mind. When we sit with what arises, without trying to change it or make something happen, we are more fully available to see what *is* happening. We discover where the sensations of breathing are most apparent, and how the in-breath feels different from the out-breath. The general label "pain" distills into "dull" or "sharp," "constant" or "throbbing," as we move from concept to direct experience. With practice, we get better at both sustained attention and focus on the details and nuance of experience. In mindfulness meditation, this is not a forced attention, but rather an exploration and cultivation of genuine interest and curiosity.

Mindfulness practice develops more sensitivity to our own experience and to the world around us, enhancing our ability to hear, see, and listen more carefully. As mindfulness promotes attunement to ourselves, it follows that we may become more resonant with and attuned to the experience of others. Refining our bodily awareness can increase our ability to tune in to patients, including non-verbal cues, and help them tune in to their own bodily experience as well (Siegel, 2007).

As the quality of mindfulness is developed with practice, the meditator's skill in making aware discrimination and choosing what to pay attention to also increases. For example, while meditating we can note "thinking," or notice the transient nature of thoughts—how they come and go. Or we can attend to recurring patterns or themes in our thought processes, noticing that they tend toward worry or future planning, for example. This kind of attention and observation is different from being caught up in the *content* of a thought or fantasy and is only possible when we are mindful and not on autopilot.

For Gestalt therapists this capacity for mindful attention is beneficial in helping us make content/process discriminations, discerning what is important to pay attention to, and sharpening what is figural. These all involve an ability to notice the current process, to see what is obvious, and to pay close attention to the details of our own and our patient's experience as it unfolds in the moment. The more sensitivity and capacity we have to attune to the specifics of what is happening with us, with our patients, and in the interaction, the more precise and impactful our interventions, and the greater the likelihood that patients will experience being seen, heard, and understood.

Seeing subtleties, or calling attention to what is obvious to the therapist, but not within the patient's immediate awareness, creates opportunity for deeper exploration of important processes, as this example illustrates.

Jayden, a shy, thirty-year-old computer programmer, came to therapy wanting more meaningful relationships and greater self-confidence. He begins this session with a moving and emotional description of an event from the past week. After reporting what happened, he seems to compose himself, looks away quickly, and starts to go right into another topic. I (Steve) feel moved by both the story and the way he told it, and I'm aware that he leaves no space for my response.

Steve: You moved very quickly past something big that you seemed to have a lot of feeling about.

Jayden: Hmm ... yeah. It had a huge impact on me.

Steve: Yes, I saw that as you talked...and I was touched too. What came up for you as you were telling me?

Jayden: I don't know. (Pause.) I feel, well ... I'm ... proud of myself and how I dealt with it all.

Steve: Yes, sounds like you took a big risk, and you really put yourself out there.

Jayden: Yeah. (Nods emphatically.)

Steve: Do you feel that pride alive in you right now?

Jayden: (Pause.) Not sure, maybe in my chest or something.

Steve: OK, you're not sure. How about checking it out? See what happens if you pay attention to your chest.

Jayden: (Pause. Laughs.) It's expanding, like something could burst out of me!

Steve: (Smiling.) Great! See if you can stay with that.

Jayden: (Big grin.) Yeah, I have a lot of pride in there! (Stops, looks away. Then looks back at me, and pauses.) And I wonder (softly) if you're maybe...proud of me, too?

Noticing the process and attending to my own and Jayden's experience let us explore the contact that was interrupted. This was the most obvious process happening in the moment, and an important enduring pattern for Jayden that has contributed to less relational depth. Attention to this opened up an opportunity for exploration and deeper connection with me; it also provided an inroad into Jayden's important therapy themes.

In Gestalt therapy this way of working is nothing new; it is basic to what we already do. Mindfulness meditation simply gives us ongoing practice that can hone and sharpen our ability to do it—to pay good attention to what is unfolding right in front of us.

Embracing Experience, Acceptance, and Equanimity

Mindfulness meditation cultivates the ability to stay with what emerges moment- to-moment, offering an open and non-evaluative attention to all experience. Whether it is an easy moment or a difficult moment, pleasant, unpleasant, or neutral, we practice being with our experience, without requiring it or ourselves to be different. This includes developing more capacity to be present for intense and highly charged emotion, physical discomfort, or pain, as we stay with what is here right now. We can develop more confidence in the stability of our body/mind in the face of our own pain. We see that waves of emotion or physical sensation can wash through and over us, and we can discover that we are not washed away no matter how strong the wave. We also learn first-hand that no matter how intensely we feel something or how difficult or painful an experience is, it does not last. We come to see that the only constant is change—as the wave crests and recedes, leaving smooth sand in its wake.

Fundamental to Gestalt therapy practice is the therapist's ability to stay steadily engaged in the moment as it is. The Gestalt therapist is well-served by the capacity for a full turning toward, the ability to welcome, explore and embrace all of our own and our patient's humanity. Sitting with ourselves and learning to be more unwavering in the face of all experience— including our grief, anger, or despair—supports us in offering this same unwavering presence to our patients. This allows us to be with them in difficult or painful emotions, or in intensely challenging moments in the relationship. We convey willingness to accompany our patients on their journey, no matter how turbulent the waters.

In mindfulness meditation we have the *intention* to meet all of what arises with acceptance. In the process we discover the ways in which we are not accepting. We notice the tendency to welcome and value some experiences or parts of ourselves, and to reject or avoid others. Our self-criticalness and our ongoing judgments of others come into sharper focus. Seeing the suffering inherent in this process and bringing non-evaluative attention to it, we naturally develop more acceptance and self-compassion. This can also translate to more acceptance of others, as we recognize our shared struggles and our shared humanity. For the Gestalt therapist, this acceptance, which is cultivated in mindfulness meditation, supports both our phenomenological and our dialogical stance.

Mindfulness practice also strengthens the capacity for equanimity. Equanimity goes beyond acceptance as we normally think of it, taking acceptance to another level. To the extent that we are able to embody and experience equanimity, it offers a spaciousness and capacity for a truly open and non-discriminatory receptivity, a grounded center from which we can be present with all arising internal and external conditions. Desires and preferences are seen for what they are so that we are not caught in being "for" one experience and "against" another. Rather than being pulled around by our experience, we maintain a sense of stability in the face of whatever comes.

For the Gestalt therapist this equanimity can enhance our ability to adhere to our phenomenological method, to explore our patient's experience with fewer preconceptions and biases. If we are less distracted by anything we think should be happening, we can be more skilled in exploring what *is* happening. Although Gestalt therapy offers guidelines for the phenomenological method's application, equanimity imbues us with the attitude that makes following these guidelines more organic, more intrinsic to who we are. The specifics of the phenomenological method and inquiry can be taught and practiced, but this attitude cannot be taught directly. However, mindfulness practice can help us develop an even more radically descriptive, non-interpretive, and non-evaluative therapeutic stance, where biases toward and evaluation of experience are diminished.

Empathy and Compassion

Compassion is the particular empathic response that arises as we directly meet our own or another's pain and suffering. This requires the capacity to remain present for pain and suffering and to meet it without resistance. Mindfulness practice cultivates not only wisdom, but compassion as well. As we sit with ourselves without our usual distractions, our own pain and suffering come up. Mindfulness meditation offers support for and practice in staying with and opening to this. This direct contact with our own grief, loss, or pain seasons us and opens our hearts, cultivating self-compassion. A more empathic and compassionate response to others is a natural extension of this. We become more permeable to others' pain, connected in the universality of human experience.

Of course, empathy and compassion are important capacities, in general, for interpersonal connection and for other psychotherapy approaches as well. For the Gestalt therapist there is a particular importance because, like the other qualities described in this section, these are aspects of both Gestalt therapy's phenomenological method and dialogical stance. To truly apprehend the other's experience, we need empathy, and when that experience is painful, we need compassion. As Gestalt therapy's phenomenological inquiry increases the patient's self-understanding and allows the therapist entry into the patient's subjective world, the therapist's capacity for empathy and compassion bring an essential heartfelt, human, and connective element. Again, these are qualities to be cultivated, rather than skills that can be taught, and mindfulness meditation offers this cultivation.

Support for Phenomenology: From Conceptual to Embodied
In mindfulness practice, we learn to explore our own experience and to observe moment-to-moment process. As we have described, this involves discerning the difference between concepts and primary experience. We attend to what we are feeling and sensing, noting rather than explaining or evaluating. This is a process of discovery as, for example, we discover that we actually do not know what the next moment will bring, and learn to more easily flow with the "not knowing."

This practice enhances the Gestalt therapist's ability to observe behavior and to attend to our own and our patient's primary experience. It supports our orienting to sensory data, and bracketing preconceived ideas and evaluation. This is the essence of Gestalt therapy's phenomenological method. In Gestalt therapy we do not rely on constructs or static diagnostic labels, even though the work does rest on theoretical scaffolding. Rather, ongoing functional diagnosis and nuanced understanding of the uniqueness of each individual patient guide the process. This calls for the therapist to meet the moment as it comes and to discover what comes next, opening to emergent contact and aliveness. Mindfulness meditation practice is itself phenomenological, and offers support and training for the Gestalt therapist in this method.

Clarifying Facets of Subjective Experience

Buddhist psychology offers a depth of exploration and understanding of the nature of human experience. Over the last 2600 years, its diversity of teachings and meditative practices has provided a rich, descriptive taxonomy of the many states, qualities, and abilities of the mind's processes. This includes fine discrimination, distinctions, and categorizations that elucidate and organize the elements of subjective experience.

Buddhist psychology's perspective on how we sense, make meaning of, and create our subjectivity can add clarity to the Gestalt therapist's understanding of the nature of experience. Just as an Inuit Eskimo may have one hundred words to describe snow in all its subtle variations, Buddhist psychology, with its precision, can help us as Gestalt therapists to hone our discernment of aspects of experience and to develop a more precise vocabulary reflecting this. Here we consider three facets of subjective experience that are seen and clarified in meditation: domains of functioning, immersion and perspective, and creation of subjective experience. Conceptualizing and recognizing these processes, as we do in mindfulness meditation, can help refine the Gestalt therapist's understanding and skills in working with these.

Domains of Functioning

Gestalt therapist John O. Stevens (1971) proposed that all experience could be divided into three zones of awareness: awareness of external stimuli, awareness of internal physical sensation, and fantasy activity. The first two zones include what is immediate and in the moment. Awareness of the outside world includes sights and sounds; awareness of our internal world includes physical sensations, like our heart beating, as well as embodied emotion. He describes these first two zones as encompassing "all that I can know about present reality as I experience it. This is the solid ground of my experience; these are the facts of my existence here, in the moment that they occur" (Stevens, 1971, p. 5). Awareness of fantasy activity includes all mental activity outside of present awareness of current experience, such as, "all explaining, imagining, interpreting, guessing, thinking, comparing, planning, remembering the past, anticipating the future" (p. 6).

In mindfulness meditation we can see more clearly the distinction between the first two zones that include our immediate experience and the third zone of our reactions, thoughts, analysis, fantasy, and assessment of experience. We become better at noticing when we have left the present moment and have shifted from being with sensation or feeling to being with thoughts of past, future, or fantasy. We start to see the shifts as they occur and to more readily recognize which of these realms we are in. Here, we refer to these as the two "domains" of functioning, one domain encompassing all immediate experience and the other encompassing these mental constructions.

Both mindfulness meditation and Gestalt therapy recognize that thinking about something is different from direct experience and takes us out of the immediacy of the present moment. As we have pointed out, the present moment is where contact happens and awareness increases. (Importantly, mindfulness of thinking, in which we notice our thinking process or note "thinking," as opposed to being caught up in the content of the thoughts, brings attention back to our present experience.) We can also notice the feeling tone or physical sensation that accompanies particular thoughts or thought pattern, sensing this connection between the domains and how they interact with and affect one another.

Developing this skill and discernment in meditation practice can help us see when our patients are connecting with primary experience and when they are not. "I feel the tears behind my eyes," is direct experience, but "I know I'm too sensitive" is not. It is thinking about experience, responding to it and judging it. There may also be a prediction or story related to what is happening or what has happened, such as, "I'm afraid if I start crying, I'll never stop." Experience with mindfulness practice allows the therapist to more readily notice the domain the patient is in and to help bring to attention to this.

The following example illustrates the benefit of the therapist's ability to discern these domains.

LeeAnn is an engaging graduate student in her late twenties. She came to therapy quite depressed, dealing with old family issues and ongoing conflict and disappointment with friends in her graduate program. In this session she describes her hurt and feelings of rejection as a result of a friend not inviting her along for a group activity with some of their mutual friends. As she tells me (Eva) about this, a lot of pain and sadness come up, and she begins sobbing, saying that she is always left out and not cared about, that she is unlovable and will always be alone.

I suggest that LeeAnn stay with and make space for these feelings that are coming up. She says, "This always happens to me. I've felt this way my whole life and it seems like I always will. This is just how it is for me, how it's always been." I acknowledge the depth of pain that this experience has tapped into and how it has brought up her worst fears and most painful feelings about herself in relationship. Then I suggest she see if she can continue to open to the feelings and stay with the pain just as it is right now and that she experiment with being with the pure feeling--separate from the thoughts about it and the past or future—just how it is for her right now.

LeeAnn nods, and within a few moments she stops crying, looks up at me surprised and says, "Without the thoughts, the intense feelings just seemed to dissolve away." When I ask her what takes their place, she considers briefly then replies slowly. "I feel ... disappointed ... about my friend ... and sad not to be invited. Now, I'm wondering why she didn't include me, and I'd like to ask her that. I couldn't imagine talking to her about it before. It seems like the real pain is not about her; it's about what happened with my family and how rejected and alone I felt with them."

For LeeAnn, the deep hurt and early introjects were embedded in her memory and fantasy, and of course these are important to explore in therapy. It was also eye opening for her to discover that the pain connected to past hurts and longstanding beliefs could separate itself out from the current situation as she stayed with her immediate feelings. This made things clearer to her and opened up the possibility for better contact with her friend, an interaction that she had not previously seen as possible. She now had more capacity and self-support for a conversation, as she was less overwhelmed, understanding what was fresh and currently relevant and what was unfinished from her past.

In subsequent sessions, LeeAnn worked with the historical bases of these issues. She explored the original introjective process in which she turned her feelings about how she was treated by others in her family into the belief, "I am unlovable." She also looked at how she now kept her distance in relationships in order to protect herself from feeling this old hurt, and how this might be contributing to her remaining an "outsider" in her friend group. She became more aware of how reflexively she saw interpersonal interactions through this lens, an enduring relational pattern that reinforced her sense of herself as unlovable and excluded by others.

Noticing the entwining of the patient's current emotion with her story and meaning-making led to the clarifying experiment. Importantly, the experiment was not suggested with an agenda for LeeAnn to move away from or lessen her pain—in fact this outcome was surprising to both of us. The intention was actually to make more space for the depth of feeling that was present. The result of the experiment was to clarify the components of her experience, highlighting the two domains and their interaction. With this clarity, each domain could be explored.

This example also reveals that introjects and other boundary processes are created and maintained by narratives that are within the domain of mental constructions. These are the building blocks of psychotherapeutic themes and character dynamics, the "second arrow" that maintains aspects of suffering. In Chapter 11 we come back to this and look at how BPGT might address these components of suffering.

Immersion and Perspective

We can be so immersed in listening to a piece of music that we lose track of time and of our surroundings. We can lose a sense of separateness at the moment of orgasm, or at the burst of flavor on our tongue as we bite into the summer's first strawberry. Diving deeply into fresh grief, it can seem we are nothing but pain. In mindfulness meditation practice, we discover that we are sometimes immersed in our present moment experience. At other times we are completely carried away with thoughts of the past or fantasies of the future, inside a mind-movie of our own making. A moment later, the thought or fantasy may segue into a completely different one. Then the sound of a car alarm or a dog barking outside brings us instantly back into the present moment. What had seemed so real is revealed as ephemeral, and bursts like a soap bubble.

Mindfulness meditation opens up another possibility for how we relate to experience. As we practice noticing what is happening as it is happening, we discover a stable awareness or consciousness that remains constant in the face of the kaleidoscope of changing emotion, sensation, story, and fantasy. Attending to and developing this capacity to observe as thoughts, feelings, and sensations, and our reactions to them, come and go, we increase our awareness of the patterns of our process. This cultivates a more stable ground from which we can attend to experience but not be immersed in it, giving us greater perspective.

The movement between immersion and perspective is an always-flowing dance, and there can be different degrees of each at different times. A high valence of emotional intensity may take all or most of our attention, with our ability to notice and observe diminished or in the background. Or observing may lead, and we see our dramas unfolding as if watching them on a stage or screen. Just remembering that perspective is possible can at times create a shift, moving us toward more balance and equanimity. "Mentalizing" is made possible by having this perspective and refers to the ability to reflect on one's experience and reactions, to consider different viewpoints, to make sense of feelings and experience, allowing them to guide actions, decisions, and choices (Wallin, 2007). Psychotherapy involves both immersion and perspective, including connecting with deep emotional experience, as well as observing, processing, clarifying, and making choices.

More familiarity with and understanding of these processes in mindfulness meditation can give us added clarity on this distinction in therapy. The therapist can consider when an intervention that supports the patient moving more fully into the experience is called for, or when to enhance perspective. For example, we might invite the patient to move more deeply into a feeling with an intervention like, "See if you can stay with your sadness." Or we might offer perspective on a current process, such as, "You seemed to connect with your sadness, then moved away from it again." To enhance perspective, we can call the patient's attention to something that seems figural but is not being addressed, or to a relevant element of the background. Therapist interventions unavoidably direct the patient's attention, and with this clarity we can be more intentional about our directing. The therapist can also be more aware of his own relational stance and choices. These choices might involve either attuning to and being with the patient in a feeling or experience, or observing, commenting on, and pointing out things that are not within the patient's immediate awareness.

Eva's work with LeeAnn illustrates both immersion and perspective, including enhancing the capacity for reflection that then informs action and contact possibilities. In addition to clarifying what is occurring in the moment for our patient, we can bring this kind of attention to our own experience and to what is happening in the interaction. Are we immersed in our patient's experience, submerged in their current world-view or their pain? Perhaps we are totally absorbed in a moment of I-Thou connection. If we are bored, frustrated, or sleepy, are we immersed in this experience or do we have a perspective that allows us to be aware of this process itself? Perspective allows reflection on what is happening for us or in the contact with our patient that might be contributing to our experience. The ability to discern these facets of experience provides the Gestalt therapist an additional clarifying lens through which to view present process.

Construction of Subjective Experience

In mindfulness meditation, as we deconstruct experience, we see the elements involved in this creation process more clearly. We begin to recognize the difference between a primary experience that is in the moment (the domain of immediate experience) and our response to or relationship with it (the domain of mental constructions). We also discover the created identification, or self-sense, in this process. Our relationship with or response to primary experience and our created identifications are more clearly revealed as mental constructs. Mindfulness also allows us to attend to and deconstruct these. We see how we attach meaning to our experience, wish for it to be different, or make a future prediction based on it. The ways we personalize experience through an identity construction are seen more clearly. This allows more awareness of the impact of mental constructs. For example, someone sitting in meditation and noticing knee pain can be aware of the direct sensation of pain and perhaps more specifically "throbbing" or burning." And there is often identification with "my pain." The person may want their experience to be different or wonder how to get rid of the pain. Fear may be present and fueled by future conjectures "What happens if I can't walk?" Self-criticism may also arise "This is my fault. I should be sitting in a chair and not trying to sit cross-legged on the floor."

These are all revealed as the constructed relationship to the primary experience of the physical pain. These constructions are discovered to be created via our thinking processes and, like everything else they are subject to change. In mindfulness meditation we see this moment-to-moment creating, and what we had previously perceived as solid, real, and unchanging, can be recognized as a flow of composite elements. We discover the ever-shifting thoughts, sensations, and feelings as they become figural, and how these create our state of mind and being.

Gestalt therapy also recognizes experience as actively created moment to moment, although we do not break it down the way Buddhist psychology does. In Gestalt therapy we look at the creation of experience in relationship to the total field. This includes the influence of memory and history, original creative adjustments and current regulation, what needs are in the foreground, what is unfinished, what is accessible to awareness, and current stimuli. Our interest is in whether currently created subjectivity is a fresh and enlivening response to the immediate situation, or if current responsiveness is restricted by a narrowed focus influenced by a limited lens of the past. We can explore how this response may ignore differences in the current situation, or what options and resources might be available that were not available at the time of the original creative adjustment.

As mindfulness meditation familiarizes us with the active creation of and components that go into our own constructions, this translates to more skill in discernment of and ability to work with these processes with our patients. Mindfulness meditation can contribute to fine-tuning attention and the capacity to recognize extracted meanings, the component parts of experience, and how solidity and identification with them is being created. The example with LeeAnn shows the subjective nature of experience, how it can be perceived as objective and unchanging: "This is just how it is." As our perspective opens up, we can recognize the elements brought to this creation, noticing that this *is* a creation and not an objective, unchanging reality.

Slowing Down and Staying With: Being Versus Doing

Slowing down, staying with, and focusing on current experience are not new for the Gestalt therapist. However, mindfulness meditation reminds us of the value of this, as we sit with what arises without doing anything about it, and our awareness increases. This experience underlines the power of sustained attention to immediate experience. Going deeply into our own experience without acting or interacting, reminds us of the possibilities and power inherent in "being" without "doing," residing in what is rather than moving toward something else. This can support doing this in therapy as well, making it easier for the therapist to sit with something and see what develops organically as a result of sustained attention, rather than moving into a more active or action-oriented intervention.

Gestalt therapy experiments can lead into action ("Imagine your father in the chair and speak to him directly") or support staying with experience as it is ("See if you can stay with the feeling that comes up when you tell me about your father"). Both are useful in leading to increased awareness and there can be a dynamic balance between them. At any point in the therapy process, we can choose one of these options. For example, working with polarities could go in either direction. Classically, we might work polarities by developing a dialogue between the two sides or positions—a more active and action-oriented experiment. As the patient alternately takes each side, giving voice to that side's perspective and feelings, this can clarify the needs and identifications of each part, bringing things to light that were out of awareness. We might also slow the process down and simply stay with what is. As a patient describes opposing forces, or competing needs, we can facilitate focused attention on how it is to sit with these opposing or competing needs or feelings in the moment. Possible interventions might be: "Notice what is happening in your body right now as you describe these pulls," or "Feel into how it is for you right now to be between the two directions," or "Without trying to solve or fix this dilemma, notice how it is to be telling me about it, and naming it right now." Staying with a more extended phenomenological investigation gives the therapist and patient space to be with and pay closer attention to the subtleties of current experiencing. This way of getting on top of the immediate experience in the moment can also open up possibilities for subsequent movement into more active experimentation.

This is not either/or. Action-oriented and contact-oriented interventions and those that are more focused on staying with awareness support one another, and an internal awareness focus may naturally generate novel contact possibilities. Importantly, undoing retroflective processes often calls for movement into action, expression, and contact.

In the following example, a patient has strong feelings of anger toward a friend. The therapist's interventions initially focus on exploring the patient's immediate experience, rather than being more contact or action-oriented.

Eric, a musician in his early thirties, came to therapy because of chronic stress and tension. He was perfectionistic and driven, appearing tightly wound, with a quality of physical rigidity. Several months into therapy, he started this session by telling me (Steve) that he was angry at his friend Sam for blowing off their dinner plans the evening before; Sam texted to cancel when Eric was already at the restaurant waiting. Eric also expressed his reluctance to confront Sam. Gestalt therapy experiments offer the possibility of working with the polarity (anger on one hand and reluctance to express it on the other) or suggesting that Eric bring Sam into the room in fantasy and express the anger or the reluctance (or both) directly. Initially, I choose instead to suggest an experiment to help Eric slow down and pay closer attention to his immediate experience.

Steve: So, you're angry at Sam, and as you're talking it sounds like there's tightness in your throat—like you're constricting. (Pause.) How about focusing in on what you're feeling right now? (Pause.) It might help to close your eyes.

Eric: (Closes eyes. Pauses.) Yeah, my throat is really tight and I have ... like a white-hot burning in my chest. I see myself sitting there waiting for Sam, then checking my phone ...

Steve: So you're tightening your throat, feeling burning in your chest. And also seeing this image.

Eric: Uh huh. (Opens eyes.) You know it reminds me of being a little kid after my parents split up. Whenever my dad was supposed to get me, half the time he wouldn't show up, but I'd just keep waiting, looking out the window, and hoping. (Chokes up.)

Steve: That's a powerful and painful image. (Pause.) And, a lot of feeling comes up as you tell me.

Eric: Yeah. I feel like crying ... and mad at myself for caring so much. I'm doing that with Sam, too, thinking this shouldn't be such a big deal. (Pause.) My throat is so tight right now.

Steve: Just stay with the tightness.

Eric: OK. (Scrunches face. Pause.) I do feel like crying. (Tears up.)

Steve: (Pause, softly.) What's happening now?

Eric: (Inhales more deeply and exhales, voice shaky, and less constricted.) I feel ... hurt. I really wanted my dad to care about me enough to show up. And I didn't want to be mad at him. I was scared if I got mad he'd stop coming around at all.

In this early part of the session, therapist interventions facilitated self-regulating in staying with each emergent aspect *of Eric's experience. This allowed Eric to access and develop more awareness of his hurt and the longing related to his dad. With this awareness, Eric could see and understand his retroflective process that involved not wanting to show or express anger and instead criticizing or blaming himself for caring too much.*

In recognizing why he needed to make this original creative adjustment, Eric felt compassion for the child who was in that bind. He made the connection between his feelings toward Sam and the anger at his dad, and he also understood why he was reluctant to let Sam know how he felt. Toward the end of this session, Eric spontaneously moved into experimenting with talking to his dad in fantasy. This work opened a door to a broader exploration of Eric's enduring sense of himself as not important to others and the ways that that played out in his relationships, including his relationship with me. In subsequent sessions we also explored more about this dynamic in relation to Sam and what Eric might want to express to him.

Gestalt therapy includes many creative intervention options. Choices are guided by the therapist's intuition, experience, preferences, training, and knowledge, as well as by the relationship with a particular patient and the unique moment. At any given time, a certain direction or intervention feels intuitively right, and if we are paying attention and attuned, all figural roads will likely lead to Rome—to what is most important and salient for the patient. In the example above, Steve had various intervention options to choose from. Mindfulness meditation practice, as part of the therapist's context and background, creates additional support for orienting toward slowing down and staying with, the "being" that can open up rich context for further exploration.

Buddhist Psychology's Heart Practices as Support for the Gestalt Therapist's Dialogical Stance

Gestalt therapy's dialogical stance involves the therapist's ability to see, appreciate, and accept the patient for all she is and all she can be. This involves holding the other as a "Thou" even when in "I-It" mode. A dialogical attitude recognizes the preciousness of human relating. As Existential-Humanistic therapist Bob Edelstein writes, "There is a sacredness in the I-Thou relationship that goes beyond the very important goals being sought in therapy, and beyond the content and process explored during therapy sessions" (Edelstein, 2015, p.441) .

Buddhist psychology recognizes the buddha nature in all human beings, and the reality of our interconnectedness. Buddhist psychology also identifies four abodes of the heart as described in Chapter 2. These qualities are cultivated not only in mindfulness practice, but also with specific meditation practices like the loving kindness or compassion practices we described in Chapter 3. **Loving kindness** is the capacity and intention to hold others and ourselves in a field of loving kindness and caring. **Compassion** involves a sense of unification as we do not keep ourselves separate from or above another's pain or suffering, recognizing the value in standing unflinchingly *with* the other, knowing suffering as a universal human experience. **Sympathetic joy** is our capacity to feel happy for another's happiness and good fortune as if it were our own. **Equanimity** allows us to accept each moment as it is, without being "for" or "against" any experience.

All of these qualities directly support the dialogic attitude, enhancing our ability to fully and open-heartedly embrace the other and the moment. Developing or cultivating these heart qualities impacts our relationship with ourselves and with others. There is a resonance between these heart qualities and Gestalt therapy's dialogic attitude. Cultivating these can support the Gestalt therapist's aspiration toward non-hierarchy, fully apprehending the other in their complete being, and holding the other as a Thou—the essential tenets of our dialogical stance. Although the concepts relating to the dialogical stance can be taught, these practices can open us to a felt sense of valuing the other and our interconnectedness, supporting embodiment of a true dialogical attitude. Accessing these qualities allows our dialogical stance to come from the heart.

You are invited to try the following experiment, prior to a therapy session, to explore one of Buddhist psychology's heart practices. As we discussed in Chapter 3, these practices cultivate our innate capacities, and nothing is forced. This exercise is to create an opportunity for opening to whatever is presently available to you, and to simply notice any effect on your experience of the patient or of yourself in the session.

Settle into a comfortable seated posture. Begin with bringing your attention to the present moment. Notice sounds and sensations, connecting with a felt sense of your body as you sit.
(Pause.)
Begin to notice the movement of breath in the body and allow your attention to rest where this movement of breathing is most apparent to you.
(Pause.)
Now bring attention to the area around the heart, breathing into the heart center, connecting with your heart. There may be a sense of an opening, warmth, or expansiveness in this area, but just allow whatever is present.
(Pause.)
Bring to mind the patient you are about to see. Consider the qualities of this person. Here is another human being with his, her, or their own unique history, strengths and limitations, doing

the best he, she or they can. Each of you is on your own jour-
ney in this life, this mystery, and you are interconnected in this
relationship. Notice the degree to which you feel open-hearted
toward your patient.

(Pause.)

Staying with the area of your heart and holding an image
of your patient in mind, silently direct a few metta phrases to
the patient you are about to see. You can make up your own
phrases based on your knowledge of the person, or use any of
the following:

May you be at ease.

May you love yourself just as you are.

May you be well.

May you embrace your own suffering with self-compassion.

Take a moment to notice the quality of your experience
before ending and going to meet your patient.

Another variant on this is to direct the following loving kindness
or compassion phrases to yourself at the beginning of your work
day or prior to a therapy session, and again to simply notice
the effect on your experience.

May I bring wisdom and compassion to my work.

May I meet the suffering of all my patients with compassion.

May I meet (patient's name) with a loving and open heart.

As these practices strengthen and allow more access to these
heart qualities, you may find it helpful to touch into them at
points of challenge or difficulty, or any time you want to access
your own capacity for open-heartedness or compassion with
your patients.

Support for the Gestalt Therapist in Recognizing the Givens of Existence

For the Gestalt therapist, Buddhist psychology's givens of existence offer a broader contextual perspective, supporting essential aspects of our work. As Gestalt therapists, we can benefit from seeing the relative level that is our ordinary point of view within the more expansive, universal perspective that Buddhist psychology provides. Our understanding of these truths, and the degree to which we directly recognize them in our own lives and through meditation practice, can allow us to meet our patients' experience with equanimity and balance, impacting the work we do and our relationship to it.

When we apprehend **impermanence**, we have perspective on our life as a whole and the reality that it will end. It also helps us see that we are afloat in a constantly changing sea of physical and emotional experience. Grounding in this truth of impermanence supports a number of foundational aspects of Gestalt therapy practice. For example, it reminds us that the field is always in flux, and that we do not have to make change happen. Instead we can notice that flow, movement, and change are *always* happening. However small or subtle the changes in our own or our patient's experience, this perspective allows us to be more primed to see these changes and to notice how no two moments of contact are exactly the same. Keeping in mind that no feeling or perspective is immutable supports our ability to stay present for and accepting of difficult interactions with patients. Realizing that no experience lasts can support us in staying with our patients in their pain, grief, or despair.

Through a Buddhist psychology lens, we see that our existence is inherently interwoven with loss, change, pain, and disappointment, as things we rely on prove unreliable, and often what we pursue does not result in what we hope for. We understand that **unsatisfactoriness** is inherent in the way things are as long as there is some attachment and a misunderstanding of the nature of reality. And since most of us are not enlightened, we can expect suffering to be part of our human experience. Remembering the universality of suffering helps us keep in mind that as humans we are subject to the pain of loss and change, and that unmet needs and desires are a natural part of life.

Seeing this bigger picture of the total human situation offers an inroad into more acceptance of and compassion for all suffering. This perspective also clarifies the difference between the pain that is unavoidable (grief at the loss of a loved one) and the mind-created "second arrow" of suffering (thinking that "grieving means I am not strong") even as we work directly with these "second arrows." This Buddhist view supports the understanding that in spite of our own and our patients' best efforts, a goal of constant happiness or contentment will most likely remain out of reach. Our acceptance of this truth means we can in turn help our patients experience less self-blame and develop more self-compassion. Even as we work with our patients in expanding their perspective and choices, we recognize that these choices are often limited by the reality of circumstance. This truth also underlines Gestalt therapy's understanding that the goal of therapy is not a particular way of being or experiencing, but increased awareness. The purpose is to feel what we do feel, to deeply know and connect with our authentic experience, and to live in the fullness of that.

Keeping in mind the truth of **not-self** can help the Gestalt therapist recognize experience as less "personal," even as we work on the personal relative level. In therapy this can help us stay present with whatever is, seeing it as simply arising from current causes and conditions. As Gestalt therapists, we already understand self-identifications as fluid, and "selfing" as a process. The Buddhist psychology view reminds us that all self-identifications are only relatively real, even though a patient may seem to be (or believe he is) stuck in ingrained patterns of behavior and reactivity.

Recognizing not-self in all experience can offer us perspective if we find ourselves caught in believing that something in the patient, the relationship, or ourselves is solid and fixed. This can also help us remain open to exploring the relationship, and how the patient experiences us, with less attachment to any viewpoint. We can more easily remain curious about ourselves, our patients' reactions to us, and the relationship as it unfolds. Less need to be seen in a certain way—for example as insightful, effective, or wise—supports our dialogical stance and our ability to bring authenticity rather than a role or persona to the therapy encounter.

Now we move from exploring the convergences of these two systems and the clinical implications of these into our integrative perspective. If we expand our psychotherapeutic approach to explicitly include Buddhist psychology's understanding and practices, what does that look like? Here, we envision a psychotherapy system that attends to the personal and relational but also incorporates working directly with Buddhist psychology's universal view. What new directions can this integration and expansion point us toward for psychotherapy practice in the 21st century?

PART IV

New Directions: Psychotherapy for the 21st Century

11

Buddhist Psychology Informed Gestalt Therapy

> *Buddhist thought ... describes ... how consciousness can be gradually purified and ... freed from ... limitations. This ... holds the promise both for individual happiness and for the evolution of our species beyond its current, all too obvious shortcomings.*
>
> —Andrew Olendzki, "The Roots of Mindfulness"
>
> *Every living thing depends on the twin dynamic principles of conservation and change.*
>
> —Gordon Wheeler and Lena Axelsson, *Gestalt Therapy*

THROUGHOUT THIS BOOK we have emphasized the convergences of Buddhist psychology and Gestalt therapy. We have also pointed to the two systems' essential differences, including differing ultimate aims. This chapter further considers these differences in exploring how integrating Buddhist psychology can expand Gestalt therapy's reach. Thus far we have not proposed any change in Gestalt therapy's theoretical perspective or method. The integration we propose in this chapter *is* new. It includes an expanded theoretical perspective, and points to new directions for practice, offering added possibilities for therapeutic focus. Although this is an expansion, it remains faithful to the core tenets of Gestalt therapy's philosophical foundations, theory, and method.

In this chapter we outline a *Buddhist psychology informed Gestalt therapy* (BPGT) that can encompass aspects of Buddhist psychology's path, practices, and aims. Informed by Buddhist psychology's understanding of the root cause of suffering, and the suggested path to liberation from it, BPGT can integrate this perspective and explore various aspects of it in therapy. The therapist can facilitate the patient's experiential recognition of the difference between pain and suffering, increasing mindfulness of the overarching processes involve in this. Meditative practices can be included within Gestalt therapy's experimental frame, both in and outside of session, to support increased awareness, and the cultivation of beneficial qualities. Considering skillful ways of being that avoid harm to oneself and others, and all aspects of the eightfold path can be explored. This exploration creates opportunity to discover cause and effect that encompasses the larger field. Buddhist psychology's expansive view of mental and emotional health, healing, and well-being can all be included in this BPGT integration.

In BPGT, Gestalt therapy's dialogical relatedness, phenomenological method, experiential and experimental focus, attention to natural regulation, and goal of increased awareness do not change. However, additional processes and another level of regulation can also be attended to. Integrating Buddhist psychology's universal understanding of impermanence, suffering, and not-self enables the work to go beyond individual psychological issues, expanding the possibilities for psychological growth and transformation. Here, we reach toward the yet-to-be-explored territory of what this unified system can offer with Gestalt therapy as a bridge between Buddhist psychology and Western psychology, enriching both and creating new possibilities for application and inquiry.

Need for This Integration

Freud once described the goal of psychotherapeutic treatment as transforming neurotic misery into ordinary unhappiness. Existential humanistic approaches, including Gestalt therapy, aimed higher with the promise that personal growth and increased self-awareness could lead to a more authentically lived and richly satisfying life. Buddhist psychology reaches further still. With its broad understanding and prescriptive path, it points us toward increased awareness of and deepening insight into what is universal in human experience. Ultimately its practices can lead to an awakened understanding that accesses deeper wisdom, compassion, peace, and happiness independent of conditions.

Western psychotherapy, including Gestalt therapy, attends to the relative level of existence. Gestalt therapy patients can develop more acceptance of themselves and of their experience as they become more aware of and deal with individual psychological issues and relational patterns, resolve internal conflict, and connect with authenticity. This process addresses the relative aspect of suffering and contributes to more well-being on this level. But from a Buddhist psychology perspective, this outcome remains limited because human suffering goes beyond individual emotional difficulties, symptoms, or relationship issues. It also involves our failure to grasp the truth of the universal givens of existence. Without this awareness and understanding, we will continue to suffer, no matter how much individual psychological work we do (Yeshe, 1998).

From this Buddhist psychology perspective, ignorance of the overarching cause of suffering, and the failure to address this aspect of human experience, are seen as an inherent limitation of Western psychology. Although external circumstances do present difficulties and challenges, psychological transformation occurs through increased awareness of our relationship with and response to these. Bringing this point of view into psychotherapy, and working directly with it, offers the opportunity for patients to reap the benefits of increased awareness of this overarching process. The BPGT approach offers patients an avenue to explore aspects of this, and to come to see these processes more clearly, just as meditative practices do.

In Gestalt therapy the patient develops a more coherent self-experience, as ego functioning and interruptions in natural regulation are brought into awareness and attended to. Conversely, Buddhist psychology's focus is on the truth of the changing nature of self-experience, the fluidity of self-identifications, and the inherent suffering in attachment to self as a reified identity. Buddhist psychology's aim is therefore freedom from all limiting and mistaken self-concepts. Gestalt therapy already aligns with an understanding of self-experience as a fluid process, and of rigidified self-concepts as limiting. We see Buddhist psychology's overarching perspective as opening up a dimension that goes beyond, but does not negate, a traditional Gestalt therapy understanding of healthy functioning. The relative level psychological work remains essential, even as we explore the universal perspective, and consider the possibility of viewing all created self-identifications as "fixed *gestalten*" that limit experience, connection, and contact. We describe how these different emphases are addressed and reconciled in BPGT in the section below on self/ego functioning and not-self/non-identification.

Several writers grounded in both Western psychology and Buddhist psychology point to the need for a psychotherapy that can bridge the two. For example, psychoanalyst Mark Epstein (2007) explains that Buddhist psychology does not have a way to focus on the particulars of individual psychodynamics or intrapsychic conflict, nor can it attend to the mind's propensity for disruption that cannot be addressed solely through meditative practices. Buddhist teacher and psychologist Jack Kornfield (1993) suggests that there is a need to complement Buddhist practice with psychotherapy as many meditation students are unable to practice traditional Insight meditation because they encounter "so much unresolved grief, fear, and wounding and unfinished developmental business from the past" (Kornfield, 1993, p. 246). The need for a holistic psychotherapy approach for meditation practitioners to address the issue of "spiritual bypassing," where one uses spiritual practice to avoid or to attempt to transcend difficult emotions, relationship challenges and psychological issues has also been addressed (Welwood, 2000).

Welwood suggests that a psychotherapy system for meditators should not be based on a medical model that pathologizes patients, nor should it rely on the limited perspective of diagnosis and cure. He proposes a transformative psychotherapy that does more than just talk, but includes methods that attend to embodied experience and to the person as a whole (Welwood, 2000). Clearly, Gestalt therapy fully meets these criteria, and as we have shown it does this within a system that aligns with Buddhist psychology and mindfulness. For Buddhist meditation practitioners, BPGT has the added benefit of offering a relational mindful approach to working directly with the processes identified in Buddhist psychology. It encompasses Buddhist psychology's universal perspective along with addressing the essential relative level of individual and relational psychological work, and includes the potential for interweaving the two, as we show later in this chapter.

It goes without saying that this work also requires that therapists have first-hand experiential understanding—through their own study, path practices, and meditation—of this perspective and these processes. In order for therapists to explore these aspects of experience with patients, we must be able to draw upon our own experience and understanding of mind-created identification and constructions, their relationship to suffering, the insubstantiality of these, and the potential for freedom that this experiential understanding holds.

Support for this Integration in Gestalt Therapy's Field Phenomenological View

Gestalt therapist Ruth Wolfert proposed that Gestalt therapy had not yet realized the full potential of its field phenomenological perspective that recognizes our active participation in creating experience via field interaction effects. She suggested that Gestalt therapy could more deeply reflect this view by articulating and emphasizing the field dependent nature of all experience as Buddhist psychology does. She saw Buddhist psychology as offering Gestalt therapy additional support for "living up to the promise of its field theory" (Wolfert, 2000, p. 77). She writes: "In the beginning is field, and ... contact in the organism environment field ... is the first and simplest reality. This radical view forms the basis for Gestalt therapy theory in Perls, Hefferline, & Goodman. There are no fixed entities interacting to produce an effect; rather there is a contactful field effect that produces us in the moment" (Wolfert, 2000, p. 77).

Although Gestalt therapy sees self-experience as fluid and field-dependent, and recognizes our limiting self-concepts as restricting awareness and contact, Buddhist psychology's radically field phenomenological understanding goes further. It sees all self-identifications as limiting. It recognizes that humans reflexively reify self, object, and experience, and that these are created constructs. Buddhist psychology's detailed investigation of this construction process has led to the destructuring not just of self-experience but of all self-referential identifications, entities, and abstractions. These are deconstructed into field phenomena consisting solely of the five co-arising, co-existing and co-vanishing aggregates that Buddhist psychology has identified: form, sense impression, perception, categorization, and consciousness (described in Chapter 2).

Buddhist psychology directs our attention to "the unaware grounds" (Wolfert, 2000, p. 81) that we take as real or given but that are themselves creations. This recognition is important in Buddhist psychology, as it helps us to see our experience as process, ultimately recognizing it as impermanent and less personal. In meditation we can observe our moment-to-moment creation of fixity, recognizing how we take our creations to be real and solid. Seeing through this helps dissolve the ground of identification, creating potential for expanded experience and transformation of suffering. We can do this in the therapy process as well. Gestalt therapy's field phenomenology is one of the bases for embracing this Buddhist psychology understanding, and for developing ways of illuminating and investigating these processes.

In the rest of this chapter we explore specifics of the BPGT integration. We consider how to reconcile the importance of healthy ego-functioning in Gestalt therapy with Buddhist psychology's not-self view. We also lay out a perspective on an expanded view of natural regulation. Next, we look at some ways to work with processes identified in Buddhist psychology including pain and suffering, as well as desire and attachment, offering several clinical examples of this approach. We describe ways of integrating meditation both in and outside of the therapy session, as well as possibilities for incorporating other aspects of the eightfold path and cultivation of heart qualities in the BPGT approach. We conclude with a consideration of an expanded field perspective. This is a beginning exploration of how Gestalt therapy's psychological understanding and methodology and Buddhist psychology's perspective and practices can be braided together, pointing toward seeing each moment as holding the possibility for a transformed reality, a radical revision of our experience of being alive.

Self/Ego Functioning and Not-Self/Non Identification

Gestalt therapy focuses on increasing awareness in the service of identification with and connection to authentic self-experience. This is the ego functioning described in Chapter 5—the capacity to identify that which is "me" or "for me" and that which is "not me," or " not for me." In contrast, Buddhist psychology's focus on increasing awareness is in the service of revealing the truth of not-self, allowing us to see through identity construction and to hold experience as less personal. This apparent contradiction is reconciled in BPGT by recognizing these processes not as mutually exclusive but rather as synergistic. From this perspective, personal psychological work on the relative level and attention to the broader view of the universal level are two sides of the same coin.

We propose that the patient's capacity to identify with and connect to self-experience establishes the foundation that clears the way for looking more deeply into the nature of self-experience and the essential insubstantiality of it. In BPGT, clarity about and relative freedom from boundary processes that interrupt natural self-regulating, and the capacity to identify with one's experience are key in pursuing the exploration that Buddhist psychology offers. Focusing on the universal perspective without this ego functioning capacity poses a risk of reinforcing introjective, projective, retroflective, confluent, deflective or egotism processes, or of the "spiritual bypassing" mentioned earlier.

Conversely, the patient's increased self-awareness and restored ego-functioning, through the therapy process, creates opportunity for deepening exploration of what self-experience actually is. The relative freedom from aspects of suffering that is a result of doing individual psychological work also supports this additional level of exploration. This can then be a next step for those who have already done in-depth personal work, and/or those who have experience with Buddhist psychology views and meditation. This focus may therefore be more often integrated in later stages of a therapy process. That said there might be times in the course of any therapy that this meta-perspective can be useful and relevant. It is also possible to move between these, focusing on individual psychological issues or this broader universal view as needed. For the patient who is not familiar with Buddhist psychology's understanding, we can integrate an educational component, as we show in a clinical example later in this chapter.

As the BPGT perspective informs the therapist's background, it may influence the therapy process in general or particular aspects of it may become more figural. A collaborative understanding and clarification of the most relevant focus for the patient remains essential. Attention to this overarching perspective is not a substitute for needed psychological work. Rather, the option of exploring this other level of understanding is always available. Gestalt therapy's focus on present process remains the doorway to working with these possibilities for transformation of self-experience.

Expanded View of Natural Regulation

A BPGT exploration may include destructuring identification and concepts, allowing early creative adjustments to be seen through this lens as well. These creative adjustments are still understood as essential adaptive responses, and *they can also be seen to have no inherent reality.* Although originally necessary for psychological survival, their current iterations in restrictive boundary processes can be recognized not only as limiting, *but also as actually insubstantial.* As the patient deconstructs the conceptual scaffolding these creative adjustments were built on, she can recognize them as created constructs. This unfolding process may allow the patient to see through this whole construction project, and to access another level of expanded awareness and freedom.

This glimpse of freedom from identifying with and taking these lifelong beliefs about oneself and one's experience as solid and unchanging is transformative, pointing to the liberation from suffering promised in Buddhist psychology. Clarity about this may even be more easily accessed in psychotherapy than in meditation, since psychotherapy can directly attend to these very psychological processes, harnessing the power of this integrative method. This work also opens the door to another aspect of what Buddhist psychology points to—the realization of our innate potential for wholeness. In these moments of clarity, freed from obscurations, all of present moment experience can be embraced without impediment or interruption.

Ruth Wolfert has also pointed to how Gestalt therapy can encompass this expanded experience. In doing so she has proposed *being* as the "final, fully lived stage of contact. *Being* signifies dwelling in moments of unity, where the splits of mind, body, and external world are healed.... According to Goodman, the final stage of full contact lies beyond therapy, that is, it is only to be experienced, not examined or otherwise explored.... *This limits Gestalt therapy unnecessarily*" (Wolfert, 2000, p. 82, emphasis added). Wolfert goes on to say that integrating a Buddhist perspective, we can extend the experience of *being* so that we can open deeper and deeper grounds, allowing moments of full contact "to flower into fuller awakenings" (2000, p.82). She suggests that one opportunity for this may be in extending the time between contact sequences—the space between final contact and the emergence of the next figure. This opening "allows us to enter a void which is pregnant with all possibilities" (p. 83). Here there is potential for firmly held constructs to loosen and to lose their valence, and for something novel to arise. This is a reality shift that encompasses the expansiveness of pure awareness "beyond content and ego... This is a time when the past is gone and the future is not yet; a time of profound newness when all things are possible" (2000, p. 83).

Buber's I-Thou moment, as described in Chapter 5, also encompasses a quality of experience similar to Wolfert's "being." These both involve sustained presence and immediacy, without the pull to a next forming figure. In both, as we are freed of thought and the usual constraints and limits of the thinking mind, we enter the fertile void, the full emptiness of surrender to the moment, to what is emergent.

Through the BPGT lens, this can be seen as *another aspect of natural regulation*. Here, we can recognize mind-created constructs and the thinking process itself as interruptions to wholeness and fuller contact with our self-experience and the world. What may emerge in experience when awareness is not limited and controlled by thought, self-identity, or rigidity? From this perspective we can see all identifications as fixed *gestalten* that limit fluidity, perceptivity, and responsiveness. Attending to this in therapy can create added freedom in the relational field in the moment, and new possibilities for novel contact and connection.

This can also be seen as another level of freedom from egotism (one of the boundary processes described in Chapter 5). Egotism involves an overarching concern with one's boundaries and identity rather than what might be contacted, an interruption in the final contact of surrender to spontaneity and novelty. This has been described as "holding back from the final release or arrival in a journey of contact...a healthy dissolution of separateness in a kind of creative union or flow" (Wheeler & Axelsson, 2015, p. 48). Freedom from this interruption may now be seen to include surrender to the expansive open awareness described above, uninhibited by identification and constructs.

Psychotherapeutic Exploration of Processes Identified in Buddhist Psychology

Gestalt therapy is well leveraged to directly explore processes identified in Buddhist psychology and illuminated through meditative practices. With phenomenological inquiry, understanding self as process, and the goal of increased awareness as essential common threads, the BPGT perspective opens the door to this exploration. In the next two sections on exploring pain and suffering, and exploring desire and attachment, we look at how aspects of experience may be clarified and deconstructed to identify and unpack the elements that comprise them.

Exploring Pain and Suffering

Recognizing when patients are connecting with present feelings and embodied experience versus when they are involved in stories and concepts is nothing new for the Gestalt therapist. One of Fritz Perls' most quoted exhortations is, "Lose your mind and come to your senses." However, Buddhist psychology's lens offers the therapist another perspective on this distinction. Differentiating present sensory experience and embodied feeling from concepts, we see that "first arrow" pain is in the former, and "second arrow" suffering is in the latter. The inevitable pain of living emerges as present sensory experience and feeling. Suffering is added through mind-made constructions. Gestalt therapy is already grounded in the value and importance of connecting with actual present moment experiencing, and in BPGT we can use this understanding in the service of exploring pain and suffering in therapy. This focus orients the therapist to paying attention to these processes more explicitly and directly, supporting increased awareness of them.

This work offers ways for the patient and therapist to

collaboratively attend to any of the following interrelated processes: 1) experientially discovering the difference between pain
and suffering; 2) recognizing the emergence of constructed concepts; 3) noticing the self-sense that co-arises with these constructions; 4) understanding what it takes to stay present with
the elements of painful experience; 5) recognizing when deeper
inquiry into psychological issues that are driving attachment is
needed.

Just as mindfulness allows us to glimpse the "second arrow"
of suffering and how it is created, so can this BPGT process. The
therapist can notice when patients are with felt experience or
when they are involved in concepts, and can also note when the
patient moves from one to the other. This can clarify whether
patients are with their emotional pain, or where elements of
suffering are present. As the patient's attention is drawn away
from present experience to past, future, or concepts, the therapist can point this out. With this awareness, the patient can
choose the focus of attention more mindfully. Bringing attention
to current embodied experience can access present pain, and
offers the potential to be with it more directly, and to experience
the elements of it more clearly. Although it is reflexive to avoid
pain, within this elemental experience we again discover the
possibility of connection with authentic experience, closure and
release. Opening to and being with our pain is where healing
and transformation begin.

The therapist can facilitate the patient's awareness of what
goes into constructions by pointing out beliefs, fantasies, or
expectations, and labeling these processes. This can clarify the
attachments and suffering contained in these. Then in bringing
attention back to current embodied experience, the patient may
discover that the thoughts are no longer compelling or do not
hold the same charge. This offers an experiential awareness of
the ephemeral and insubstantial nature of thoughts that tend

to be treated as solid and "real," and more ability to see the thinking process for what it is. Another possible experiment may then be to suggest that the patient see if she can intentionally go from her embodied experience back to thoughts, to increase awareness of this process itself. The ability to move between these aspects of experience also points to the insubstantiality of the constructs as they arise and recede.

In this relational mindful process, the therapist offers presence and support and makes observations to help bring attention to details of experience, increasing awareness of all of these processes. Gestalt therapy's experiential paradigm and descriptive phenomenology make it a natural fit for this mindful exploration.

The following is an example of how this process allows the patient to clarify her own experience of the difference between pain and suffering.

Grace is in her mid-fifties; she has been in therapy for almost a year and has done some meditation practice. Typically very intellectual, Grace has been able to access more feelings in therapy and has seen how suffering results from some of the ways she reflexively thinks of herself. She has just gone through losing a long-term relationship that she had hoped would last. In this session the therapist initially suggests she attend to how she is experiencing the grief as she talks about it.

This brings up more emotion, and Grace describes aching and heaviness in her heart area and feels the tears on her face. At a certain point she moves into a future prediction: "I know I'll always be alone," and along with that the introject of "It's my fault Cara left; I knew I wasn't good enough for her."

This is a therapeutic "fork in the road," a choice point for therapist focus. The therapist could choose to focus on these enduring therapy themes and related feelings. Alternatively, this offers an opportunity for Grace to see that there is a difference between connecting with the present pain of her loss, and the suffering in her future predictions and self-blame. Here, the therapist points out this process, supporting Grace in staying more with the pain. Grace becomes aware of how the constructs--predictions and self-blame--cut her off from the "pure" pain of losing Cara.

This work helps to illuminate the in-the-moment creation of suffering and its components. Rather than remaining out of awareness, this process itself then becomes figural, and Grace can see it more clearly; she has perspective rather then being embedded in it. From this vantage point, the difference between the inevitable pain and grief in response to her loss and the added suffering is revealed.

Another way to see this process clearly is with a patient dealing with physical pain or illness. The therapist can help the patient differentiate between pain in the body ("first arrow") and mind-created suffering ("second arrow"). As in the previous example, the therapist directs the patient's attention to the actual physical sensation as a starting point and suggests ways to attend more closely to the details and qualities of this experience. For example, the therapist can suggest that the patient discover if a pain is sharp or dull, constant or throbbing, consistent or intermittent. Also, whether it changes or stays the same as the patient attends to it.

The therapist can also draw the patient's attention to any aversion to the painful sensation, perhaps manifesting in tightening around the pain or restricted breathing. The therapist can explore aversive thoughts, such as the patient "arguing" with what is or being reluctant to feel or pay attention to the pain, which can be expressed as: "I'm too young to be having this much pain," or "Isn't it better to just ignore it?" Fearful thoughts are also a natural response to pain and are often about the future: "Will I always have this pain? Will it get worse?" or "I think I'll have to have surgery." Again, the patient can discover the difference between what is actually here right now and the thoughts about it, the difference between staying with present experience and jumping to the unknown future. The patient can also experiment with shifting attention between these two domains to discover more about the difference.

Sometimes with physical pain, as with emotional pain, the aversion is worse than the pain itself, or it makes the pain worse. To increase awareness of this, the therapist can direct the patient's attention to noticing any physical "resistance" to the pain. As the patient does this, he may discover holding or tension. If he is able to sustain attention, there may be a natural release, allowing opening to and softening around the pain, creating more space for it. This may lessen the experience of pain itself, or the perceived intensity of it, which may in turn decrease the aversion to it. This work supports the patient staying with what is, allowing discernment of the difference between the pain and what is added, potentially resulting in more freedom from suffering.

With patients who are not familiar with the Buddhist psychology understanding of pain and suffering, we can still bring this perspective to the work. This does mean briefly explaining this difference, as Steve does in the following example.

Cody is in his mid-forties, and has been divorced for two years after ten years of marriage. He came to therapy because he couldn't resolve his strong feelings of hurt, anger and betrayal involving his ex-wife. She'd had multiple affairs, including one with a friend of his, and lied to him about this throughout their marriage, while continuing to profess her commitment to him and the family. Only after she was caught did she admit to lying. Cody "just couldn't get over" this, and it was interfering with his new relationship.

In our sessions, Cody presented many details of how his ex betrayed him. He could barely stand being around her when he saw her at a school event, or when he dropped their children off at her house. With me, he talked as if he were presenting a case to a jury, determined to prove her guilty. It was difficult for Cody to be with any feelings other than anger, but over time we did touch on his hurt, sense of loss, and longing for the intact family he'd had. Often he ended up circling back to "making his case" about his ex to me. We then talked about this process in which Cody felt like he was "spinning his wheels." He did not know what he wanted from me as he did this. He did recognize the difference between his feelings, like hurt or sadness and "talking about" his ex.

I decide in this session to experiment with presenting the Buddhist psychology perspective on pain and suffering to him. I go over what we have already clarified in our work—that there is a difference between his feelings, and the thoughts and stories about his ex and what she did. I then add the perspective that in Buddhist psychology this is the difference between pain (being with primary feeling) and the added suffering (the concepts and stories). This is immediately clarifying for Cody and offers him support and motivation to stay with the sadness around his loss, rather than going into the "wheel spinning" that is the mind-created suffering. Doing this, Cody recognizes more clearly that there is no way around his pain, but that the added suffering is in the endless loop of wishing things had been different, and blaming his ex. Cody quickly "gets it" that he is perpetuating his suffering in this process, and sees that focusing on his ex keeps him from dealing with his own pain. We then experiment with a few "rounds" of moving between Cody touching his pain and feelings of loss, and then going back to a story. There is soon less energy and "charge" in the story. Cody also notices that in connecting with his pain, he feels more connected with and understood by me, something he had not previously recognized as a need, and now does.

At the next session Cody tells me that he's been thinking about his ex much less, and that he isn't as angry. He's also been more able to stay with his sadness about the loss of his family, and as he has done that, he feels more accepting of how things are now. A few weeks later Cody reports, with some surprise, that he saw his ex sitting alone at his son's soccer game while he was there with his new girlfriend. He actually felt sorry for her and imagined inviting her to sit with them—something he previously would not have thought possible.

This example shows that there can be potential benefit for some patients of bringing this Buddhist psychology perspective to the therapy process while maintaining Gestalt therapy's experiential and experimental focus. Although a conceptual understanding of the difference between pain and suffering can be useful, in BPGT we want this understanding to be grounded in the patient's actual experience.

Identification and Non-Identification in This Exploration

Gestalt therapy theory recognizes self as process rather than as a solid or reified entity. Although this recognition informs Gestalt therapy method, in Gestalt therapy we do not work directly with increasing the patient's awareness of this. In BPGT however, we have a perspective that gives us reason to include this work. Informed by Buddhist psychology, we see that identification is the ground for the grasping, clinging, craving, or aversion that creates the attachment that leads to suffering. Any time there is identification and attachment, even with positive or pleasurable experience, this can become suffering as we cling to it, crave more of it, or fear its loss. An aspect of working with suffering involves attending to this process of created identification.

The BPGT view suggests the possibility of exploring identification by looking at "selfing" in therapy, just as we do in meditation. This is the process in which fluidity and impermanence are mistaken for a fixity that is then identified with. From this perspective, any reified self-identification can be recognized as created, not inherently permanent or solid. Exploring this in therapy first requires that the therapist recognize all self-views and constructions as insubstantial, impermanent, and only relatively real. Then the therapy can include this exploration with patients.

Again we can direct the patient's attention to primary present experience, allowing the patient to discover the elements that make it up; the ongoing flow of physical sensation, sensory experience, and embodied emotion. The more the patient mindfully deconstructs experience into these elements and sees them as phenomena that arise and pass away, the more he can see the insubstantiality of any assumed or created "I." The longer the patient is able to sustain this awareness of present phenomena, the more a space is opened for experience less bounded by concepts and identification. Conversely, thoughts and constructs always involve a created "I."

In one way of experimenting with these contrasting experiences, the patient can begin with any primary experience, for example physical pain. She can experiment with saying "my knee hurts" and notice what this is like. Next, the therapist can direct the patient's attention to simply *noticing* the specific sensations in her knee more closely, letting go of *thoughts* about it. She can then experiment with noting/saying "sharpness," or "aching," or "painful sensations are arising."

The same can be done with emotional experience. For example the patient can experiment with saying, "I'm sad," versus attending directly to the elements that make up sadness in the mind and body, and noting, "Sadness is arising." What is the sense of self or "ownership" in the first experience, contrasted with the second? Is there an "I" to be found, or is there only whatever is arising along with awareness of it? Can the connection with direct experience—without the identification and the personalizing or "owning"—be discerned as the difference between unavoidable pain and added suffering? Experiments like this can allow patients to begin to see how identification can dissolve in paying attention to what is actually here. In this way patients can learn to uncover the pieces of constructed identity in a therapeutic process, just as they might in meditation practice.

Again and importantly, this work requires that the patient first have the capacity to know, connect with, and "own" her experience. This is not a way to distance from, detach, or attempt to disown anything. Rather, as good ego functioning supports it, this is an added level of awareness to experiment with in order to further illuminate this element of the difference between pain and suffering.

Field Influences in This Exploration

As we attend to these processes, the important role of field influences involved in the development of any construction is clarified. These field influences are the causes and conditions from which the constructions emerge. This includes all of the patient's background, such as history and creative adjustments, and also what is foreground, such as an immediate situation, something unfinished, or current relational interaction and needs. As patients become increasingly aware that these constructions are actively created based on field effects—that are themselves created subjectivities—they can begin to get the flavor of their insubstantiality, as pointed to by Buddhist psychology.

Impermanence in This Exploration

In paying attention to present phenomena, it is easier to see impermanence and to recognize experience as transitory. Here, we are in the flow of a natural process of movement and change in which closure naturally leads to newly emergent figures. When we are embedded in concepts, these can be experienced as solid and unchanging, masking the truth of impermanence. The actual insubstantiality of these constructs and the reality of movement and change can be more easily and directly apprehended as the patient stays with embodied experience, or moves between embodied experience and created constructs, with awareness.

The following example shows how the above processes are explored with a patient who is interested in more clarity regarding her own experience of pain and suffering.

Kristin is a psychologist in her late forties. She has more than a decade of meditation experience and an in-depth understanding of Buddhist psychology. She has also done extensive therapy work. She begins the session tearfully telling me (Steve) that she is again experiencing recurrent physical symptoms that include extreme fatigue, weakness, and headaches. She is finding it hard to function today because of this. She doesn't know why this happens periodically (no medical diagnosis), and she seems overwhelmed and anxious as she talks about it. She tells me her catastrophic predictions—her fears about the symptoms getting worse, and about what the underlying yet-to-be-discovered cause might be. She also feels shame for her own emotional reaction. This shame relates to her history; growing up in her family, things were not supposed to trouble her, and there was little support for her emotional needs.

Initially I support her in being with these feelings, and in letting me in on them. Then we begin exploring how we might look at and clarify both the pain and the suffering in her current experience. I initially point out her aversion to the physical symptoms, a natural response to the pain and discomfort. There is also longing for more vitality and a more energetic "self." As we explore this, she recognizes the attachment, and that there is added suffering in her shame--rejecting the emotional response she is having. She also sees that her fear is understandable as she imagines future frightening possibilities, and this awareness brings more self-compassion.

Kristin then notices how she is caught in her thinking process, and that what she is feeling is in response to the thoughts. She is not aware that she has omitted attention to, or focus on, the physical sensations (symptoms) she is having right now, or her feelings about these.

Steve: I notice we haven't attended to the actual physical experience that you're having right now, or your feelings about it. That would be the more primary experience, the "pain."

Kristin: (Pause.) Oh...that's true. I mostly go into my thoughts...and then the feelings are about them.

Steve: So, let's slow things down a bit. Close your eyes if you want to, and pay attention to your body, the sensations, what you're aware of...what's present right now.

Kristen: (Closes eyes. Long pause, deep sigh.) Very tired... so tired.

Steve: So...just stay with that...

Kristen: Heaviness, and foggy in my head, kind of weak... (Pause.) Now...there's sadness coming up, I feel it in my throat... and chest...deep sadness (Starts crying.)

Steve: Yes...there is a loss for you in this....

Kristen: (Crying harder.)

Steve: Just allow all of what you're feeling...

Kristen: (Eyes still closed. Gradually stops crying and continues silence for another minute. Her face looks calmer, and relaxed.)

Steve: What's happening now?

Kristen: The experience of space...just space...

Steve: OK—stay with that...

As we sit mostly in silence, I inquire once or twice about her experience. Kristen stays with the spaciousness, occasionally noting a thought coming in and then seeming to dissolve. After a time she opens her eyes, and she seems grounded, brighter, and present with me.

Kristen: So...powerful.

Steve: Yeah, for me too...quite something...

We spend a few minutes just absorbing, and assimilating this shared experience.

Kristen: Hmm...now I'm wondering... if I'm just avoiding all those other feelings that I came in with.

Steve: Well, you can experiment with going back to those thoughts and feelings, the fear...we can work more with that...

Kristen: I know (Pause.) And that's just not where I am now. I want to stay with this...let it be what it is right now.

Steve: Sure. And we can always come back to any of those thoughts or feelings as they come up ...

As we continue to process her experience, Kristen says that moving into the actual physical sensations in the moment and connecting with and staying with her sadness opened up the spaciousness. She describes how in that "space" there were moments of non-identification, just pure awareness, a sense of freedom and expansiveness.

In this session there was a clear experiential distinction between the initial mind-created suffering, and being with the pain—first physical then emotional—more directly. The therapeutic process facilitated this in several ways. Processing her fear and the psychological issues related to lack of entitlement to her own emotional experience, paved the way for this work.

My pointing out what was omitted--that Kristen was not attending to her embodied experience—was also key, and she needed support in order to do that. Being with this experience allowed closure, and as there was not another immediately emergent figure she naturally moved into the open spaciousness.

This can be seen as an example of Wolfert's "being;" what she described as pure awareness without ego-identification or content in the extended time between final contact and the emergence of the next figure. This also reflects the natural regulation that we described earlier in this chapter, free of the interruptions that impede a full openness to experience and contact in the moment.

Exploring Desire and Attachment

Gestalt therapy's understanding of the figure formation/destruction (FFD) cycle includes recognizing that it is basic to human functioning for wants and needs to arise, along with a natural reflex to act on and satisfy these. Seeking safety, pleasure, or comfort and avoiding danger and pain is part of this process, and essential to survival for all sentient beings. Humans experience desire for many different things, starting with necessities like food and water and expanding from there. Our wants can be endless and may include wanting material things, pleasure of all kinds, physical and emotional connection and relatedness, artistic or creative expression, novelty, learning, recognition, or power.

Although natural and built into us, from a Buddhist psychology perspective, the arising of desire always has the potential to become attachment that leads to suffering. Pleasure and enjoyment are not themselves problematic, but we can grasp onto these, turning them from a source of happiness into a source of suffering and dissatisfaction (Yeshe, 2001). And in any experience of attachment, if we attend mindfully to it, we can make the direct experiential connection to suffering. Including this understanding in therapy helps us see patients' suffering in their clinging, craving, and grasping, or aversion. There might be attachment to wanting to be what they are not, or to wanting a different experience from the one they are having. They may be craving or grasping for something, or clinging to something they are afraid of losing. They may have aversion to aspects of themselves or their experience. Created identification drives both hope for satisfaction and fear of loss in this process, as the patient is pulled between these poles.

This can be explored in BPGT just as it is in mindfulness meditation. And just as in meditation, this exploration is not to try to get rid of wants. It is rather to look into the nature of desire, and the experience of wanting. This can allow a fuller understanding of this process, more mindfulness of its arising, and recognition of the possibility of freedom from being caught in the attachment that begins with the arising of desire, and that can ultimately result in suffering. Awareness of the arising of desire and mindful attention to it allows a want to be present without it capturing us. Then it is simply an aspect of experience to pay attention to, to notice, and to sit with. In this mindful process, we are not identified, not attached, not suffering. Instead we are aware that "desire is arising."

Simply noticing in-the-moment attachment, and recognizing the resulting suffering, can also become a doorway to more freedom. Attachment can be as subtle as wanting the grocery line to move faster. The suffering may then arise in the form of irritation with the checker who is taking her time, chatting with a customer ahead of us. Or particular attachments can pervade our life in the form of ubiquitous disappointment, or envy of others who seem to have what we wish for ourselves. Generally we are in an ongoing process of attachment that involves identification and striving that is out of our awareness.

The antidote to being caught in this reflexive cycle is increased awareness of and perspective on this process itself.

Here we point to possibilities for how to explore this in BPGT, including increasing awareness of wanting as a naturally and endlessly arising phenomenon. This *is* the FFD process that Gestalt therapists are practiced at attending to. Informed by this broader perspective, we have the option to work with this process directly just as we can in mindfulness meditation. Again, this is never a therapist-driven agenda, but rather something to consider as an area of exploration if and when it is relevant for the patient.

The "How" of this Exploration in Psychotherapy

In one way of working with this process of desire and attachment, the therapist may suggest an intentional turning of the "flashlight beam" of the patient's attention away from the external, the object of desire "out there," and toward internal experience. This allows "wanting" to become the lively figure of interest. As this forming figure clarifies, the patient can experience the wanting more clearly, including its attendant bodily sensation, feelings, and thoughts. In Gestalt therapy we often direct attention to embodied experience, suggesting that the patient focus inside, however here we are interested in an even more elemental deconstruction of this experience. The therapist can support the patient in remaining open to and curious about what the wanting is like, guiding the patient in deconstructing the experience into its elements. This is a facilitated phenomenological investigation of the experience of "wanting" as it is directly sensed in the moment. In much the same way as clarifying pain and suffering, the patient can begin to experientially differentiate the embodied elements of desire and the constructions and identification that create attachment. More clarity about the nature of wanting itself can emerge in this

process, along with less personalization and therefore less identification. Coming back to, staying with, and attending to what
is present in the elemental experience is the entry point to this
increased awareness.

Paying attention in this way to the details of the experience
of wanting can, in itself, transform the relationship to it. At
times, wanting is only contained in thoughts, and it dissolves
as we focus on present embodied experience. The patient may
also learn to directly link attachment and suffering, whether it
is as subtle as a slight leaning away from current experience and
into a future perceived as being more satisfying, or whether it
is as painful as a sense of desperation that if she does not get
what she wants, she cannot survive. Making this connection
may at times loosen or dissolve the attachment, allowing more
ease in being with what is and all attendant feelings. When this
happens, it is a naturally unfolding and organic process, not a
false or forced detachment.

At other times, staying with the experience of wanting
can clarify and increase awareness of what drives the attachment. Sometimes attachment and identification are strong and
multi-determined, for example, "If I don't get this promotion,
I'm a failure and my whole life is a sham. Maybe my father
was right when he said I'd never amount to anything." Here
the therapist can help the patient more deeply investigate these
forces behind the desperation, looking at unfinished business
and unresolved psychological issues. This traditional work
also creates opportunity for further exploration of these beliefs
as mind-created constructs. These aspects of experience are
interwoven, and this again points to the value in the therapist
having the tools, skills, and perspective to attend to both of
these levels.

In this exploration, the attention is not focused on action
and contact in the FFD cycle. Instead the therapist helps the

patient remain with the experienced "wanting." Staying with the beginning part of the FFD cycle can increase awareness of the thoughts, feelings, and sensations that comprise this experience. This allows the patient to look at and deconstruct wants and emotional needs, not reflexively taking them as adequate motivation for action (Wolfert, 2000), which opens up greater choice and flexibility. The patient remains mindful of this present experience itself rather than moving further into identification, or toward action.

Because this work can lead to "uncoupling" of the desired object or experience and the wanting itself, this can also offer one way to work with patients dealing with addiction. An essential skill for these patients is the capacity to tolerate the experience of craving, without reflexively acting on it. With addiction, there is a strong pull toward the substance or activity, the external "object," and attention tends to be focused on the substance or experience "out there." The impulse to action is often driven not only by the want, but also by a wish to avoid the aversive experience of craving itself. Turning the focus of attention from the external to the embodied internal experience supports the patient in being with the craving, and attending mindfully attend to it. It may be helpful for the patient to note, "This is what craving is like right now." This mindful attention, along with the therapist's support can then change the patient's relationship to the experience, decreasing aversion and increasing the ability to sit with it.

Directly experiencing the link between craving and suffering may also dissolve the craving, or result in it losing some of its "charge." Or this work can reveal and clarify other significant wants and feelings. The craving for the substance or activity may be in response to other longings that are out of awareness, like a wish for comfort, companionship, or emotional support. Underlying anxiety-related feelings that are being avoided might emerge. The "sitting with" can allow these to become figural and then to be attended to in the therapy process.

This is one example of working with desire and attachment in this way.

Antonia, a tall, elegantly dressed woman in her late twenties, arrives at her session preoccupied with thinking about a watch she just saw in an online ad. The experience of wanting to buy something she doesn't need and can't afford is familiar, with origins in a childhood of emotional and material deprivation. She is pleased that she has not yet acted on the impulse to buy the watch. This is new for her, as therapy has helped her become aware that buying expensive things is a way of avoiding old feelings of worthlessness, envy of others, and a sense of deprivation.

She has recently developed more ability to avoid or delay acting on these impulses and to be with her feelings when they arise. In this process she has dealt with shame about growing up in poverty and the pain of not feeling valued. She has also seen that her impulsive buying has offered only temporary solace, and has actually made her life more stressful, getting her into debt that meant taking on a second job

In this session with me (Eva), Antonia describes being "caught" in thinking about the watch and imagining buying it. Although she is clear that she won't act on the impulse, she wants to understand more about how she gets caught in this process. Antonia recently attended her first meditation retreat, so she has some familiarity with bringing mindful attention to experience, and she has seen how her attachment can lead to unskillful action and suffering. She wonders if there is a way for her to have more freedom from this frequent internal struggle of being pulled by and resisting these impulses.

Traditional Gestalt therapy work might begin with something like exploring Antonia's current experience of being" caught," or with a dialogue between the "impulse" and the "resisting," and then attending to whatever emerges. This might be unfinished business, or a current situation that triggered the want. Because Antonia has done much of this work, and is aware of these issues, we agree to explore this in a different way.

I ask Antonia to close her eyes and intentionally turn her attention from the object "out there"—the watch—and the fantasy of buying or having it, to her present internal experience of the wanting. Focusing in on her bodily sensations, she describes tightness in her chest, and an empty hollowness in her stomach, "almost like a physical hunger."

Rather than focusing in on and further exploring these particular sensations, I suggest she just sit with "this is what wanting is like right now" to allow a mindful perspective on her experience. Sitting with this requires that she tolerate the feelings coming up for her. This is uncomfortable, and she sees why she wants to get away from it, recognizing the strong impulse to "do something." With support she is able to stay with this, even as it is challenging. I encourage her to also notice whatever thoughts are arising along with the physical sensations and feeling tone. As she is able to do this, I then suggest that she experiment with "breathing with" whatever is here, noticing if there is possible softening around or opening to it, and just making space for whatever is present for her.

Antonia then reports a shift, that the tightness is easing, and that the impulse to get away or to do something is gone. She describes a loosening of "the pull" on her and more of a sensation of fullness in her bodily experience. At this point she opens her eyes.

Antonia: So, that whole thing with the watch…completely lost its charge. It's like there was a de-coupling between it and me … my experience. They seemed so glued together before.

Eva: Yes. What's your sense of how you did that?

Antonia: Something about focusing inside...and paying attention to my body and the particular sensations, the need... or want, or whatever, stopped being this solid "thing." There was a feeling of release....

Eva: As you're talking right now, I get a sense of that.

Antonia: And whatever power the watch had ... it's like seeing the man behind the curtain revealed. You can't see it the same after that.

Prior to this session, Antonia had already done much of the hard work of dealing with these issues, and the powerful underlying needs and feelings driving the related attachment. The work in this session was, in a way, "icing on the cake." On the other hand, Antonia's ability to work with her craving in this process, deconstructing the elements that made up her experienced wanting, importantly allowed her to recognize this wanting as less "real" and solid. This experience offers another level of awareness and a new skill in dealing with her craving as it arises.

Often the attachment that we work with in therapy reflects enduring relational patterns that began in significant early relationships. Unmet developmental needs that result in lifelong pain and longing can drive our strongest identification and attachment. The following example is a combination of exploring pain and suffering and looking at the attachment involved in the suffering.

Mia, a participant in our training program, is in her late thirties. In one of the trainer demonstration sessions, she wants to work on her relationship with her father. She begins by telling me (Steve) that she has worked on this in therapy before, and has tried to deal with her hurt and anger about her father dismissing her and not acknowledging any of her positive qualities or accomplishments. Although she has told him how she feels, nothing changes. Her interactions with him are frustrating because he never acknowledges how he treats her, and he blames her for being "too sensitive." Mia sees how she holds on to wanting him to be different, thinking he will change, or believing that she can do something to get him to treat her differently.

Mia wants to explore this from the perspective of attachment and suffering that we have been discussing in the training. We agree to approach the session with this in mind, while staying open to working with whatever becomes figural.

Mia: So, I'm thinking about my last conversation with my dad, just replaying some of the hurtful things he said.... I'm always wondering if there was something I could have done or said to get him to actually see me. (Pause.) But really I don't think I'm ever going to get what I want from him (tearfully).

Steve: I see that's painful for you. (Pause.) Just stay with what you're feeling.

Mia: I'm sad about that ... and I want to tell you what he said, so you can see what an asshole he is.

Steve: Uh-huh. So, you're feeling sad ... and you want me to know what an asshole your dad is.

Mia: (Nods.) Yeah.

Steve: OK. Telling me what he said might help me under-stand what an asshole he is. And right now I can see your sad-ness ... and that you feel hurt by him.

Mia: (Nods.) You know when you say that, I realize it's not about you getting it that he's an asshole. It's about what you just said ... you seeing me...understanding how I feel. That's what I don't get from him. (Tears up again.)

Steve: Right. See if you can just stay with what's coming up now....

Mia: (Pause. Closes eyes.) I'm just sad. It hurts not to get that from him. He is my dad ... and I've never gotten it. (Crying.)

Steve: Yes, a lot of sadness... and hurt.

Mia: (Opens eyes, looks at me.) I just want him to care

about me, maybe even to be proud of me. I don't think that's so much to expect.

Steve: No, it's not. And still you don't get it from him.

Mia: (Pause) You know as soon as I hear you say that, these familiar thoughts start coming up. (Wipes tears, stops crying.) "I'm not good enough. If I'd just try harder." I start to think of what I can do, something he'd be impressed by.

Steve: Yeah, so those thoughts are pretty reflexive ... and are you aware you moved away from the feeling ... the sadness as you went into those?

Mia: Oh. Yeah, I see that. (Pause.) I guess it is hard to just be with the hurt ... and sadness. (Crying.) Such old and deep feelings ... (Stops crying, reaches for tissue).

Steve: (Pause.) What's happening now?

Mia: Just ... seeing a little more clearly ... all the trying, blaming myself and waiting for him to be different, clinging to that hope, thinking I'm not good enough. There's the suffering right there ... the wanting it to be different. (Pause.) The pain, well ... it just hurts.

Steve: (Nods) Yeah, it just hurts.

Mia: But right now I'm OK with that. Being more clear feels good. And (smiling) I can see you're here with me, too.

Although in many ways this looks like traditional Gestalt therapy work, the added perspective that both therapist and patient brought to the work allowed Mia the opportunity to see the "optional" or mind-created suffering more clearly, as this emerged in how she related to the pain with her dad. Also, she discovered that coming back to and staying with her pain offered a way out of this suffering in the moment, and led to more clarity.

Broader View of Desire

Exploring both desires and attachment can also allow patients to look at what their actual aims are, and to consider more deeply the consequences of particular actions. As we consider with patients what they hope to achieve, we might help them clarify the "bigger picture," as supported by Buddhist psychology view. This means enabling the patient to recognize whether what he is pursuing is really consistent with his overarching values and aims.

For example, in a therapy session with me (Eva) Miguel talks about wanting to take on a big extra project at work. Initially he sounds excited about it. But as we talk further, he recognizes that he is actually ambivalent. In slowing down and attending directly to the experience of the wanting as described above, Miguel discovers that it is driven by fear, competitiveness, and a desire for approval. Staying with this, he sees that if he takes on this project, it will not lead to what he really wants but to more stress, pressure, and continued striving. It will reduce time with his family—something that he actually values more highly than his professional accomplishments. In this exploratory process, Miguel accesses a deeper wisdom based less on a particular identification and attachment. Seeing that his family will also benefit from him turning down the project, he feels a sense of integrity within himself, and the interconnection between his family's well-being and his own.

This kind of exploration does not prevent us supporting and working with patients to take needed action guided by their circumstances and aspirations. It does mean that we may help them consider more clearly the true motivation for their actions and choices, and whether these are in line with their higher values. Here, patients can begin to recognize what Buddhist psychology calls "wholesome desires," those aspirations that lead to less (rather than more) suffering for others and for ourselves, such as the desire to live with more ease, to practice generosity, or to cultivate more compassion for others.

Once again, this work requires that psychological issues and related boundary processes have been worked through, or that there is enough awareness of them to notice if they are coming into play. For example, if a patient has introjected "What I want doesn't matter" or "I should sacrifice my needs for others," these introjected beliefs and related feelings must be attended to, so that this additional way of exploring wants and attachment does not support or reinforce these. For example, Miguel's decision to forego taking on the work project and to have more time with family is importantly not based on overriding his own wants and needs, but is based on clarification of what is actually important to him. Within the BPGT framework, interruptions in contacting and lack of clarity about identification with self-experience can continue to be attended to.

Meditation in BPGT

Gestalt therapy's experimental method lends itself to a seamless and creative integration of experimenting with meditation both in and out of session. The Gestalt therapist's familiarity with designing, suggesting, and collaborating with patients to create relevant experiments can be applied in this process. These meditation experiences can be tailored to address particular patient issues or interests and to support different aspects of awareness and therapeutic work. As with all experiments, we are not looking for any particular result or outcome. Rather, we are interested in whatever emerges that may allow additional exploration.

Meditation in the Therapy Session

Generally in Gestalt therapy, it is preferable to have the patient start the session to see where the patient wants to begin without the therapist influencing a direction. This also ensures that what is initially figural for the patient becomes the focus. However, the therapist offering the option for the patient to spend some time in silence at the beginning of or early in the session can also be useful at times. This can allow patients space to check in and to connect with themselves and current feelings, and to arrive more into the body and present moment experience. And it allows the therapist to do the same. This time may be guided with prompts from the therapist, such as, "Just notice your experience right now," or "See what comes up for you as we sit together." It can be useful to specifically direct the patient's attention to embodied experience. This can also lead into "See what interests you right now and what you want to explore today." With some patients the added direction of "Rather than looking for something to talk about, just allow whatever emerges for you as you pay attention to your experience" is useful. Once this process has been introduced, patients may spontaneously start their sessions this way or request this brief check-in at the beginning of or during a session.

Guided meditations of ten to fifteen minutes can also be integrated into a session. This may involve teaching a particular practice, such as mindfulness or loving kindness. Or, it may focus on or highlight a particular aspect of experience. For example a patient who is describing feeling anxious or depressed may benefit from a guided mindfulness process of attending more directly to bodily sensations and the details of the experience. When an experience is unpleasant, this process can support staying with it, as well as highlighting whether or how the patient avoids it. What emerges from this can lead to and open up possibilities for subsequent work.

Silent meditation can also be incorporated with some preliminary instruction to the patient. Or this can be an "out loud" meditation, where the patient reports on experience as it emerges. As these offer patients perspective on current processes, they may notice things like their frequent fantasizing about the future, or trying to solve a problem. These can then be explored in the therapy session. Longer silent meditations can also allow something that is in the patient's background to emerge clearly enough that it can then be worked with. For example, a pervasive feeling of fear, sadness, or excitement may reveal itself with this space, silence and focused attention.

Meditation experiences in session can also be specifically tailored to the patient and the situation. For example, a patient dealing with a tragic loss, such as the death of a child, may feel alone in this very particular and searing pain. At the right time, a meditation offering the possibility of feeling connected with the countless other mothers or fathers in the world or throughout time who have also lost their child, can be a way of touching into interconnectedness. This may also allow patients more access to compassion and self-compassion, and added support for staying with their own pain.

Another opportunity for in-session meditation is in couple's therapy. For example--with some couples--an opportunity for loving kindness (*metta*) practice at the beginning of the session can help them connect with an intention to have goodwill toward one another, and a wish for their partner's happiness, even in the face of conflict. This can allow access to more open-hearted feelings toward one another, or help bring awareness to how they are not open hearted. Re-visiting this later in the session can be useful in addressing this aspect of their relational experience when this is relevant.

In Chapter 10 we described how therapists might make use of directing *metta* to patients prior to a session. We can also work with *metta* directly in the session itself, by setting up an experiment in which the therapist says the *metta* phrases out loud to the patient. This can be done with eyes closed, or while making eye contact, with the patient simply receiving the therapist's words. We can use either the traditional phrases, or use phrases tailored specifically for the particular patient that also reflect the therapist's authentic wishes. In keeping with Gestalt therapy's dialogical and non-hierarchical model, another experiment might be for the patient to also offer the *metta* phrases to the therapist. Whatever emerges from experimenting with these powerful and novel ways of making contact (the result of the experiment) is fertile ground for further exploration. Possibilities include the impact on the relational connection, the patient's experience of the therapist, the therapist's experience of the patient, and the experience of giving or receiving. Of course, all feelings about, difficulty in, or obstacles to giving or receiving in this way--like possible embarrassment or vulnerability--would be attended to as they would with any experiment. And as with experiments generally, this must be directly related to the work, what is present for the patient in the moment, and the therapy themes and issues being addressed. This could also be a powerful process to experiment with in a group therapy setting.

Any of these in-session meditation experiments offer rich opportunity for weaving together the meditative experience, intrapersonal exploration, and interpersonal contact.

Meditation Outside of the Therapy Session
Implicit in Gestalt therapy is the expectation that the power of directing attention to and increasing awareness of present experience in therapy will generalize to the patient's capacity for doing this outside of therapy as well. However, anyone who tries to bring attention to present experience in an ongoing way discovers how challenging this actually is. We are reflexively lost in thoughts of the past, fantasies, or future planning, or just going through motions on autopilot. To more explicitly link attention to the present moment in therapy, and how this can generalize to the patient's life, the therapist can support the patient experimenting with formal mindfulness meditation

practice or with intentionally bringing more attention to present moment experience in daily life. These practices then offer the patient continuity with this process between therapy sessions. This can also enhance the therapeutic work allowing the patient to bring more attentional capacity, and the increased awareness it supports, to the therapy experience as well.

For patients who come to therapy with specific interest in feeling more grounded, slowing down, or connecting more with bodily experience, working with this in meditation outside of sessions can be directly relevant. For patients who "take" to meditation and experience the benefits of it, this can increase their sense of agency and responsibility for their own well-being as they work in therapy.

Both Gestalt therapy and Buddhist psychology recognize that connecting with actual present moment experience is an antidote to suffering. For the BPGT therapist who wants to support the patient's increased awareness of where freedom from suffering can be found, one way to do this is encouraging the patient's meditative practice outside of session. Mindfulness practice is designed to help us find more freedom from the ongoing commentary on our experience; the worrying, planning, and getting lost in anticipating the future. It offers a way to connect directly with immediate experience instead. In daily life, even a moment of mindful presence--noticing a tree's changing colors or the crispness of fall air on the walk to work from the bus stop, rather than focusing on the future and worrying about being late to a meeting--offers a brief respite from suffering.

The BPGT therapist can support the patient who experiments with meditative practices outside of the session by exploring the patient's experience of these, along with the obstacles that arise in practice. A patient working with disordered eating, for example, who experiments with mindful eating will inevitably develop new awareness and experience challenges in this process. These experiments outside of session may reveal important issues that can then be addressed in therapy.

Creative collaboratively developed meditation experiments to be done outside of session can also be designed to address particular patient issues. Mindful eating is one example of this. So is *metta* meditation as we describe below in the section on cultivating heart qualities. A body scan meditation may help a patient who wants to gain more awareness of physical sensations and embodied experience. For patients with anxiety symptoms, meditations that help focus closely on noticing the details of actual embodied experience, like paying attention to breathing, can also be useful when they are experiencing anxiety. Any meditation that we experiment with in session can be a springboard and support for the patient to continue to work with it out of session. For any patient who wants to pursue meditation or learn more about Buddhist psychology, the therapist can also offer resources, such as those listed at the end of this book.

For the BPGT therapist, maintaining Gestalt therapy's experimental perspective in this process is key. The patient's meditation practice (or non-practice) does not become a therapist agenda. The therapist offers support, direction, and exploration only when it is the patient's interest. Just like any other homework experiment, the result of the experiment may be that the patient does not do it. This then offers an avenue of discovery and exploration for the patient to choose to pursue or not.

Path Practices and Cultivating Heart Qualities in BPGT
In addition to meditative practices, other elements of Buddhist psychology's eightfold path (described in Chapter 2) offer fertile ground for therapeutic exploration. As Gestalt therapists we know that how and where we focus attention can shift

the figure and transform experience. Buddhist psychology offers additional ground for the "how and where," extending the reach of Gestalt therapy's interest in expanded human potential. Buddhist teacher Dipa Ma referred to this path as "a journey of transformation in which the mind's cherished beliefs and self-imposed limitations are challenged at every turn" (Schmidt, 2005). BPGT's transformative holistic exploration can include Buddhist psychology's path practices, and the cultivation of heart qualities (see Chapter 3). Here we consider some possibilities for this additional ground of exploration.

Exploring the Eightfold Path

Buddhist psychology is pragmatic when it comes to understanding how to live one's life. It holds that living ethically, being oriented toward service to others, compassion, and non-harming are essential to our own emotional and mental health. Current happiness research also aligns with this perspective in finding that we derive more satisfaction and happiness from giving to or doing for others than from only pursuing our own individual gain. The intertwined eightfold path is not a set of rules to follow. Rather, as with everything in Buddhist psychology, it is an invitation to explore and discover what leads us to a sense of peace and well-being and what leads us away from it. The path points us to the freedom and joy that are possible, even in the face of life's inevitable difficulties.

Aspects of the Buddhist psychology path can offer opportunity for exploration in therapy. For example, an overarching perspective of this path is the law of cause and effect or *karma*. This perspective can be explored to help patients gain a clearer experiential awareness of how their thoughts and actions have direct consequences; how the consequences for them can impact others and how the consequences for others can impact them. To explore this, the therapist might suggest that the patient experiment with paying closer attention to the immediate result of any thought or action. Particular aspects of the path can be usefully explored for patients addressing specific issues.

For example, a patient who engages in fantasies of revenge toward someone who has hurt him can attend more directly to how this affects his bodily and mental state, rather than staying caught in the fantasy. Another example is a patient who is harsh and punitive with her employees when they make a mistake. She is aware that this reflects how she was treated growing up, and she does not want to continue this pattern. The therapist might offer the perspective of the path practices of right livelihood (since this is related to her way of engaging at work) or more generally of right action, to explore this more deeply. Taking up one of these practices can support this patient's increased attention to and awareness of the impact of these actions. She may discover the effect in her own body in the moment, and also how she ends up feeling about herself afterward. She could choose to pay closer attention to the effect on her employee, for example the look on his face when she does this, and what their interaction is like the rest of the day. For a patient who is unhappy that he blames and criticizes his teenage daughter when he is angry, taking up the practice of right speech might be both a support and a way to explore this. He could start with the intention to communicate with his daughter more skillfully. In this process he will likely discover what gets in the way of his doing this, which can then also be addressed in therapy. Taking responsibility for having more mindful interactions with his daughter might result in greater awareness of what type of communication leads to a more desirable outcome. A patient who discovers he is "stingy" with praise for or acknowledgment of others may want to consider practicing more generosity in speech and action.

These path practices can offer both added support for the patient and a way to increase awareness, as well as opportunity for further creative experimentation. In this process patients can discover whether their thoughts, speech and actions lead to desired consequences or not, and this awareness may increase clarity and choice. As understanding is strengthened, this can guide intention, aspiration, and action, and offer possibilities for further therapeutic exploration.

Cultivating Heart Qualities and Psychotherapeutic Work
Cultivating the heart qualities of loving kindness, compassion, equanimity, and sympathetic joy can be seen as an aspect of personal development in BPGT, just as they are in Buddhist psychology. Importantly, these qualities are not fabricated or added to who we are; rather they can be discovered and explored just as other aspects of self-experience are in Gestalt therapy work. Their cultivation allows them to be more easily accessed, and allows them to more fully flower.

We can see this cultivation in the same way that we see the enhanced connection with any self-experience in Gestalt therapy work. As Gestalt therapists we are always interested in where there may be unrecognized supports, and in BPGT we have another place to look for these. Having more access to these qualities offers the patient a previously untapped source of self-support for moving into challenging emotional territory, increasing awareness, and deepening psychological work. The patient can explore this both in and outside of therapy.

For example, just as the therapist might direct the patient's attention to posture, breathing, or language as aspects of self-support, we can also propose experiments that help the patient access more equanimity or self-compassion. As the patient discovers that this is available, she can deepen connection to it more intentionally. Accessing these qualities in session can support opening to and staying with experience, particularly if it is painful, organically shifting the patient's self-experience in the moment. This often brings new awareness and a fresh way of being with experience, as well as an opportunity for novel contact with the therapist. The patient may then want to explore mindfulness, loving kindness, or compassion practices (see Chapter 3) outside of session to continue to access and cultivate these.

Connecting with an image of oneself as a child often evokes self-compassion. This happened in the work with Anna (Chapter 5) for example, as she identified with the young part of her that was on the receiving end of her self-hatred and rejection. The organic emergence of self-compassion offers an opportunity for the therapist to point it out as something that can be purposefully accessed and nurtured. In the work with self-compassion, we do not bypass other authentic experience or suggest superimposing compassion. Rather, we can look for opportunities to support authentic connection with and cultivation of this heart quality.

Loving kindness meditation (described in Chapter 3) can be a useful practice for someone who has unresolved feelings toward another person, and who wishes added freedom from anger or resentment. For example, a mother struggling with her son's addiction and homelessness is angry at him and wants to set clear limits and boundaries, but also does not want to shut him out of her heart. *Metta* practice outside of sessions gives her a way to connect with her genuine heartfelt wishes for her son's happiness, and to work with her own heart opening in an ongoing way. Along with this practice, she continues work in therapy with her anger as it comes up, as well as with her grief, fear, and disappointment.

Although practices of cultivation can point us toward how we might aspire to be in relationship, our developmental relational history and psychological issues often make this manifestation challenging or, at times, impossible. In psychotherapy we can address the particular relationship difficulties and conflicts that may impede this aspiration. Within BPGT's experimental method, we have rich opportunity for exploring this intersection. For example, a patient who is working with cultivating loving kindness in his Buddhist practice might discover and clarify in therapy the barriers to opening his heart to others, like fear or self-protectiveness. As he uncovers and clarifies what he is actually experiencing in relationship to others, this in turn may lead to the possibility of more heart opening. Another example is a patient who struggles with feelings of chronic envy of and competitiveness with others. We might work with this by experimenting with the patient imagining feeling happiness for another's success. Sensing this as a possibility can help the patient more deeply understand the envy and its impact on his own well-being, as well as seeing the potential freedom in his release from it.

In BPGT we can explore both the cultivation of heart qualities and the barriers to the kind of relationships and self-experience that we aspire to. In this way the processes of cultivation and psychotherapeutic inquiry can work together to develop increased awareness and potential for relational connection.

Expanded Field Perspective

Although patients typically come to therapy to improve their own lives, the work they do on themselves also impacts others. A mother's discovery in therapy that she is treating her children in the same harsh way she was treated growing up benefits her children. A patient who begins to take responsibility for his own behavior rather than blaming others, contributes to the well-being of those others. The binge drinker who seeks treatment improves the work lives of the co-workers who were covering for her absences and mistakes. Still, although this may motivate some, most patients seek therapy to benefit themselves, not others.

Unlike Western psychotherapy, Buddhist psychology emphasizes that our practice is not only for our own well-being. All aspects of the path help us recognize our interdependence and that the things that benefit us benefit others and vice versa. A life of peace, ease, and emotional balance is impossible if we are driven by hatred or greed, and if our motivations are only self-serving. This is not a moralistic judgment about right and wrong. It is rather based in the truth of interdependence and the recognition that our happiness is inextricably interconnected with the welfare of others, our extended communities, and our planet. From this perspective, all of our actions, large and small, can be recognized as having far-reaching consequences. And because our well-being is linked to the field we are part of, any positive effect we have on it comes back to us as well.

Focusing on this interconnection and considering the consequences of actions in terms of their broader impact has traditionally been in the realm of politics, religion, or spirituality. However, Gestalt therapy's field understanding aligns with considering the consequences of actions, as every part of the field is understood to influence every other. Gestalt therapy's field perspective generally comes into play as we consider the field influences on the patient, (described in Chapter 5) recognizing the impact of broader familial, socio-cultural, community, economic, institutional, political, and environmental contexts. However, in BPGT we may expand this field understanding to explore influences in the other direction. That is, we can consider the ways patients' own well-being may rely on their ability to recognize interconnectedness, and to consider the impact of their actions.

Expanding Gestalt therapy's field perspective in this way opens a door to exploring this in therapy. Can we think of our patient's taking up practices of non-harming as a necessary part of their own well-being, personal growth, and transformation?

Can we see emotional and psychological health as more broadly rooted in recognizing the impact of all of our actions and ways of being, as Buddhist psychology does? Can patients appreciate how the work they do on themselves also benefits those they are in relationship with? How might this be an added support and motivation for the work itself? Importantly, as with all things Gestalt, this is never a therapist agenda; but it can inform the therapist's background and be brought forward as it is useful and relevant.

Engaged Buddhism (Nhat Hanh, 1987) suggests the importance of applying the insights of meditation practice and the teachings of the *dharma* for the benefit of all in working for social justice. This work always begins in our own hearts, so that we can bring skillfulness and purer motivation to it. Working on ourselves, and contributing to others' welfare supports an aspiration to live our lives in ways that lead us to love and care for ourselves and others equally, and to deeply recognize our interconnectedness. In Gestalt therapy, individual psychological well-being is also linked to the wider field. Paul Goodman (1991) saw effective therapy as helping recover lost aliveness and spontaneity, yet recognized that the quality of a person's life was inevitably dependent on what is available in the broader society and culture. He also thought that social activism would be an organic consequence of individual liberation through therapy. Both perspectives envision the natural outgrowth of our own evolution and deeper understanding as pointing us toward an aspiration to make a positive impact on the field as a whole. In BPGT, this perspective may be made more explicit and be seen as an essential aspect of emotional and psychological health, personal growth, and transformation.

Support for and increased capacity to meet rather than to avoid our own pain means we are less likely to create suffering. Discovering the illusion of a separate self brings freedom from greed, hatred, and delusion, making these less likely to manifest in destructive ways. Nurturing ourselves in these practices, and cultivating our own equanimity and self-compassion means we have more to give to others. We start to see that we can find freedom in the most trying of circumstances, or feel imprisoned no matter how fortuitous our situation. Recognizing this lets us grow toward that light of more freedom.

Here we have explored what we see as only the beginning of the continued development of the integration of Buddhist psychology and Gestalt therapy, and of a Buddhist psychology informed Gestalt therapy (BPGT) approach. We propose this as a *psychotherapy for the 21st century*, because it expands our understanding beyond the relative level of our existence to encompass a universal perspective, including but extending beyond our individual psychology.

Our planet's habitability is clearly at risk, a result of runaway greed. Globally, we see that human caused suffering and destruction are rampant. Our technological advances, devices and the ever-faster pace of our lives, are leading us away from, rather than toward, more ease, joy, and love in our lives. In the midst of this there is also a surge of interest in cultivating the capacity for stillness and silence, and for compassionate social engagement. There is ongoing exploration of Eastern wisdom practices, and their place in Western psychology. The clear need for our species to evolve in the direction of a higher wisdom, and to deeply recognize that we live in an interconnected and interdependent world is apparent. In embracing Buddhist psychology's 2600 year-old wisdom tradition, and allowing it to inform our psychotherapy approach, we can not only align with but perhaps also contribute to this evolution.

12

Integrated Training Model

> *If human connection and social interaction are the most potent agents of emotional healing, then training programs should help students to cultivate their personal qualities and interpersonal abilities so that they can connect ... with clients in an effective way.*

—David Elkins, *The Human Elements of Psychotherapy*

BUDDHIST PSYCHOLOGY VIEWS and meditation practices have had such a profound influence on each of us, both personally and in our work, that we were inspired to develop a model that allowed integrating Buddhist psychology and meditation practices in Gestalt therapy training. This model evolved out of an interest in giving therapists a perspective on the convergences of these systems, the potential of their integration, and the skills to apply this understanding in their work.

An ongoing experiment, the model has continued to evolve. We began with integrating teaching basic Buddhist psychology concepts, presenting the convergences of the two systems, and including guided meditation in the training sessions. As we developed the BPGT approach, we began incorporating this in the training as well. In this chapter we outline this model and what we see as the benefits of it. We also point out some of the challenges in it, and how these may be addressed. We hope that this outline offers a jumping off point for further exploration of the potential of this dynamic integration for

Gestalt therapy trainers. Our model was originally based on an introductory training that consisted of six weekends over two years. However, we see the potential for its adaptation to any training structure.

Integrated Curriculum Overview

This model follows a structure that is typical of Gestalt therapy training in general in that it includes both didactic and a variety of experiential learning opportunities. Didactic components include reading, brief lectures, and discussion on Gestalt therapy theory and method. Its experiential components include trainer demonstrations, paired exercises, trainer-supervised practicum work, and client role-plays. The didactic and experiential come together as concepts are illustrated in demonstrations and role-plays, and are practiced by participants. These experiences help bring theory to life and support further discussion and clarification of both theory and method. Observing and participating in demonstrations, working under trainer supervision, and participating in patient-therapist dyads offers trainees active, in-the-moment learning experiences as patient, therapist, supervisee, and observer.

The integrated model adds a number of both didactic and experiential elements to the structure described above. We have found that beginning with Gestalt therapy's philosophical foundations and their alignment with Buddhist psychology (described in Chapter 5) is a clarifying starting point for presenting the intersection of these two systems. Including this in the didactic presentation and discussion during the first weekend of training offers a big picture perspective on the essential convergences of the two systems. Then, in subsequent sessions, in addition to teaching Gestalt therapy concepts, Buddhist psychology views as well as mindfulness and other practices (as outlined in Chapters 1 through 3) are presented, as are the convergences of view and method (outlined in Chapters 7 and 8). Like Gestalt therapy, Buddhist psychology requires experiential learning. In this model, meditation experiences are an additional experiential component of each training session. The first two weekends are somewhat more heavily oriented toward the didactic and content to give trainees a basic understanding of and vocabulary for each system. Subsequent weekends then have more time allotted for the experiential elements of the training.

Over the course of the training, we bring in elements of both Chapters 9 and 10. We might look specifically at the relational mindfulness aspects of work that is demonstrated in a training session, for example how the work translates aspects of mindfulness into the therapist's stance, what the therapist pays attention to and what the therapist does. We also explore both conceptually and experientially how Buddhist psychology views and practices enhance and support Gestalt therapy work. For example, in supervising trainees' work in the group, the trainer might point out where and how the trainee could bring the type of "bare attention" cultivated in mindfulness practice to the particular phenomenological exploration with the patient. Or, where there might be opportunities to slow a process down and stay with experience, rather than moving into an action-oriented intervention. This does not replace the elements generally focused on in Gestalt therapy training supervision, such as identifying process, clarifying what is figural, and using experiments, but rather expands on these.

Later in the training, aspects of the BPGT integrative perspective can be included in lecture and discussion; this perspective is also brought in experientially. For example, the trainer might demonstrate how to focus on facilitating the patient's awareness of her primary experience and of where and how constructed concepts enter in. The discussion might then include the Buddhist psychology perspective of "first arrow" pain, "second arrow" suffering, and constructed identification. As trainees have more of their own meditation experience and become more familiar with Gestalt therapy's experimental method, we can also explore the specifics and variety of experiments (described in Chapter 11) that involve incorporating meditation into their work with patients.

Meditation Practice in the Training

Incorporating meditation in the training experience is an essential part of this integrated model. For example, at our first meeting with a new group—after introductions, orientation to the training, an overview, and a few basic meditation instructions (see Chapter 3)—we offer an opening meditation to support arrival into the present moment and into embodied experience. This is an invitation to settle in, to check-in with ourselves, and to begin paying attention to present experience. Starting the weekend with this meditation sets the tone and offers support for continuing to stay with a sense of embodied presence throughout the training session, as we move through different activities in our time together. In subsequent group meetings, we generally begin with an opening meditation to give trainees the opportunity to connect with themselves before checking in with one another.

We generally start each morning with a guided meditation as well. These may be specifically chosen to highlight a particular aspect of practice that relates to the training focus or theme for the weekend, for example, mindfulness of the body or cultivation of compassion or loving kindness. We also end the weekend with a brief meditation, after the group closure process. Thus, these meditations (or variations of them) become the "bookends" of the training experience.

Opening Meditation

The following is an example of an opening meditation for the beginning of a training session.

Finding a comfortable and supported posture ... allow yourself to arrive a little more into your body ... and into the present moment. You may close your eyes if you wish, or keep a soft-focus gaze downward and in front of you. If you'd like to, you can take a few slower, deeper breaths ... then allow your breathing to return to its natural rhythm. There is no right or wrong way to be breathing, so just allowing the breath to be as it is.

(Pause.)

Settling into stillness ... and silence, notice the support your body receives from what you are sitting on. Feeling your feet on the floor if they are, sensing the earth we rest on.

(Pause.)

See if you'd like to surrender a bit more to a sense of being supported, of being held to earth by its gravitational pull, letting go of any unnecessary holding or tension that you become aware of.

(Pause.)

Now, opening to also sensing the space around you, finding yourself in this balance of grounding and spaciousness.

(Pause.)

Bringing attention to present moment sensation ... just listening to the body and what you notice right now. As much as possible allow the experience to be just as it is, with nothing different required.

(Pause.)

As we bring attention to the present moment and to the body, we can also more easily notice the flow of the movement of breath—the sensations of breathing. Allow your attention to rest in this movement of breath.

(Pause.)

Noticing how it is right now for you to be here in this space ... sitting ... and breathing.

(Pause.)

As you attend to present moment experience, you may also notice emotions...or thoughts arising. You may find aspects of this experience either pleasant, unpleasant, or perhaps just neutral.

(Pause.)

As much as possible, just notice, open to, and allow what is here ... without requiring your experience to be any different than it is.

(Pause.)

Any time you notice you have lost the thread of connection to present experience, this noticing is a moment of mindfulness.... You can simply bring attention back to the body, to present sensation, to the movement of breath.... It is always here, always available, a home base to return to again and again.

(Pause.)

(Bell.)

Closing Meditation

The following is an example of a closing meditation for the end of a training session.

With eyes opened or closed, take a moment to be with your experience just as it is right now as we come to the end of our time together.

(Pause.)

You might want to take this opportunity to appreciate yourself and the work you have done here—risks you have taken and support you have offered—appreciating your contribution to the others here who are on this learning journey with you.

(Pause.)

You may want to extend this appreciation to the others here

... for what they have contributed to your experience. Just allow any sense of gratitude or appreciation that is present for you, again not requiring your experience to be any different than it is.

(Pause.)

If you'd like to, you can extend this appreciation further to include gratitude for those outside of the group who support your being here, and all of the causes and conditions that allow us to come together for our growth and learning.

(Pause.)

May the work and practice that we have done here together increase our capacity for compassion, and further our own understanding, healing, and transformation.

(Pause.)

May this not only benefit us, but all of those we work with and come in contact with in our lives, so that the benefit extends outward in ever widening circles of care and compassion like ripples in a pond ... and ultimately be for the benefit all beings.

(Pause.)

(Bell.)

Meditation and Paired Exercises

Guided meditations can also be a lead-in to exercises in which trainees work together in therapist-patient pairs. After the meditation, trainees move directly to these dyads for a brief practice session (fifteen to twenty minutes). This offers an opportunity for the trainees in the role of therapist to notice the impact of the meditation experience on their work and the relational interaction. For example, a concentration meditation may carry forward into the trainee therapist's ability to pay more attention to the details of his experience as he is with the trainee patient or to notice subtleties of the interaction. In another paired exercise we choose the patient-therapist pairs first and then do a loving kindness meditation (described in Chapter 10). During this meditation the trainee who will be therapist has the opportunity to direct the silent *metta* phrases to their designated patient, offering the therapist an opportunity to notice any effect of this connecting, heart opening practice.

In our experience, the trainee in the role of patient is also affected by these meditations prior to their session. For example, a mindfulness meditation before the session may deepen or clarify what they are able to bring to the session as a patient. The experience of receiving the *metta* phrases from the therapist prior to the session often results in more open-heartedness and access to vulnerability.

In a variation on this exercise, we ring a bell during these patient-therapist sessions. At the sound of the bell, both patient and therapist pause, stop talking, and close their eyes, each spending a few moments noticing and attending to their present experience. When the bell is rung a second time, the pair returns to their interaction. This mindful pause offers an opportunity for both patient and therapist to notice their embodied experience—what they are presently aware of and what is happening for each of them. This can allow one or both of the participants to access a new awareness, or a deeper level of understanding or of connection. Often something that was actually figural but not focused on can now be attended to. This experience can also function as a support for trainees to integrate a mindful pause as needed and when appropriate while working, whether in the training group or with their own patients.

Benefits of this Integrated Model

We have found this integrated training model to have a number of benefits. These benefits are a result of both teaching the Buddhist psychology views in the training, and of including meditation experience in the training.

Benefits of Buddhist Psychology Views in the Training
Understanding Buddhist psychology views offers a broad perspective on the human condition. Introducing these views offers trainees this expanded perspective on their personal experience as well as on their work; for example, the understanding that there is a difference between inevitable pain and optional suffering can be highlighted as we observe work in the training. As we have pointed out, Buddhist psychology's three givens of existence support fundamentals of Gestalt therapy practice. In the training we point to **impermanence** as support for the trainees' ability to remain open and flexible, and to have faith in natural self-regulating that is based in movement, growth and change. Remaining mindful that **unsatisfactoriness** and suffering are part of life, we can use this perspective to support trainees in learning to stay with the patient's experience rather than getting caught in trying to fix something, change the patient, or to make things better. Exploring the Buddhist psychology **not-self** view, gives trainees the opportunity to experiment with holding both their own and their patients' identifications more lightly, contributing to more fluidity and flexibility in their work as they practice throughout the training experience.

Benefits of Meditation in the Training
The meditation practices are the doorway to the essential experiential recognition and understanding of the Buddhist psychology views. Specific benefits of meditation in the training are in the following three areas: the therapist's personal development, the therapist's relational qualities and skills, and the overall training experience.

Therapist Personal Development
Training to be a Gestalt therapist requires not only skill acquisition but also awareness of and access to one's own

emotional experience. The "person of the therapist" is key, including the therapist's capacity to be self-aware, relationally attuned, and available for an engaged connection with patients. In Gestalt therapy training, one aspect of therapist development is doing personal work as a patient in the context of the training group. Here we add the additional component of participating in meditation, which offers added opportunity for personal growth and increased self-awareness throughout the training experience.

Exposure to meditation in the group also gives trainees an opportunity to discover what it offers. The meditation experiences in the training provide trainees an immediate experiential understanding of the power of directed attention to increase their awareness. These meditative experiences also allow the trainee to glimpse the inner refuge that can be available to them. These experiences also provide support to start, continue, or deepen their own meditation practice outside of the training. The combination of meditation in and out of the training sessions then contributes to development of more capacity for presence, self-compassion, self-awareness, and equanimity—all essential aspects of trainees' personal growth and development. As meditation sessions in the training bring up new awareness, or clarify personal psychological issues, this also augments the personal work trainees can do in the group, further enhancing personal growth and transformation.

Enhancing the Therapist's Relational Qualities and Skills

In Chapter 10 we detail the ways Insight meditation practices can make us better Gestalt therapists, and how what is cultivated in meditation can increase the capacity for contact and relatedness with patients. It has been suggested that relational capacities are intertwined with mindfulness even at the level of brain structure. So as mindfulness promotes the development of resonance circuits, and as we become more attuned to the nuances of our own experience, we are likely to increase our capacity for attuning to others at this level as well (Siegel, 2007). Exposure to meditation and meditation experience in the training allows trainees to cultivate a number of qualities, capacities, and skills that cannot be directly taught.

The guided meditations offered in the group give participants practice in focusing their attention in the present, noticing what is, and sensing direct, embodied experiences. Trainees can make the experiential connection between the way we pay attention and what we pay attention to in meditation and this same process in Gestalt therapy. They can bring these developing capacities to their work as therapists in the training group, as they access more depth of presence with themselves and others. As participants are learning Gestalt therapy, they see the value of acute observational skills, attention to the nuances of experience, present focused attention, and authentic relatedness. At the same time, they are also engaging in meditative practices that build the "muscle" for and support these very capacities; this is a powerful combination. Trainees also gain deeper access to their own emotional experience as mindfulness meditation in the group offers support for staying with experience as it is, even if it is difficult or painful. This can increase the trainee's ability to stay present for a patient's difficult emotional experience and to trust being in the moment, enhancing the possibility for deeper and more authentic engagement as they work as therapist in the group and in their own practices.

Meditating in the group also establishes the experiential foundation for participants to expand their experimental repertoire in work with patients to include meditation, both in session and as homework experiments (described in Chapter 11). Exploring the meditations in the training allows trainees to grasp both the benefits of practice and the challenges and difficulties that emerge in meditation. For those who want to incorporate meditative practices with their patients, understanding the benefits and challenges of these practices is essential.

Enriching the Overall Training Experience

Gestalt therapy training involves intensive learning experiences. This includes the trainee's own personal work, watching and participating in others' work, working as therapist under supervision and receiving feedback. All of these can be both emotionally and intellectually challenging. Including meditation in the training sessions creates space for trainees to sit with and assimilate their experiences. The trainers and trainees alike find that the meditations contribute to being more grounded and present during the training, and to feeling more refreshed at the end of a training session. This also supports trainees in including this self-care into their own workdays.

Meditation sets a tone of presence and mindful attention in the group and offers trainees a shared experience. This enriches the co-created field, contributing to group depth and cohesiveness. As group members become more mindful, and loving kindness and compassion are cultivated, this spills over and strengthens the sense of connection in the group, and the interpersonal bonds between group members. After a group meditation experience, trainees can share what came up for them personally during the meditation, offering another way for group members to make contact with one another. Trainees can bring up what they find challenging, ask questions about practice, and get support. Both the trainers and trainees can respond to questions and share resources for study and practice. This added dimension of the training contributes to a supportive learning community, which in turn increases the trainee's ability to take risks and to do deeper personal work in the group.

Challenges of the Model

This model offers certain challenges for Gestalt therapy trainers and trainees. Here we outline what we see as some of these
challenges and offer possible ways to address them.

One challenge of the model is that in order for Gestalt therapy trainers to adopt (or adapt) this training model, trainers
must themselves have first-hand knowledge of Buddhist psychology and meditation experience. Of course, trainers interested in
this model will likely have some of this background. For those
whose experience and knowledge is more limited, there may be
ways to supplement it, allowing this integration. For example,
trainers could include this book and other Buddhist psychology
reading material in the reading for the training. Trainers and
trainees might attend talks and guided meditation experiences
offered by local Buddhist teachers if available, or a Buddhist
teacher from the community might be invited to give a guest
talk and guided meditation. Many talks and guided meditations
are also available online, and these could be integrated into the
training curriculum. Some trainees may have extensive Buddhist
psychology and meditation background themselves, and this can
be tapped as well, creating a collaborative learning experience.

A second challenge is simply the time constraints of teaching
two systems, where experiential learning is essential for both.
Finding the balance between didactic and experiential learning
can also be a challenge when there is a lot of conceptual material
to present. This can be partially addressed by having reading
material available to trainees prior to the training sessions so
that the experiential parts of the learning are not short-changed.

A third challenge is for trainees with little or no previous
background or experience in Buddhist psychology and meditation or with Gestalt therapy. Learning both of these systems
"from scratch" can be a lot to integrate and assimilate. One
possible structure to address this challenge is to offer trainees an

introduction to the basics of Gestalt therapy prior to their participation in a program that includes the Buddhist psychology and meditation components. Another possibility is to introduce this integrated model with more advanced trainees who already have fluency with Gestalt therapy.

Gestalt therapy training, like Gestalt therapy itself, is always creative, alive, and evolving. Because of the consilience of these two approaches, bringing them together in training opens the door to many creative possibilities. In spite of the challenges, we hope that Gestalt therapy trainers will be encouraged to explore this model (and to develop your own) and the many ways these ideas and practices might be included to enrich and support Gestalt therapy training, and to open the door to training therapists in a BPGT approach.

RESOURCES

Audio Dharma
www.audiodharma.org

Dharma Seed
www.dharmaseed.org

Sounds True
www.soundstrue.com

UCLA Mindful Awareness
   Research Center
Los Angeles, CA
www.marc.ucla.edu

Insight Meditation Society
Barre, MA
www.dharma.org

Insight Retreat Center
Santa Cruz, CA
www.insightretreatcenter.org

Spirit Rock Meditation Center
Woodacre, CA
www.spiritrock.org

British Gestalt Journal
www.britishgestaltjournal.com

Gestalt Journal of Australia and
   New Zealand
www.ganz.org.au

Gestalt Review
www.gisc.org

Inquiring Mind
www.inquiringmind.com

New Gestalt Voices
www.newgestaltvoices.org

The Gestalt Therapy Page
www.gestalt.org

REFERENCES

Atwood, G., Brandchaft, B., & Stolorow, R. (1987). *Psychoanalytic treatment: An intersubjective approach*. New York: Routledge.

Beisser, A. (1970). The paradoxical theory of change. In J. Fagan, & I. L. Shepherd (Eds.), *Gestalt therapy now* (pp. 77–80). New York: Harper Colophon.

Bien, T. (2006). *Mindful therapy: A guide for therapists and helping professionals*. Somerville, MA: Wisdom Publications.

Bodhi, B. (1994). *The noble eightfold path: The way to the end of suffering*. Onalaska, WA: Pariyati Publishing.

Bodhi, B. (2005). *In the Buddha's words: An anthology of discourses from the Pali canon*. Somerville, MA: Wisdom Publications.

Brach, T. (2012). *True refuge: Finding peace and freedom in your own awakened heart*. New York: Bantam.

Brazier, D. (1995). *Zen therapy: Transcending the sorrows of the human mind*. New York: John Wiley & Sons.

Breshgold, E. (1989). Resistance in Gestalt therapy: An historical theoretical perspective. *Gestalt Journal*, 12(2), 73–102.

Breshgold, E., & Zahm, S. (1992). A case for the integration of self psychology developmental theory into the practice of Gestalt therapy. *Gestalt Journal*, 15(1), 61–93.

Buber, M. (1958). *I and thou* (R. G. Smith, Trans.). New York: Scribner.

Davis, D. M., & Hayes, J. A. (2011). What are the benefits of mindfulness? A practice review of psychotherapy–related research. *Psychotherapy*, 48(2), 198–208.

Edelstein, B. (2015). Frames, attitudes and skills of an existential–humanistic psychotherapist. In J. K. Schneider, J. F. Pierson, & J. F. T

Bugental (Eds.), *The handbook of humanistic psychology: Theory, research, and practice* (pp. 435–450). Thousand Oaks, CA: Sage.

Elkins, D. (2016). *The human elements of psychotherapy: A nonmedical model of emotional healing.* Washington, DC: American Psychological Association.

Epstein, M. (2007). *Psychotherapy without the self: A Buddhist perspective.* New Haven, CT: Yale University Press.

Epstein, M. (2013). *Thoughts without a thinker: Psychotherapy from a Buddhist perspective.* New York: Basic Books.

Feldman, C. (2006). *The Buddhist path to simplicity: Spiritual practice for everyday life.* New York: Harper Collins

Fosha, D. (2000). *The transforming power of affect: A model for accelerated change.* New York: Basic Books.

Frew, J. (2008). Gestalt therapy. In J. Frew, & M. Spiegler (Eds.), *Contemporary psychotherapies for a diverse world* (pp. 228–274). Boston, MA: Lahaska Press/ Houghton Mifflin Company.

Fronsdal, G. (2006). *Dharma talk.* Woodacre, CA: Spirit Rock Meditation Center.

Fronsdal, G. (2005). *The issue at hand: Essays on Buddhist mindfulness practice.* Third edition.

Fronsdal, G. (2009). *Dharma talk.* Boulder Creek, CA: Vajrapani Institute Retreat Center.

Fronsdal, G. (2011). *Dharma talk.* Woodacre, CA: Spirit Rock Meditation Center

Fulton, P. (2005). Mindfulness as clinical training. In C. K. Germer, R. D. Siegel, & P. R. Fulton (Eds.), *Mindfulness and psychotherapy* (pp.55–72). New York: The Guilford Press

Germer, C. K. (2005). Mindfulness: What is it? What does it matter? In C. K. Germer, R. D. Siegel, & P. R. Fulton (Eds.), *Mindfulness and psychotherapy* (pp.3–27). New York: The Guilford Press

Gilbert, P. (2010). *Compassion focused therapy: Distinctive features.* New York: Routledge.

Goodman, P. (1991). *Nature Heals: The psychological essays of Paul Goodman* (T. Stoehr, Ed). Gouldsboro, ME: Gestalt Journal Press.

Greenberg, L.S. (2002). *Emotion–focused therapy: Coaching clients to work through their feelings.* Washington, DC: American Psychological Association.

Hayes, S. (2007, Sept/Oct). Hello darkness: Discovering our values by confronting our fears. *Psychotherapy Networker.*

Heidegger, M. (1962). *Being and time.* New York: HarperOne.

Hycner, R. H. (1985). Dialogical Gestalt therapy: An initial proposal. *Gestalt Journal,* 8(1), 23–49.

Jacobs, L. (1992). Insights from psychoanalytic self psychology and intersubjectivity for Gestalt therapists. *Gestalt Journal,* 15 (2), 25–60.

Jacobs, M. (2012). Critiquing projection: Supporting dialogue in a post–Cartesian world. In T. Bar–Yoseph Levine (Ed.) *Gestalt therapy: Advances in theory and practice* (pp. 59–69) New York: Routledge.

Jacobs, L. (2017). Hopes, fears, and enduring relational themes. *British Gestalt Journal,* 26, 1, pp. 7–16.

Joko Beck, C. (1995). *Now Zen.* New York: HarperSanFrancisco.

Johnson, S. M. (2004). *The practice of emotionally focused couple therapy: Creating connection.* New York: Brunner–Routledge.

Joyce, P., & Sills, C. (2014). *Skills in Gestalt counselling & psychotherapy.* London: Sage Publications.

Kempler, W. (1973). Gestalt therapy. In R. Corsini (Ed.) *Current Psychotherapies* (pp. 251–286). Itasca, IL: F. E. Peacock

Kornfield, J. (Ed.) (1996). *Living dharma: Teachings of twelve Buddhist masters.* Boston, MA: Shambhala Publications.

Kornfield, J. (Ed.) (1996). *Teachings of the Buddha.* Boston, MA: Shambhala Publications.

Kornfield, J. (2008). *The wise heart: A guide to the universal teachings of Buddhist psychology.* New York: Bantam.

Latner, J. (1973). *The gestalt therapy book.* New York: Bantam.

Levine, N. (2007). *Against the stream: A Buddhist manual for spiritual revolutionaries.* New York: HarperCollins.

Lewin, K. (1952). *Field theory in social science: Selected theoretical papers by Kurt Lewin.* London: Tavistock.

Melnick, J. & Nevis, S. M. (2005). Gestalt methodology. In A. Woldt &

S. Toman (Eds.), *Gestalt therapy: History, theory, & practice*, (pp. 101–114) Thousand Oaks, CA: Sage Publications, Inc.

Merleau–Ponty, M. (2014). *Phenomenology of perception*. New York: Routledge.

Nhat Hanh, T. (1998). *The heart of the Buddha's teaching: Transforming suffering into peace, joy, and liberation*. New York: Broadway Books.

Nhat Hanh, T. (1998). *Interbeing: Fourteen guidelines for engaged Buddhism*. Berkeley, CA: Parallax Press

Olendzki, A. (2005). The roots of mindfulness. In C.K. Germer, R. D. Siegel, & P. R. Fulton (Eds.), *Mindfulness and psychotherapy* (pp. 241–261). New York: The Guilford Press.

Parlett, M. (1991). Reflections on field theory. *British Gestalt Journal*, 1: 115–120.

Perls, F., Hefferline, G., & Goodman, P. (1951). *Gestalt therapy: Excitement and growth in the human personality*. New York: Dell Publishing Co., Inc.

Perls, F. (1969). *Gestalt therapy verbatim*. Moab, UT: Real People Press.

Perls, F. (1970). Four lectures. In J. Fagan, & I. L. Shepherd (Eds.), *Gestalt therapy now* (pp. 77–80). New York: Harper Colophon.

Perls, F. 1992). *Ego, hunger, and aggression: A revision of Freud's theory and method*. Highland, NY: The Gestalt Journal Press.

Perls, L. (1992). *Living at the boundary: Collected works of Laura Perls*. Highland, NY: The Gestalt Journal Press.

Polster, E., & Polster, M. (1973). *Gestalt therapy integrated: Contours of theory and practice*. New York: Brunner/Mazel.

Polster, E., & Polster, M. (1976). Therapy without resistance: Gestalt therapy. In A. Burton (Ed.), *What makes behavior change possible* (pp. 259–277). New York: Brunner/Mazel.

Polster, E. (1987). *Every person's life is worth a novel*. New York: W. W. Norton.

Polster, E. (1995). *A population of selves: A therapeutic exploration of personal diversity*. San Fransisco: Jossey–Bass.

Polster, E., & Polster, M. (1999). *From the radical center: The heart of Gestalt* therapy. Cambridge, MA: GIC Press.

Resnick, R. (1995). Gestalt therapy: Principles, prisms, and perspectives. Robert Resnick interviewed by Malcolm Parlett. *British Gestalt Journal*, 4(1), 3–13.

Robinson, M. (2004). *Gilead.* New York: Farrar, Straus, and Giroux.

Schmidt, A. (2005). *Dipa Ma: The life and legacy of a Buddhist master.* New York: BlueBridge.

Seligman, M. E. (2002). *Authentic happiness: Using the new positive psychology to realize your potential for lasting fulfillment.* New York: Simon & Schuster

Siegel, D. J. (2007). *The mindful brain: Reflection and attunement in the cultivation of well-being.* New York: WW Norton & Company.

Stevens, J. (1971). Awareness: Exploring, experimenting, experiencing. Moab, UT: Real People Press.

Tirch, D., Silberstein, L. & Kolts, R. (2017). *Buddhist psychology and cognitive–behavioral therapy: A clinician's guide.* New York: The Guilford Press.

Tobin, S. (1990). Self psychology as a bridge between existential–humanistic psychology and psychoanalysis. *Journal of Humanistic Psychology*, 30(1), 14–63.

Watson, G. (2000). I, mine and views of the self. In G. Watson, S. Batchelor, & G. Claxton (Eds.), *The psychology of awakening: Buddhism, science, and our day–to–day lives* (pp.30–39). Boston, MA/York Beach, ME: Weiser Books.

Wallin, D. J. (2007). *Attachment in psychotherapy.* New York: Guilford press.

Wegela, K. K. (2014). *Contemplative psychotherapy essentials: Enriching your practice with Buddhist psychology.* New York: WW Norton & Company.

Welwood, J. (2000) Realisation and embodiment: Psychological work in the service of spiritual development. In G. Watson, S. Batchelor, & G. Claxton (Eds.). *The psychology of awakening: Buddhism, science, and our day–to–day lives* (pp.137–166). Boston, MA/York Beach, ME: Weiser Books.

Wheeler, G., & Axelsson, L. (2015). *Gestalt therapy.* Washington, DC: American Psychological Association.

Wolfert, R. (2000). Self in experience, Gestalt therapy, science, and Buddhism. *British Gestalt Journal*, 9(2), 77–86.

Yeshe, T. (1998). *Becoming your own therapist: An introduction to the Buddhist way of thought.* Boston, MA: Lama Yeshe Archive

Yontef, G. (1981). Mediocrity or excellence: An identity crisis in gestalt therapy training. ERIC/CAPS, University of Michigan (Ed.), 214062.

Zahm, S. (1998). Therapist self–disclosure in the practice of Gestalt therapy. *The Gestalt Journal*, 21(2), 21–52.

INDEX

Ingram Content Group UK Ltd.
Milton Keynes UK
UKHW041449120423
420045UK00004B/142